OECD Studies on Water

Reform of Water Supply and Wastewater Treatment in Lithuania

PRACTICAL OPTIONS TO FOSTER CONSOLIDATION OF UTILITIES

OECD
BETTER POLICIES FOR BETTER LIVES

The activity "Reform of the water supply and wastewater treatment sector of Lithuania by consolidation of utilities" was co-funded by the European Union via the Structural Reform Support Programme REFORM/IM2020/004. This publication was produced with the financial assistance of the European Union. The views expressed herein can in no way be taken to reflect the official opinion of the European Union.

Please cite this publication as:
OECD (2022), *Reform of Water Supply and Wastewater Treatment in Lithuania: Practical Options to Foster Consolidation of Utilities*, OECD Studies on Water, OECD Publishing, Paris, https://doi.org/10.1787/f966a980-en.

ISBN 978-92-64-60110-9 (print)
ISBN 978-92-64-85253-2 (pdf)
ISBN 978-92-64-69880-2 (HTML)
ISBN 978-92-64-37441-6 (epub)

OECD Studies on Water
ISSN 2224-5073 (print)
ISSN 2224-5081 (online)

Photo credits: Cover © Marina J/Sutterstock.com.

Corrigenda to publications may be found on line at: www.oecd.org/about/publishing/corrigenda.htm.

Acknowledgements

The Lithuanian Ministry of Environment called on the OECD in 2020 to facilitate a national policy dialogue focused on consolidation of utilities as a condition to set water supply and sanitation services on a sustainable path. The OECD is grateful to have had the opportunity to support an ambitious reform agenda.

The report captures the main analyses and policy discussions, which informed the policy dialogue on water in Lithuania. The analyses were initially clustered in several project outputs, compiled here as chapters of the report. Some analyses and policy discussions are likely to be relevant for countries considering options to enhance the performance and financial sustainability of water supply and sanitation services.

The active and constant support of the Ministry is acknowledged. Special thanks go to Irmantas Valūnas, Monika Sakalauskaitė and Agnė Kniezaitė-Gofmanė for the time and expertise allocated to this project. The Ministry was particularly successful in engaging with a range of stakeholders, through co-presence or virtual meetings. The OECD Secretariat convened meetings with regional stakeholders, in Kaunas and Marijampole; the active participation of local authorities and utilities of these regions was a most valuable addition to test the practicalities of consolidation scenarios and accompanying measures.

The project was undertaken in collaboration with – and with the financial support of – the European Commission DG Reform. This collaboration has been particularly fruitful, with special thanks to Mauro Sibilia for his support throughout the process.

The project was undertaken by the OECD Environment Directorate (Tatiana Efimova), with substantial contributions from the OECD Centre for Entrepreneurship, SMEs, Regions and Cities: Oriana Romano shared her in-depth understanding of the governance of water utilities and Maria Salvetti contributed her extensive knowledge of aggregation processes in Europe and beyond. Tim Keyworth (Keyworth Consulting) plaid a pivotal role, in particular in relation to tariff policy, economic regulation and benchmarking the performance of water utilities; the OECD Secretariat benefitted from insightful discussions on these and related issues. Pierre Strosser, Gloria Depaoli and Youssef Zaiter (Acteon Environment) facilitated engagement with regional authorities and provided useful feedback in later stages of the project. Aukse Kaziulioniene (PV Grupe) was instrumental in collecting and analysing disaggregated data at regional level and in facilitating regional consultations. Xavier Leflaive, the OECD Environment Water Team Leader, co-ordinated the process and contributed his vision on consolidation options and sustainable water services. Ines Reale provided impeccable support to the project. The work was conducted under the overall supervision of Walid Oueslati, Acting Head of the Environment, Transitions and Resilience Division of the OECD's Environment Directorate. The Lithuanian Ministry of Environment called on the OECD in 2020 to facilitate a national policy dialogue focused on consolidation of utilities as a condition to set water supply and sanitation services on a sustainable path. The OECD is grateful to have had the opportunity to support an ambitious reform agenda.

Table of contents

Tables

Figures

Boxes

Executive summary

Consolidation was introduced in the legal framework for water supply and sanitation in Lithuania in 2006, and reflected in the Implementation Plan of the Government Programme, with a view to ensure higher operational efficiency and to reduce the disparity in prices for water supply and sanitation services. Still, progress has been slow. In practice, concerns have emerged, from smaller municipalities, which fear their interest will not be properly represented in consolidated utilities, and from well-managed utilities, whose customers will have to pay higher water bills to absorb less cost-effective ones.

In that context, the Lithuanian Ministry of Environment and the OECD endeavoured to operationalise the national strategy to enhance the sustainability of the water supply and sanitation sector and compliance with the EU acquis. Two pilot regions - Kaunas and Marijampole - were selected by the Lithuanian Ministry of Environment to explore and test the feasibility of consolidation scenarios and accompanying measures.

Analyses and discussions in the two pilot regions emphasised that consolidation can contribute to addressing enduring challenges, and help to:

- Increase the number of inhabitants connected to the water supply and wastewater treatment networks
- Make better (efficient) investment decisions which leads to economies of scale
- Decrease operation costs
- Improve water supply efficiency and decrease leakage.

Discussions were also instrumental in stressing that merging is neither the only solution, nor the unavoidable point of arrival of the consolidation process. Building on international good practices, alternative scenarios were discussed, such as coordinating or mutualising a range of functions, which can translate into flexible governance arrangements for water utilities. Work in the two pilot regions also established that the preferred outcome may differ, reflecting regional specificities, such as the existence of a strong urban centre that can provide resources and capacities to manage select functions.

Several measures should accompany the preferred scenario for consolidation. One set of measures relates to tariff policy for water supply and sanitations services. Particular attention was devoted to the depreciation method in the tariff setting methodology. This technical issue can serve different policy objectives. The prevailing method is adjusted to the Lithuanian context. However, there seems to be benefits in supplementing it with a possibility for accelerated depreciation for utilities, which demonstrate efforts to transition towards some form of consolidation.

Moreover, international experience suggests that consolidation does not need to necessarily lead towards harmonisation to tariff across municipalities, at least in the short term: decoupling both processes can actually help address some political concerns. Another consideration suggests that there are limits to how much water ills can finance environmental policies that benefit large communities (beyond water users). This issue deserves further attention and concertation across the Lithuanian government. It resonates with similar considerations at EU level.

Another set of measures relate to benchmarking the performance of water utilities, moving beyond the comparison of costs in Lithuania. The benchmarking of costs is an important tool that is available to regulators. More sophisticated processes capture multiple dimensions of utilities' performance. International good practices emphasise that attention to performance indicators should be completed by attention to the benchmarking process itself, and how utilities are clustered for performance comparison and information sharing. Less well-known, but very appropriate in the Lithuanian context, is benchmarking of business planning, to encourage more efficiency-enhancing consolidation activity: the tool can ensure that a range of (consolidation) options have been explored and duly assessed in the context of development and investment planning.

It is noteworthy that the Ministry has the capacity to set targets and a deadline for a move towards some form of consolidation. Should such targets not be meet ahead of the set deadline, a more top-down approach could be considered. Suspending or revoking licences of service providers which fail to achieve set level of performance by an agreed-upon deadline is a relevant tool in the Lithuanian context, assuming the thread is considered serious by municipalities and utilities.

On these and related issues, experience sharing among Baltic states and across Europe can be a source of inspiration. An international workshop in the course of the project revealed the breadth and depth of experience with forms of consolidation for water supply and sanitation service provision, both in terms of end point and in terms of processes for getting there. Lithuania has a lot to share, building on recent experience and the on-going reform. This confirms the distinctive value added of peer learning supported by DG Reform.

1 Report with a robust analysis of the state of play

Guided by a questionnaire drafted by the OECD Secretariat, Lithuanian authorities collected data and information on the state of play for water supply and sanitation in the country. That background information provides the common knowledge on which to identify pending issues and areas for further work.

1.1. Background and objectives

The Ministry of the Environment of Lithuania jointly with other governmental bodies, the European Commission –DG Reform, and the OECD are partnering to enhance the sustainability of water supply and sanitation services in Lithuanian. The Project will support the consolidation of the water utility sector, a requisite for improved services, a sustainable and socially acceptable financing strategy, and a broader water sector reform in Lithuania. See the Detailed Project Description, for more information on background, scope and process.

The specific objectives of this Project are:

- to support the initiatives of national authorities to design reforms according to their priorities, taking into account initial conditions and expected socioeconomic impacts
- to support the efforts of national authorities to define and implement appropriate processes and methodologies by taking into account good practices of and lessons learned by other countries in addressing similar situations
- to assist the national authorities and water utilities in enhancing the efficiency and effectiveness of human-resource management, inter alia, by strengthening professional knowledge and skills and setting out clear responsibilities.

The report presents background information compiled by Lithuanian authorities on the state of play, and on previous attempts to agglomerate water utilities in the country. Data and information were collected on the basis of a questionnaire developed by the OECD Secretariat (see Appendix), and then shared with the water utilities and national and local government bodies by the Ministry of Environment of Lithuania. The questionnaire covers the following areas:

- Legislation, institutional and regulatory framework
- The organisation of service provision
- The performance of service providers
- Tariff setting
- Inter-agency co-ordination and cooperation for WSS service provision
- Mapping WS service coverage and recent trends in service provision
- WSS strategic policy making and financing water supply and sanitation
- Experience with consolidation of municipalities and/or service providers.

Propositions unfold on key issues that deserve further analysis in the context of this project. The analyses are meant to document possible courses of action and options to facilitate agglomeration of water utilities in Lithuania. They were discussed with Lithuanian stakeholders at the kick-off meeting. The outcome of the discussions are reflected in an Issue paper (Chapter 3). The initially proposed programme of work for the project covers 12 months (in line with the Detailed Project Description) from 27/07/2020. Governmental changes in Lithuania in the autumn 2020 and a delay with collection of responses to the questionnaire triggered adjustments of the project implementation plan.

1.2. The state of play

Lithuania has implemented a massive investment programme over the past two decades to catch up with EU standards for water supply and wastewater collection and treatment. Progress is remarkable. More than 90% of the population is connected to safe water supply across the country, reflecting a high level of compliance with the Drinking Water Directive (DWD). However, there is room for improvement as regards the Urban Wastewater Treatment Directive (UWWTD). Moreover, recently built assets now need to be properly operated and maintained, to ensure lasting service provision and performance and avoid costs related to premature decay of existing infrastructures.

1.2.1. Access to water supply and sanitation services in Lithuania

Lithuania has undertaken significant investments to reach compliance with the EU water *acquis* on water supply and sanitation (WSS). The constructed public water supply and sewerage systems require consistent maintenance and new investments. Unfortunately, the present fragmentation of water companies, where the majority are micro-companies, prevents access to the funds required for investments and to the qualified workforce for maintenance of equipment while offering water services at affordable tariffs.

It should be noted that due to the infringement procedure on non-compliance with Directive 91/271/EEC on urban wastewater treatment (hereinafter – UWWTD) until 2023 the main priority is implementation of the requirements of the UWWTD construction of sewage networks infrastructure in the remaining non-compliant agglomerations; connection to existing centralized sewage infrastructure, reconstruction of Kėdainiai WWTP, improvement of planning, management and control of individual appropriate systems.

After setting the measures for full implementation of UWWTD, it is planned to focus on smaller agglomerations. Services provided in settlements of any size must meet environmental protection, water quality, service continuity and other requirements.

Figure 1.1. WSS services in Lithuania

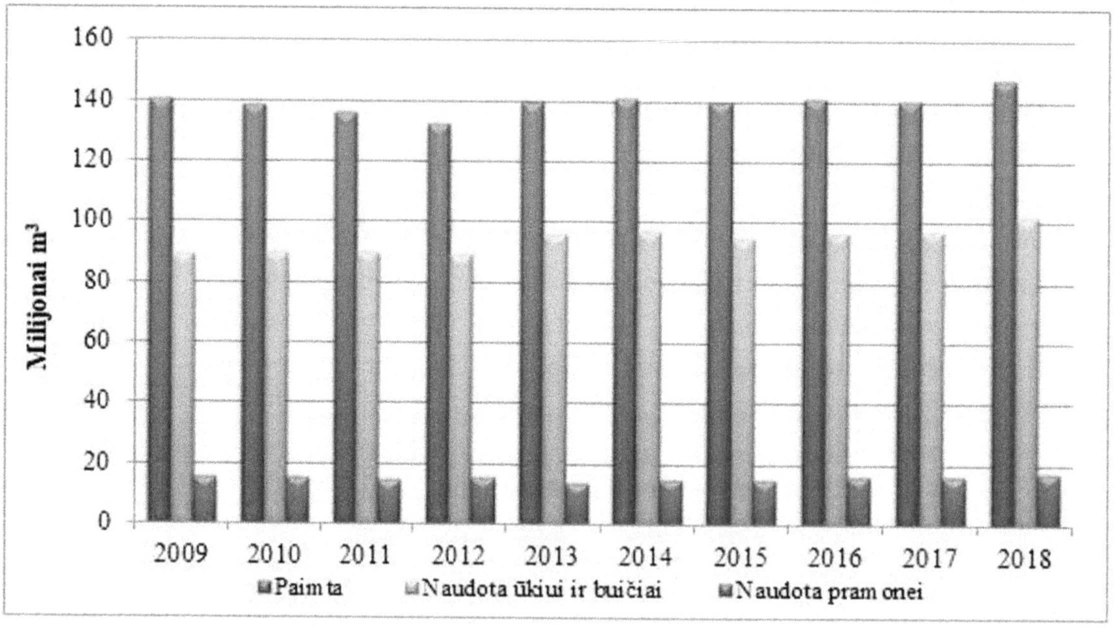

Translation: Taken; Used for household; Used for industry; Millions
Source: http://gamta.lt/cms/index?rubricId=4516f985-6445-4904-9192-db8999b6567d .

1.2.2. Institutions in charge of policies that affect water supply and wastewater management

Institutions in charge of designing and implementing policies that affect water supply and wastewater management include the Government of the Republic of Lithuania, Ministries of Environment and Health of the Republic of Lithuania; the State Food and Veterinary Service; the State Energy Regulatory Council and the State Consumer Rights Protection Service. Municipal authorities also take part in policy making for WSS management.

More specifically, the Government:

- formulates the policy of state regulation of drinking water supply and wastewater management;
- approves the licensing rules for drinking water supply and wastewater treatment;
- approves the standard terms and conditions of the public contract for the supply of drinking water and / or wastewater treatment;
- approves the description of the procedure for payment for the supplied drinking water and the provided wastewater treatment services;
- approves the description of the procedure for redemption of drinking water supply and wastewater treatment infrastructure objects.

The Ministry of the Environment:

- approves legal acts establishing environmental requirements for the extraction, use and treatment of drinking water, supervise the implementation of these requirements;
- approves the rules for the preparation of plans for the development of drinking water supply and wastewater treatment infrastructure;
- establishes the procedure for the accounting of extracted drinking water, discharged wastewater and pollutants;
- approves the rules for the preparation of activity plans of drinking water suppliers and wastewater managers;
- establishes quality requirements for drinking water supply and wastewater treatment services;
- approves the rules for the use and maintenance of the Drinking Water Supply and Wastewater Treatment Infrastructure;
- approves the Wastewater Management Regulation and the Surface Wastewater Management Regulation;
- establishes the requirements for the connection of new subscribers and consumers to the drinking water supply and wastewater treatment infrastructure;
- approves the description of the procedure for the installation, operation and control of sewage storage tanks and septic tanks;
- approves the description of the procedure for the design, installation, conservation and liquidation of wells for the supply of drinking water;
- co-ordinates the allocation of financial support from the state budget, European Union funds and other sources of financing for the renovation and development of drinking water supply and wastewater treatment infrastructure;
- co-ordinates the activities of other state and municipal institutions in order to implement the requirements of this Law;
- approves the criteria for the delimitation of agglomerations.

The Ministry of Health:

- establishes public health safety and quality requirements for drinking water.

The State Food and Veterinary Service performs state control of the safety and quality of drinking water in accordance with the procedure established by the Law of the Republic of Lithuania on Drinking Water Supply and Wastewater Management (further the Law on Water Supply). It also examines complaints of subscribers and consumers regarding the safety and quality of drinking water.

The State Energy Regulatory Council:

- approves the methodology for setting the prices of drinking water supply and wastewater treatment services and supervise its application;
- approves the methodology for setting the prices of surface wastewater treatment services and supervise its application;
- coordinates the prices of drinking water supplied by drinking water suppliers and wastewater managers and the wastewater treatment services provided and supervise the application thereof;
- coordinates the prices of surface wastewater treatment services and supervise their application;
- has the right to unilaterally set the prices of drinking water supply and wastewater treatment services, the prices of surface wastewater treatment services for the drinking water supplier and wastewater manager, the surface wastewater manager in the cases specified in Paragraphs 15 and 16 of Article 34 of the Law on Water Supply;
- approves the requirements and (or) method and (or) model and technical tasks of the regulatory accounting system;
- in accordance with the Licensing Rules for Drinking Water Supply and Wastewater Management, issues drinking water supply and wastewater treatment licenses, register them, warn of possible suspension and / or revocation of the license, revoke the licenses, suspend the validity of the licenses, revoke the suspension of the licenses, supervise , compliance with the conditions of the licensed activity;
- establishes the methodology for setting the prices of services for temporary disconnection from (connection to) drinking water supply networks and supervise the application;
- establishes rules for the imposition of sanctions, impose sanctions for violations of the provisions of this Law;
- approves the description of the procedure for assessment of the technological, financial and managerial capacity of service provider;
- approves the accounting separation rules for drinking water supply and wastewater treatment and the set of requirements related to accounting separation;
- approves the rules for the provision of information by the service providers;
- approves the description of the procedure and conditions for the performance of the drinking water supply and / or wastewater treatment;
- approves the description of the procedure for calculating the price of wastewater treatment for increased and specific pollution and supervise its application;
- approves the description of the comparative analysis of drinking water supply and wastewater treatment services;
- by 31 December each year, assesses whether the amount paid monthly by consumers for drinking water supply and / or wastewater treatment services after the establishment of new prices will not exceed 4 per cent of the average monthly family income;
- approves the methodology for calculating the fee for the acquisition, installation and operation of drinking water metering devices and supervise its application;
- performs inspections of the activities of drinking water suppliers and wastewater managers, surface wastewater managers;
- in accordance with the principles of transparency, objectivity and non-discrimination and criteria for assessment of investment efficiency, payback period and reasonableness, approve the

description of investment assessment and coordination procedures, coordinate investments (to be included in the tariff) of service providers.

Municipalities:

- Councils approve infrastructure development plans for the drinking water supply and sanitation;
- the directors of the administrations are in charge of the preparation of infrastructure development plans;
- when approving the infrastructure development plans, the councils should determine the boundaries of agglomerations and public drinking water supply territories by a decision;
- Councils appoint public service providers of drinking water supply and sanitation;
- Councils appoint rain water managers;
- Councils approve the action plans of public service providers;
- Councils, in accordance with the methodology for setting the prices of drinking water supply and wastewater treatment services established by the SERC, determine the prices of drinking water and wastewater treatment services supplied by public service providers;
- Councils, in accordance with the methodology for setting the prices of rain water management established by the SERC, shall establish the prices of rain water management services;
- Councils organize the redemption or use of drinking water supply and wastewater treatment infrastructure objects necessary for public drinking water supply and wastewater management;
- Councils, in accordance with the methodology for calculation of the acquisition, installation and operation fee for drinking water metering devices established by the SERC, approve the fee for the acquisition, installation and operation of drinking water metering devices;
- Councils or the institutions authorized by them, in accordance the Law on Water Supply and other legal acts, organize the supply of drinking water supply and sanitation, rainwater management services in the territory of the municipality;
- Councils perform the rights and obligations of the owner of the drinking water supply and wastewater treatment infrastructure needed for public drinking water supply and wastewater treatment;
- directors of administrations or their authorized persons supervise performance of public service providers and ensure the implementation of solutions of infrastructure development plans;
- directors of administrations or persons authorized by them shall coordinate and supervise the supply of drinking water, rainwater management services in the territory of the municipality;
- directors of administrations or persons authorized by them shall ensure the establishment of protection zones for wells in accordance with the procedure established by legal acts;
- directors of administrations or their authorized persons shall, during spatial planning procedures, ensure that the objects of drinking water supply and wastewater treatment infrastructure and their protection zones are located in communication corridors or that the right to exercise easement is required when maintenance, modification and other use of drinking water supply and wastewater treatment infrastructure facilities;
- directors of administrations or their authorized persons provide information on the implementation of the requirements of the Law on Water Supply and its implementing legal acts and inform the public service providers, rainwater managers, quality of supplied drinking water and wastewater (including surface wastewater) treatment services, conditions and prices.

1.2.3. Legislation and regulatory framework

The key pieces of legislation of Lithuania for WSS services are:

Law of the Republic of Lithuania on Drinking Water Supply and Waste Water Management

The purpose of this Law is to establish general requirements for the provision of drinking water supply and wastewater treatment services, organization and planning of drinking water supply and wastewater management in order to avoid adverse effects on human health and the environment, ensure uninterrupted provision of drinking water supply and wastewater management services, adequate development of drinking water supply and wastewater treatment infrastructure. The Law on Water Supply determines that the supply of drinking water and wastewater management, with the exception of storm water management and wastewater transportation is licensed.

In accordance with the provisions of the Law and the Law on Local Government drinking water supply and wastewater treatment services in the territories of municipalities are organized and coordinated by municipal institutions. Pursuant to the Law on Local Government provisions, organization of drinking water supply and wastewater management - independent (established (assigned) by the Constitution and laws) functions of municipalities, in the implementation of which municipalities have the freedom of initiative, adoption and implementation of decisions established by the Constitution and laws and are responsible for performing independent functions.

The Law on Water Supply establishes that a public drinking water supplier and wastewater manager is an enterprise controlled by the state or a municipality (municipalities). The public supply of drinking water and / or the treatment of wastewater (except surface water) is carried out by the public drinking water supplier and the wastewater manager. In the territory of the municipal public drinking water supply, another (non-public) drinking water supplier and / or wastewater manager may supply drinking water and / or provide wastewater treatment services in cases of exceptions provided for in the Law on Water Supply.

Surface wastewater in the territory of the municipality is managed by a public drinking water supplier and wastewater manager or another enterprise managed by the municipality by a decision of the municipal council. Surface wastewater is treated in accordance with the Surface Wastewater Management Regulation.

The Law on Water Supply stipulates that the drinking water supply and wastewater treatment infrastructure for public drinking water supply and wastewater management must be owned by the municipality or the public drinking water supplier and wastewater manager, except for the cases specified in the Law on Drinking Water.

The surface water treatment infrastructure must be owned by the municipality or the surface water manager, except in the cases specified in this Law.

Drinking water supply and / or wastewater treatment infrastructure owned by others and necessary and appropriate for public drinking water supply and / or wastewater treatment and / or surface water treatment infrastructure owned and operated by others necessary and suitable for surface wastewater management, shall be transferred to the municipality or public drinking water supplier and wastewater manager or surface wastewater manager at the initiative of the municipal institution in accordance with the procedure established in the Description of Drinking Water Supply and Wastewater Management Infrastructure Redemption Procedure.

The competence and financing procedure of the State Energy Regulatory Council in the field of regulation of drinking water supply and wastewater management are established by law. The State Energy Regulatory Council approves the Methodology for Pricing Drinking Water Supply and Wastewater Treatment Services, the Methodology for Pricing Surface Wastewater Treatment Services and oversees their application; coordinates the prices of drinking water and wastewater treatment services provided by drinking water suppliers and wastewater managers, supervises, their application and performs other functions. WSS services are licenced activity. The Council evaluates technological, managerial and financial capabilities of water utilities and if these capabilities meet the minimum criteria, the licence is issued. The Council has the right to take measures if the conditions of the licensed activity are not complied with.

The Law on Water Supply establishes the conditions for ensuring the safety and quality of drinking water supplied to the market, used in food enterprises and individually in private households by exercising the right of the residents of the Republic of Lithuania to consume healthy and clean drinking water and receive information on its safety and quality.

Law of the Republic of Lithuania on the Protection of Objects of Importance to Ensuring National Security

The purpose of this Law is to ensure that objects (enterprises, facilities and assets and economic sectors) important for ensuring the national security of the state and property and territory located in protection zones of enterprises, facilities and assets important for national security and critical information infrastructures the transactions of managers are protected from all risks that could jeopardize the interests of national security, and the causes and conditions of such factors are eliminated.

1.2.4. The organisation of WSS services. Accountability of municipalities

The Lithuanian Law on Water Supply provides that enterprises engaged in water, wastewater and storm water belong to local governments and are not privatized. Private enterprises can offer different water services only in limited cases. According to the Law on Water Supply, water companies owned by local governments must provide public water supply services to at least 95% of consumers in the service area. Therefore, private enterprises cannot provide services to more than 5% of consumers in areas with public water supply.

WSS infrastructure must be owned by a public service provider or a municipality, but a portion of the infrastructure is still owned by others or does not have owner.

Lithuanian municipalities are the main administrative-territorial unit in Lithuania after the restoration of independence in 1990. Since 2009 there are 60 municipalities. At the moment no change is foreseen.

Figure 1.2. Map of municipalities of Lithuania

The Law on Water Supply stipulates that the public water supply and wastewater management infrastructure is owned by the municipality in the territory of which the public water supply and sanitation services are provided or by public service provider (Water Utility controlled by municipality). If the drinking water supply and / or wastewater treatment infrastructure required and suitable for public WS and WW treatment is necessary and suitable but is owned by others, it must be transferred to the municipality or the public supplier. If no agreement can be reached on the redemption and transfer of infrastructure, contracts must be concluded on the initiative of the municipal authority for the use of drinking water supply and / or wastewater treatment infrastructure (lease, use, joint activities) and the provision of drinking water supply and / or wastewater treatment services.

The process of taking the ownership of the infrastructure needed for the public services is quite slow. The Law on Water Supply also provides exception, that drinking water supply and wastewater management infrastructure may also be owned by other persons. If it is not clear what part of infrastructure is owned by others, or what infrastructure is needed for public services, an inventory should be performed.

Figure 1.3. Ownership for WSS infrastructure by regions

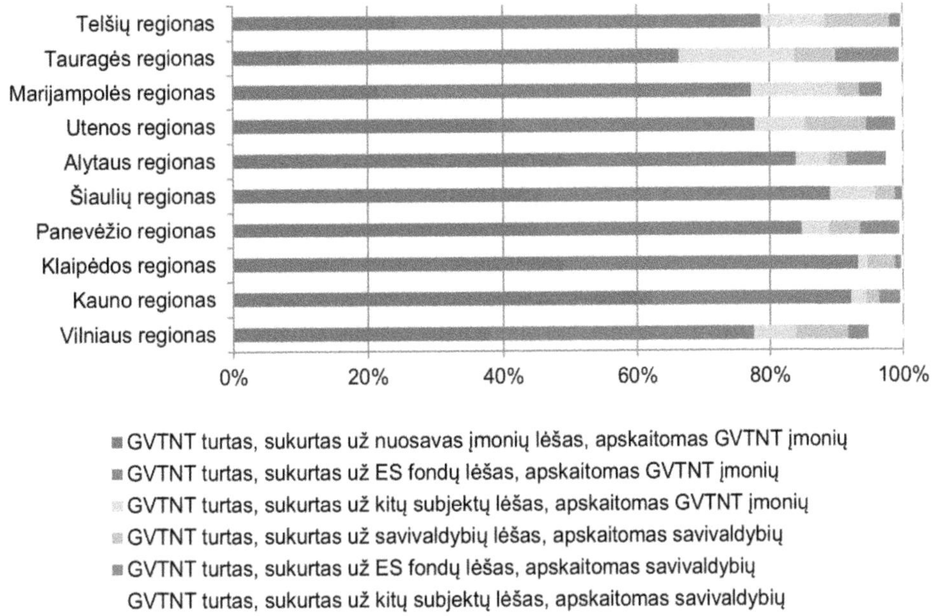

Source: Ministry of Environment of Lithuania
Translation:
GVTNT turtas, sukurtas už nuosavas įmonių lėšas, apskaitomas GVTNT įmonių, en. Drinking water supply and wastewater treatment assets created with the companies' own funds are accounted for by Drinking water supply and wastewater treatment companies;
GVTNT turtas, sukurtas už ES fondų lėšas, apskaitomas GVTNT įmonių, en. Drinking water supply and wastewater treatment assets created with EU funds are accounted for by Drinking water supply and wastewater treatment companies;
GVTNT turtas, sukurtas už kitų subjektų lėšas, apskaitomas GVTNT įmonių, en. Drinking water supply and wastewater treatment assets created at the expense of other entities are accounted for by Drinking water supply and wastewater treatment companies
GVTNT turtas, sukurtas už savivaldybių lėšas, apskaitomas savivaldybių, en. Drinking water supply and wastewater treatment assets created with municipal funds are accounted for by municipalities;
GVTNT turtas, sukurtas už ES fondų lėšas, apskaitomas savivaldybių, en. Drinking water supply and wastewater treatment assets created with EU funds are accounted for by municipalities;
GVTNT turtas, sukurtas už už kitų subjektų lėšas, apskaitomas savivaldybių, en. Drinking water supply and wastewater treatment. assets created at the expense of other entities are accounted for by municipalities.
Names of regions along the Y axis are provided in Lithuanian.

Figure 1.4. Acquisition value of WSS infrastructure by regions

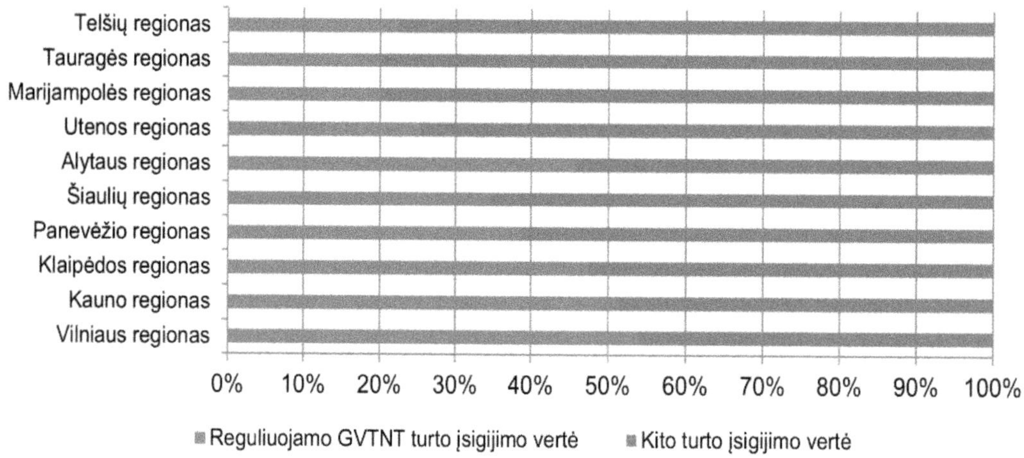

Source: Ministry of Environment of Lithuania
Translation:
Acquisition value of regulated Drinking water supply and wastewater treatment assets; Acquisition value of other assets.
Note: names of Lithuanian regions are provided in Lithuanian.

Most Lithuanian water companies have one owner, which is a local authority. There are also exceptions to the system, and there are cross-local government water companies. For example, the owners of UAB "Vilniaus vandenys" are the city of Vilnius and the municipalities of Vilnius, Šalčininkai, and Švenčionys. The majority of the Lithuanian water and wastewater network is managed by the 50 largest water companies, with the number of inhabitants in their service areas varying from 3,000 to 500,000 (UAB "Vilniaus vandenys").

The management of water companies is organized through the general meetings of the owners, the supervisory board, the management board and the general director. Owners of water companies, i.e., municipalities, and cities, participate directly in the management of water companies by appointing their representatives to the general meetings of owners and the supervisory boards and management boards of enterprises. In addition to enterprises owned by local governments, Lithuania has a large number of smaller private water companies: water cooperatives, holding enterprises, agricultural enterprises, etc.

Municipal authorities are obliged to ensure that all residents of the municipality receive drinking water and sanitation services that meet safety and quality requirements or have access to individual drinking water and sanitation in accordance with the infrastructure development plan. In agglomerations, centralized drinking water supply and centralized sewage collection systems should be planned.

Individual Appropriate Systems (IAS) may be planned in exceptional cases where the environment does not benefit from the installation of centralized sewage collection systems or the installation of centralized drinking water supply systems and / or centralized sewage collection systems is not justified due to high cost of installation of such a system. IAS should insure the same level of environmental protection as it is required for the agglomeration.

"Agglomeration" means an area of public drinking water supply and sanitation in urbanized areas where population equivalent of 2 000 or more occurs and where drinking water is supplied or intended to be supplied by a centralized drinking water supply system or is extracted individually; the generated or potentially generated wastewater is collected by centralized wastewater collection systems or treated by wastewater treatment / storage facilities.

The municipal public drinking water supply and sanitation area includes the territory of the municipality which meets at least one of the following criteria:

- Drinking water supply and / or sanitation services are provided to at least 50 persons who have declared their place of residence in the area;
- There is a suitable drinking water supply and / or sanitation infrastructure belonging to the municipality or Water Utility managed by the municipality;
- Urbanized and planned to be urbanized areas identified in the special planning documents.

Designation of public drinking water supply and sanitation service providers

The municipal council appoints a public service provider in the area of the municipal public drinking water supply and sanitation and licences it to provide services.

The municipal council may - in agreement with other municipalities in one public drinking water supply region - merge the Water Utilities into a regional public drinking water supply and sanitation service provider through reorganization. It then licences it to carry out public services in the public drinking water supply areas of these municipalities. A regional public drinking water supplier established by way of reorganization may be designated as a regional public drinking water supplier.

Organization of drinking water supply and wastewater treatment

Drinking water supply, sanitation and rainwater management in the territory of the municipality and in the public drinking water supply area are organized by municipal institutions.

In the public supply area of a municipality the public drinking water supply and / or sanitation (except for rainwater) management shall be performed by the public service provider (Water Utility). In the municipal public drinking water supply area, another (non-public) drinking water supplier and / or wastewater manager may provide services only if it complies with the requirements of legal acts and it has a drinking water supply and wastewater treatment license issued in accordance with the requirements.

The public service provider is obliged to supply drinking water and provide wastewater treatment services in the municipal public drinking water supply area, except for parts where provider provides wastewater treatment services or performs individual extraction, use and / or individual wastewater treatment in accordance with the requirements of legal acts.

Since July 29, 2011, a quality assurance system for water companies has been set up with the aim of ensuring cost-effective, high-quality drinking water. In addition, all water companies in Lithuania must comply with the requirements (No. D1-639) for drinking and wastewater quality, established by the Ministry of the Environment and entered into force in 2016. The quality of drinking water must also comply with generally set quality requirements such as Hygiene Norm of Lithuania (HN 24: 2003 "Safety and quality requirements of drinking water"). If necessary, the water company does not have to monitor the water quality requirements during the maintenance period, but the customers must be informed thereof in advance. There are also nationally regulated codes of conduct in the event that consumers' water supply has been interrupted for more than 12 hours. In such situations, the water company must ensure that customers are supplied with 30 litres of water per day (for example, via mobile containers). Some Lithuanian water companies have themselves implemented environmental and quality assurance systems that comply with LST EN ISO 14001 and LST EN ISO 9001 standards.

Municipalities, implementing the provisions of the above-mentioned legal acts, are responsible for planning and organizing the drinking water supply and sanitation services throughout the territory of the municipality.

Municipal institutions are responsible for the planning of drinking water supply and sanitation, development of drinking water supply and sanitation infrastructure in their municipality's public drinking water supply areas by preparing drinking water supply and sanitation infrastructure development plans (Infrastructure development plan -spatial planning document). In those plans agglomerations and public drinking water supply and sanitation areas should be established with directions for the development of drinking water supply and sanitation infrastructure, indicating the stages of implementation (priorities, progress, and timing) and financing of the planed infrastructure. The development of rainwater infrastructure is planned and envisaged in the Infrastructure development plan or in another spatial planning document.

Regional Cooperation

Municipalities located in one public drinking water supply region (administrative region) may seek the appointment of a regional public service provider in the public drinking water supply region in accordance with the procedure established by the legal acts.

A municipal institution may initiate the merger of a Water Utilities managed by municipalities in the same region by reorganization when:

- the activities of public service provider do not comply with the criteria set out in the description of the procedure for assessment of technological, financial and managerial capacity of drinking water suppliers and sanitation providers approved by the State Energy Regulatory Council;
- the amount paid by consumers every month during a calendar year for drinking water supply and / or wastewater treatment services provided by a drinking water supplier and / or wastewater manager exceeds 4 per cent of the average monthly family income. Such an assessment is made taking into account the average monthly family income of persons living in the territory of the municipality and the amount of funds paid by consumers per month for drinking water supply and / or sanitation services provided by the public service provider.

Municipal institutions may initiate the merger of their Water utilities, if there are other circumstances related to the increase of the efficiency of drinking water supply and sanitation, by the decision of municipal councils.

There is currently no cooperation between municipalities in providing WSS, except in a few cases - the largest Lithuanian drinking water company UAB "Vilniaus vandenys", whose shareholders are four municipalities, therefore UAB "Vilniaus vandenys" operates in four municipalities. Also, AB "Klaipėdos vanduo" provides services in the city and district municipalities.

Currently public drinking water supply and sanitation services are state owned monopolistic services delegated by the Law to municipalities. Legal form of Water utilities can be described as follows:

- 58 Closed Stock Companies (whose shares belong to municipality);
- 2 municipal companies;
- 1 public institution (established by the municipality);
- 1 Joint Stock Company (whose shares belong to several municipalities).

There are some private companies that provide services (in very small area, not as public service provider), but this is a small part. As of 31 December 2018, there were 70 licensed drinking water supply and wastewater treatment companies. The distribution of companies by region is presented in the table below.

Table 1.1. Public service providers (Water utilities)

S. No.	Company name	Territory of licensed activity
1.	UAB „Visagino energija"	Visaginas municipality
2.	UAB „Ukmergės vandenys"	Ukmergė city ir Ukmergė disc. municipality
3.	UAB „Kelmės vanduo"	Kelmė city ir Kelmė disc. mun.
4.	UAB „Šiaulių vandenys"	Šiauliai city ir Šiauliai disc. mun.
5.	UAB „Jonavos vandenys"	Jonava city ir Jonava disc. mun.
6.	UAB „Druskininkų vandenys"	Druskininkai municipality
7.	UAB „Molėtų vanduo"	Molėtų city ir Molėtų disc. mun.
8.	UAB „Širvintų vandenys"	Širvintos city ir Širvintos disc. mun.
9.	UAB „Varėnos vandenys"	Varėna disc. mun.
10.	UAB „Šilutės vandenys"	Šilutė disc. mun.
11.	UAB „Zarasų vandenys"	Zarasai disc. mun.
12.	UAB „Dzūkijos vandenys"	Alytus disc. municipality
13.	UAB „Utenos vandenys"	Utena disc. mun.
14.	UAB „Kretingos vandenys"	Kretinga disc. mun.
15.	UAB „Aukštaitijos vandenys"	Panevėžys city ir Panevėžys disc. mun.
16.	UAB „Palangos vandenys"	Palanga city municipality
17.	UAB „Neringos vandenys"	Neringa municipality
18.	UAB „Tauragės vandenys"	Tauragė disc. mun.
19.	UAB „Švenčionių švara"	Švenčionys disc. mun.
20.	UAB „Kėdainių vandenys"	Kėdainiai disc. mun.
21.	UAB „Giraitės vandenys"	Kaunas disc. mun.
22.	UAB „Prienų vandenys"	Prienai disc. mun.
23.	UAB „Pasvalio vandenys"	Pasvalys disc. mun.
24.	UAB „Vilniaus vandenys"	Vilnius c., Vilnius disc., Šalčininkai disc. ir Švenčionys disc. municipalities
25.	UAB „Nemenčinės komunalininkas"	Vilnius disc. mun.
26.	UAB „Plungės vandenys"	Plungė disc. mun.
27.	UAB „Kuršėnų vandenys"	Šiauliai disc. mun.
28.	UAB „Šilalės vandenys"	Šilalė disc. mun.
29.	UAB „Joniškio vandenys"	Joniškis disc. mun.
30.	UAB „Biržų vandenys"	Biržai disc. mun.
31.	UAB „Ignalinos vanduo"	Ignalina disc. mun.
32.	UAB „Pakruojo vandentiekis"	Pakruojis disc. mun.
33.	UAB „Nemėžio komunalininkas"	Vilnius c., Vilnius disc., municipality
34.	UAB „Eišiškių komunalinis ūkis"	Šalčininkai disc. mun.
35.	UAB „Rietavo komunalinis ūkis"	Rietavas municipality
36.	UAB „Telšių vandenys"	Telšiai disc. mun.
37.	UAB „Didžiasalio komunalinės paslaugos"	Ignalina disc. mun.
38.	VšĮ Velžio komunalinis ūkis	Panevėžys disc. mun.
39.	UAB „Raseinių vandenys"	Raseiniai disc. mun.
40.	UAB „Anykščių vandenys"	Anykščiai disc. mun.
41.	UAB „Birštono vandentiekis"	Birštonas municipality
42.	UAB „Radviliškio vanduo"	Radviliškis disc. mun.
43.	AB „Klaipėdos vanduo"	Klaipėda c. ir Klaipėda disc. mun.
44.	UAB „Kupiškio vandenys"	Kupiškis disc. mun.
45.	UAB „Jurbarko vandenys"	Jurbarkas disc. mun.
46.	UAB „Vilkaviškio vandenys"	Vilkaviškis disc. mun.
47.	UAB ,,Kauno vandenys"	Kaunas r. ir Kaunas c. municipalitys
48.	UAB „Sūduvos vandenys"	Marijampolė disc. mun.
49.	UAB „Lazdijų vanduo"	Lazdijai disc. mun.

S. No.	Company name	Territory of licensed activity
50.	UAB „Trakų vandenys“	Trakai r. ir Vilnius disc. mun.se
51.	UAB „Pabradės komunalinis ūkis“	Švenčionys disc. mun.
52.	UAB „Mažeikių vandenys“	Mažeikiai disc. mun.
53.	SĮ „Simno komunalininkas“	Alytus disc. mun.
54.	UAB „Kazlų Rūdos komunalininkas“	Kazlų Rūda municipality
55.	UAB „Kaišiadorių vandenys“	Kaišiadorys disc. mun.
56.	UAB „Akmenės vandenys“	Akmenė disc. mun.
57.	UAB „Tvarkyba“	Šalčininkai disc. mun.
58.	UAB „Elektrėnų komunalinis ūkis“	Elektrėnai municipality
59.	UAB „Rokiškio vandenys“	Rokiškis disc. mun.
60.	UAB „Skuodo vandenys“	Skuodas disc. mun.
61.	UAB „Šakių vandenys“	Šakiai disc. mun.
62.	UAB „Kalvarijos komunalininkas“	Kalvarija municipality
63.	UAB „Pagėgių komunalinis ūkis“	Pagėgiai municipality

Table 1.2. Private companies providing drinking water supply and/or sanitation service

S. No.	Company name	Territory of licensed activity
1.	Jotainių socialinės globos namai*	Panevėžys disc. mun.
2.	Prūdiškių socialinės globos namai*	Vilnius disc. mun.
3.	UAB ,,Didma“ *	Pakruojis disc. mun.
4.	UAB Gargždų plytų gamykla*	Klaipėda disc. mun..
5.	Pravieniškių pataisos namai – atviroji kolonija*	Kaišiadorys disc. mun.
6.	UAB „Baisogalos bioenergija“ *	Radviliškis disc. mun.
7.	Skemų socialinės globos namai*	Skemiai, Rokiškis disc. mun.

In 2010 in Lithuania, the management of the water supply and wastewater treatment sector was highly fragmented, with a total of about 460 companies providing services. In 2014, when the Law established the obligation to have a license in order to provide a service, the number of companies decreased significantly - from 359 to 64 public suppliers owned by municipalities, later it became 63 in 2018, and currently 62 public suppliers) or in total 70 licensed entities (public and private suppliers).

Voluntary consolidation of water utilities is almost non-existent, only the companies serving Klaipėda city and Klaipėda district have merged. Thus, there are several cases where the company operates in several municipalities, but has not fully taken over all activities (for example, UAB Viliaus vandenys operating in Vilnius city, Vilnius district, Šalčininkai, Švenčionys, Švenčionėliai, Pabradė, Širvintos municipalities; UAB Kauno vandenys operates in Kaunas city and Kaunas district municipality). There are also municipalities where two companies operate (e g. Švenčionys and UAB “Vilniaus).

1.3. Concerns about the sustainability of the state of play

While the quality of WSS services markedly improved over the last couple of decades, stakeholders share concerns about the sustainability of the current level of performance.

First, demographic trends affect the financing needs and capacities of water utilities. On the one hand, urbanisation drives investment needs in urban settlements. On the other hand, a decreasing population can affect the revenues of utilities and lead to oversized infrastructures, which will be costly to operate. These contrasted trends need to be properly reflected in infrastructure and service development.

Second, the economic and fiscal situation deteriorates. It is unlikely that public funds, which account for the lion’s share of investment finance in the country, can be sustained in the long run. This calls for a revision of financing models, which need to harness other sources of finance, including (but not limited to) revenues from tariffs.

Finally, cause and consequence of the concerns above, the performance of water utilities seems to be very fragile. Financing sustainability, in particular is an issue: capacity to finance the operation, maintenance, renewal and (potential) upgrade of existing services; creditworthiness and capacity to access commercial finance to cover investment costs. Other potential weaknesses reflect the lack of technical and financial capacities to cope with a range of operational and strategic issues (such as efficient use of water resources, or energy efficiency).

As a result, there is a risk that performance of the service to the population (or selected settlements) deteriorates in the coming years/decades. As an early signal, it is noteworthy that compliance with the EU acquis on water is lagging, in particular as regards the Urban Waste Water Treatment Directive.

1.3.1. Demographic trends

According to the data of the Lithuanian Department of Statistics and Eurostat, it is forecasted that in 2028 the Lithuanian population will be 11.5 percent or 332,000 people less than in 2018; and in 2050 - 22.5 percent or 633,000 less.

It is projected that in 2028, 2050 the largest part of the population will live in three regions: Vilnius, Kaunas and Klaipėda regions:

- In 2028, about 32 percent of the total population of Lithuania will live in the Vilnius region; this share is projected to reach 45% by 2050.
- In 2028, about 20 percent of the total population of Lithuania will live in the Kaunas region; 20.5% by 2050.
- In 2028, about 12 percent will live in the Klaipėda region, and about 12.5 percent in 2050.

Table 1.3. Population of Lithuania (2020 and historical)

Year	Population	Yearly % Change	Density (P/km²)	Urban Pop %	Urban Population
2020	2,722,289	-1.35 %	43	71.3 %	1,940,986
2019	2,759,627	-1.49 %	44	70.4 %	1,943,693
2018	2,801,264	-1.55 %	45	69.5 %	1,946,762
2017	2,845,414	-1.53 %	45	68.6 %	1,951,399
2016	2,889,557	-1.44 %	46	67.8 %	1,959,170
2015	2,931,880	-1.26 %	47	67.2 %	1,971,134
2010	3,123,816	-1.35 %	50	66.8 %	2,085,346
2005	3,344,268	-0.92 %	53	66.6 %	2,228,451
2000	3,501,839	-0.70 %	56	67.0 %	2,345,732

Table 1.4. Lithuania Population Forecast

Year	Population	Yearly % Change	Density (P/Km²)	Urban Pop %	Urban Population
2020	2,722,289	-1.47 %	43	71.3 %	1,940,986
2025	2,591,273	-0.98 %	41	74.4 %	1,929,035
2030	2,484,803	-0.84 %	40	77.3 %	1,919,747
2035	2,381,867	-0.84 %	38	80.2 %	1,909,316
2040	2,284,293	-0.83 %	36	83.2 %	1,899,816
2045	2,197,745	-0.77 %	35	86.0 %	1,890,982
2050	2,121,397	-0.70 %	34	88.6 %	1,879,932

Source: Demographic trends since 2000: https://www.worldometers.info/world-population/lithuania-population/

Between 2028 and 2050, only one region will grow in terms of population - Vilnius, due to the capital. Given the trends in municipalities in 2011-2018, a population decline of more than 50% is forecasted for 6 regions: Alytus, Marijampolė, Panevėžys, Šiauliai, Tauragė and Utena.

Figure 1.5. Population decline forecast by regions

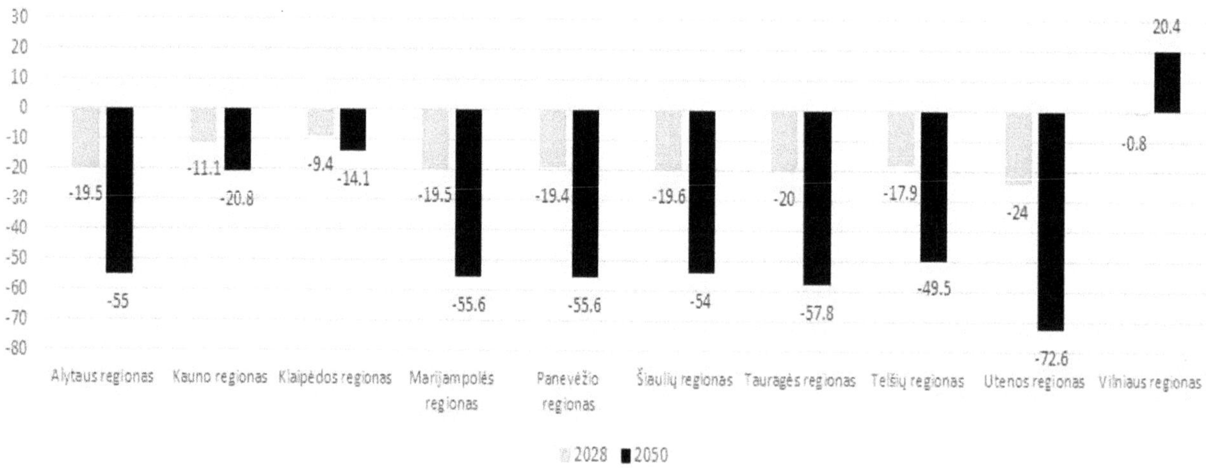

Figure 1.6. Maps of population decline by regions by 2028 and 2050

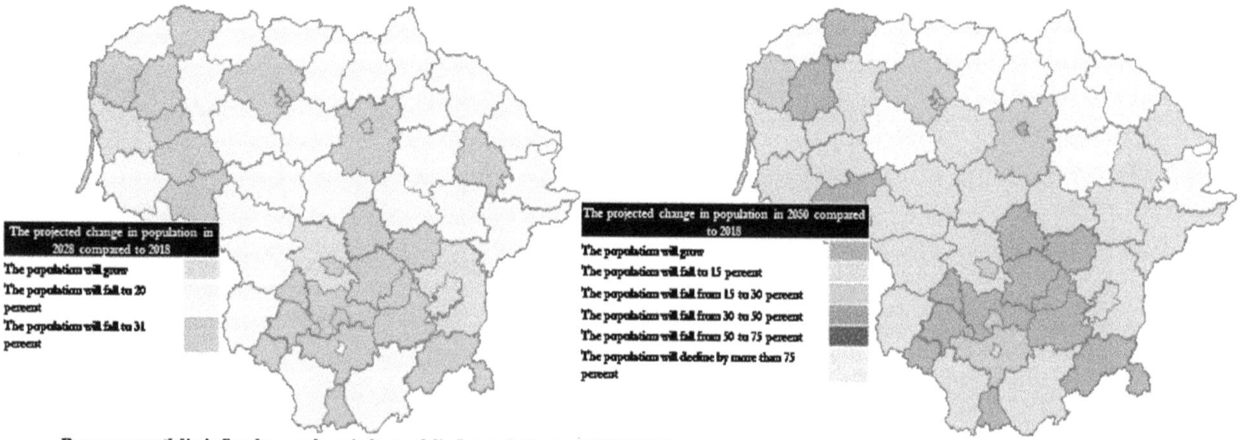

Data source: compiled by the Consultant according to the data provided by Statistics Lithuania and VERT (2018)

1.3.2. Economic and fiscal situation

In 2020, Lithuania is going through a health crisis with far-reaching economic effects, because of which the GDP is projected to decrease. As this crisis is more acute for population with lower incomes, the government ensures adequate social protection measures. As a consequence, COVID-19 created further stress on public budget expenditures.

The budget deficit of previous years has made it more difficult for the government to help the economic sectors. This affects provision of public budget guarantees and/ or direct financing of new investments in infrastructure.

Figure 1.7. Lithuania Gross Domestic Product (GDP, billion USD)

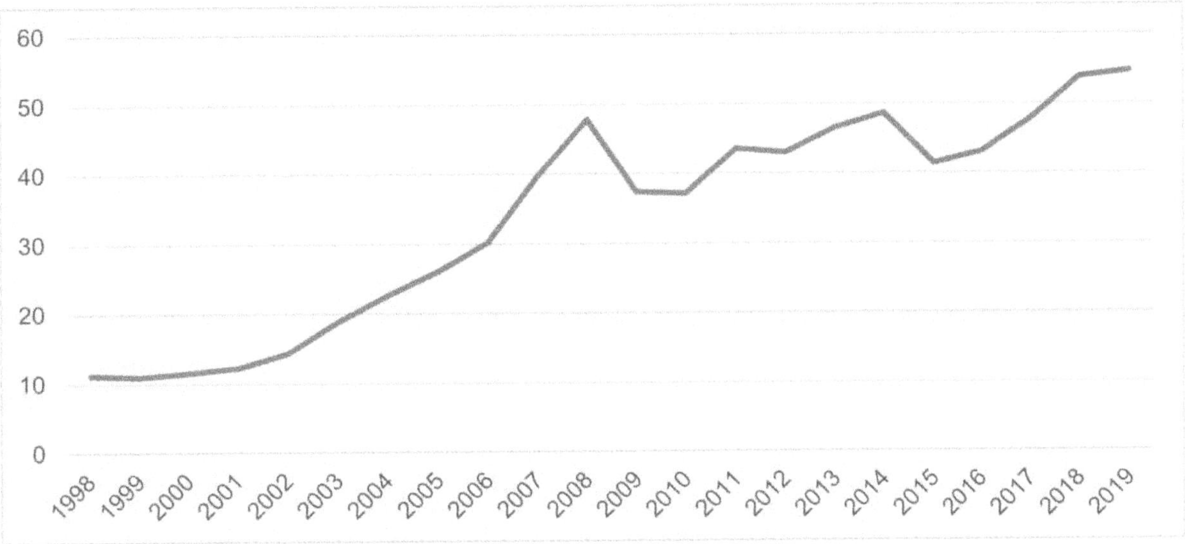

Data: https://data.worldbank.org/indicator/NY.GDP.MKTP.CD?end=2019&locations=LT&start=1999 .
GDP growth projections: https://www.lb.lt/uploads/publications/docs/25859_df03d2f842b2efeb19fefe204e73e4fe.pdf .

1.3.3. Accountability of local governments for local infrastructure

Decentralised ownership for local infrastructure creates issues with accountability for service provision. Water companies and local governments are responsible for the provision of water services in cities and settlements; the Ministry of the Environment is responsible for sustainable access to WSS services in the state as a whole. The allocation of tasks and responsibilities across institutions is blurred, on some issues. These institutional arrangements raise a few questions:

- Are responsibilities equally clear and understandable to each party?
- Do all of the parties agree to the performance of the functions and obligations assigned to them?
- How are some obligations and functions financed? Is this allocation fair from the viewpoint of all parties and does it treat all of them equally?

There may be disputes and misunderstandings between the Ministry of the Environment, the local governments and water companies about who should be responsible if a policy goal is not achieved. For example:

- Who should guarantee the WSS access in areas of over 2,000 p.e. to the sewerage system?
- Who should pay the fine for non-compliance with the EU directives, should it occur?

Questions also arise when major disruptions and problems occur in the provision of the water service in a densely populated settlement. For example, if a major problem occurs, and drinking water no longer complies with requirements, so that an advanced water treatment is to be put in place; or if treated wastewater does not comply with norms, and a solution requires major investments, and minor operational improvements cannot solve the problem. Who bears responsibility to the citizens and/or the Ministry of Environment – the local government or the water company?

In that context, the utilities boards' roles, responsibilities and capacity to deliver on the tasks devolved to them seem uneven across the country.

1.3.4. The performance of utilities

Water utilities' performance is measured and monitored by licenses. The licencing process provides some guidance on minimal requirement and capacities to operate water services.

According to the Law of the Republic of Lithuania on Drinking Water Supply and Wastewater Management:

- Article 24. Licensing of drinking water supply and wastewater treatment: Drinking water supply and wastewater treatment, with the exception of rainwater and wastewater transportation, are licensed.
- Article 25. Principles for issuing licenses for drinking water supply and wastewater treatment: Drinking water supply and wastewater treatment licenses are issued in accordance with the following principles:
    - security - this principle means that uninterrupted, stable and safe drinking water supply and wastewater treatment activities must be ensured, the health and safety of workers and bystanders must be ensured, and the negative impact of activities on the environment must be reduced;
    - reliability - this principle describes the frequency and duration of interruptions in the provision of drinking water and wastewater services to subscribers and consumers;
    - efficiency -this principle describes the amount of costs required for the provision of drinking water supply and wastewater treatment services and the ratio of the achieved result (EUR/m3);
    - non-discrimination -this principle means that it must be ensured that services are provided on equal terms and at the same prices to all subscribers and consumers in the same category.
- Article 26. Conditions for licensed activities for drinking water supply and wastewater treatment: The drinking water supplier and wastewater manager must comply with the following conditions of the licensed activity:
    - carry out the activities specified in the license;
    - to ensure the development of the used drinking water supply and / or wastewater treatment infrastructure, to connect the subscriber and consumer facilities located in the public drinking water supply area under its supervision to the drinking water supply and wastewater treatment networks in accordance with the Drinking Water Supply and Wastewater Treatment Infrastructure Use and Maintenance Rules requirements for the connection of new subscribers and consumers to the drinking water supply and wastewater treatment infrastructure;
    - to supply drinking water and provide wastewater treatment services at prices calculated in accordance with the procedure established in Article 34 of this Law;

  - ensure that the inspection of the reports on regulated activities and the inspection of the regulatory accounting system are performed in accordance with the provisions of Paragraphs 9–15 of Article 33 of this Law;
  - to supply drinking water and provide wastewater treatment services in accordance with the quality requirements for drinking water supply and wastewater treatment services;
  - to provide state and municipal institutions with the information necessary for the performance of duties established by laws and other legal acts. The drinking water supplier and the wastewater manager must provide the necessary information within 10 working days from the date of receipt of the request, unless the drinking water supplier and the wastewater manager indicate reasonable reasons for state and municipal authorities to set a longer deadline for providing information;
  - to inform and consult subscribers and consumers in accordance with the procedure established by legal acts.
- Article 27. Conditions for issuing drinking water supply and wastewater treatment licenses: 1. Licenses for the activities referred to in Article 24 of this Law shall be issued for an indefinite period to legal persons who meet the requirements set out in Paragraph 3 of this Article. 2. One license shall be issued to a public drinking water supplier in the municipal public drinking water supply territory. Licenses shall also be issued to other legal persons entitled to carry out drinking water supply and / or wastewater treatment activities in accordance with Paragraphs 4 and 10 of Article 13 of this Law. 3. Licenses for the provision of drinking water supply and wastewater treatment services shall be issued to legal persons under 2 conditions. The person 1) does not have tax arrears to the budget of the Republic of Lithuania, municipal budget or funds to which taxes are administered by the State Tax Inspectorate (except in cases where payment of taxes, interest, fines to a legal person tax dispute is taking place) and are not indebted to the budget of the State Social Insurance Fund; 2) has the technological, financial and managerial capacity to supply drinking water and / or provide wastewater treatment services in a certain municipal territory in accordance with the requirements of legal acts, in compliance with the conditions of the licensed activity. Technological, financial and managerial capacities shall be assessed in accordance with the description of the procedure for assessment of technological, financial and managerial capacities of drinking water suppliers and wastewater managers in accordance with the criteria specified in paragraph 3 of Article 14 of this Law.

A legal person seeking to obtain a drinking water supply and wastewater treatment license shall, in accordance with the procedure established in the Drinking Water Supply and Wastewater Management Licensing Rules, apply to the State Energy Regulatory Council.

The State Energy Regulatory Council, in accordance with the Licensing Rules for Drinking Water Supply and Wastewater Management, issues licenses for drinking water supply and wastewater treatment, registers them, warns about possible suspension and / or revocation of the license, revokes the licenses, suspends the licenses, revokes the suspension of licenses, monitors compliance with the conditions of the licensed activity.

The performance of licenced service providers is monitored. In particular, pursuant to the Description of the Procedure for Assessing the Technological, Financial and Management Capacity of Economic Entities (hereinafter - the Description) approved on 29 January 2009 by Resolution No. O3-6, sub-clause 4.6, the Council conducts an annual assessment of the financial capacity of water utilities.

When assessing the total financial capacity of water utility, the Council determines and applies the lower value of the normative indicator of the financial capacity of the drinking water supply and wastewater treatment sector (Item 17 of the Description). Item 15 of the Description stipulates that the financial capacity of water utility is assessed as sufficient if (i) the overall financial capacity of water utility in the reporting year is higher than the lower value of the normative indicator of financial capacity of the relevant sector set by the Council (Sub-paragraph 15.2.1); (ii) the ratio of the entity's equity to the authorized capital complies with the requirements of the Law on Companies (Sub-paragraph 15.2.2 of the Description).

According to the Law of the Republic of Lithuania on Drinking Water Supply and Wastewater Management - Inspections of drinking water supply and wastewater treatment and surface wastewater treatment companies, the State Energy Regulatory Council, in accordance with the provisions of this Law and the Law on Public Administration of the Republic of Lithuania, has the right to review the activities of a drinking water supplier and a wastewater manager, via operational inspections. Personal data must be processed and stored in accordance with the procedure established in the legal acts regulating the processing and storage of personal data.

When performing inspections, the State Energy Regulatory Council has the right to:

- receive all information, personal data, documents (regardless of the medium in which they are stored), copies and extracts thereof necessary for the inspection;
- receive oral and written explanations from persons related to the activities of the inspected drinking water supplier and wastewater manager, surface wastewater manager, to demand that they come to the premises of the State Energy Regulatory Council to provide explanations;
- receive information, personal data and documents necessary for the inspection, their copies on the assets and income of legal persons, economic, financial and other operations from state and municipal institutions, as well as from the Bank of Lithuania, commercial banks and other credit and financial institutions, auditors , other legal and natural persons, regardless of whether the information is considered confidential or not, to receive information from registers or databases managed or maintained by the state or other legal persons;
- obtain conclusions from the examination institutions in accordance with the inspection material;
- use specialists and experts to perform the inspection;
- enter into agreements with audit companies, other legal or natural persons whose services will be used by the State Energy Regulatory Council in performing inspections;
- when performing an inspection, use all information available to the State Energy Regulatory Council, including information obtained during other inspections;
- exercise other rights granted by law.

Civil servants and employees of the administration of the State Energy Regulatory Council authorized by the State Energy Regulatory Council, working under employment contracts, ensuring the performance of tasks and functions assigned to them during inspections, shall have the following rights exercised on behalf of the State Energy Regulatory Council:

- to freely enter the premises or territory used by the drinking water supplier and wastewater manager, surface wastewater manager and other legal persons and to perform inspection activities during the working hours of legal persons and not during working hours - if there are reasonable suspicions of violating the law in the presence of a legal person's representative, the owner of the premises, territory or his authorized representative. Civil servants and employees of the administration of the State Energy Regulatory Council authorized by the State Energy Regulatory Council and employed under employment contracts may enter the premises or territory used by other legal persons only with the permission of a court or with the consent of the legal person;
- to record factual circumstances;
- to use technical means during the inspection;
- to use the persons specified in items 5 and 6 of Paragraph 1 of this Article to perform inspection activities;

- to check the documents confirming the identity of persons;
- to use law enforcement institutions to perform their functions in accordance with the procedure established by legal acts.

The drinking water supplier and wastewater manager being inspected must:

- appoint authorized responsible persons who would participate in the inspection and co-operate with the State Energy Regulatory Council;
- submit to the State Energy Regulatory Council all information, data and documents necessary and necessary for the performance of the inspection (regardless of the medium in which they are stored), copies thereof and extracts thereof;
- provide oral and written explanations at the request of the State Energy Regulatory Council, to provide explanations to the State Energy Regulatory Council

1.3.5. Compliance with the EU acquis on water

Coherent implementation of the EU *acquis* on water would help to enhance cost effectiveness of new water investments. A comprehensive monitoring of water quality and setting treatment standards based on expected environmental impacts can better inform investment decisions by features of the receiving water body. A robust cost-benefit analysis (particularly, in case of diffuse pollution) can support agri-environmental actions to improve the ecological status of rivers.

Compliance with UWWTD, in particular, needs to be analysed in more details. Distance to compliance may depend in the size of the settlements and the status of receiving water bodies. In this context, prioritisation of new investment, taking into account the total cost for O&M costs over the lifetime of the investment, is to be done.

1.4. Pending issues

This section sketches issues that need to be analysed to address the concerns listed above on the sustainability of water supply and sanitations services in Lithuania.

Pending issues in the Lithuanian WSS sector include:

- in smaller towns and rural areas, many households are not connected to the public water supply and sewerage system. This is an issue as the quality of service may not be monitored properly. Moreover, this situation affects the utilities' revenues. The driver for such behaviour (e.g. the cost of connection, the structure of the tariff, or else) should be identified to consider appropriate responses
- many water companies (especially smaller ones) operate at a loss and cannot independently carry out investments. This issue will intensify as needs to renew and upgrade infrastructure grow; it will be exacerbated by demographic trends in municipalities where the population declines;
- WSS tariffs are very different from region to region. This is an issue if differences reflect more than differences in the capital and operating costs of the service;
- Affordability of water bills is an issue in several municipalities. Water companies in Lithuania are mandated to plan their investments in such a way that the price of water would be lower than 4% of households' net income. However, in certain regions, this criterion cannot be met without the support of local authorities.

The Lithuanian Ministry of the Environment emphasizes the importance of the formation of water companies with a larger customer base. According to the Lithuanian Ministry of the Environment, this would stimulate the economy and prevent tariffs from rising. The new Water Law adopted in 2015 provided for the consolidation of water companies. However, merger is voluntary only and water companies have shown little appetite for agglomeration of water services. As a consequence, there has in fact been no consolidation. Therefore, Lithuania is expected to propose a number of steps to expedite consolidation of enterprises in the near future.

1.4.1. Access to WSS services

According to 2019 data, 83,1% of the country - nearly 2.890 million people - received drinking water supply services; and about 76,5% of the population - 2.670 million people – received wastewater collection and treatment services.

In order to achieve the goal of 95 per cent of the country's population having access to drinking water supply and wastewater treatment services, 274,000 inhabitants still need be connected to drinking water supply systems and 302,400 inhabitants to wastewater treatment systems (based on the 2018 population and the Environmental Protection Agency). According to the data of 2018, up to 50 percent of the population receives centralized drinking water supply services in 6 municipalities, and wastewater treatment services in 32 municipalities.

9 municipalities (Akmenė, Alytus, Kaunas, Klaipėda, Neringa, Palanga, Panevėžys, Vilnius, Visaginas) cover more than 95% of the population on their territory.

Table 1.5. Municipalities providing drinking water supply and wastewater treatment services for 95 percent and more population (2018, per cent)

	Availability of drinking water supply services 95%. and more	Availability of wastewater treatment services 95 percent. and more
Akmenės r. sav.	95%	no data
Alytaus m. sav.	95%	95%
Kauno m. sav.	100%	100%
Klaipėdos m. sav.	98%	98%
Neringos sav.	100%	100%
Palangos m. sav.	99%	99%
Panevėžio m. sav.	100%	100%
Vilniaus m. sav.	no data	98%
Visagino sav.	97%	97%

*Lithuanian Drinking Water Supply and Wastewater Management Company Management Improvement Plan

1.4.2. Water losses

According to the audited annual reports of licensed drinking water supply and wastewater treatment companies in 2018:

- 135,865 thousand cubic meters of groundwater was extracted;
- 131,938 thousand cubic meters of water were supplied;
- 105,158 thousand cubic meters of water were sold.

The amount of water sold averaged about 77 percent of the total amount of water extracted per year in the country. The national average masks regional discrepancies. The lowest amount of sold drinking water (compared to extracted) is in the Marijampolė region water supply and wastewater treatment company (44 percent) (see the figure below).

Figure 1.8. Drinking water production by regions

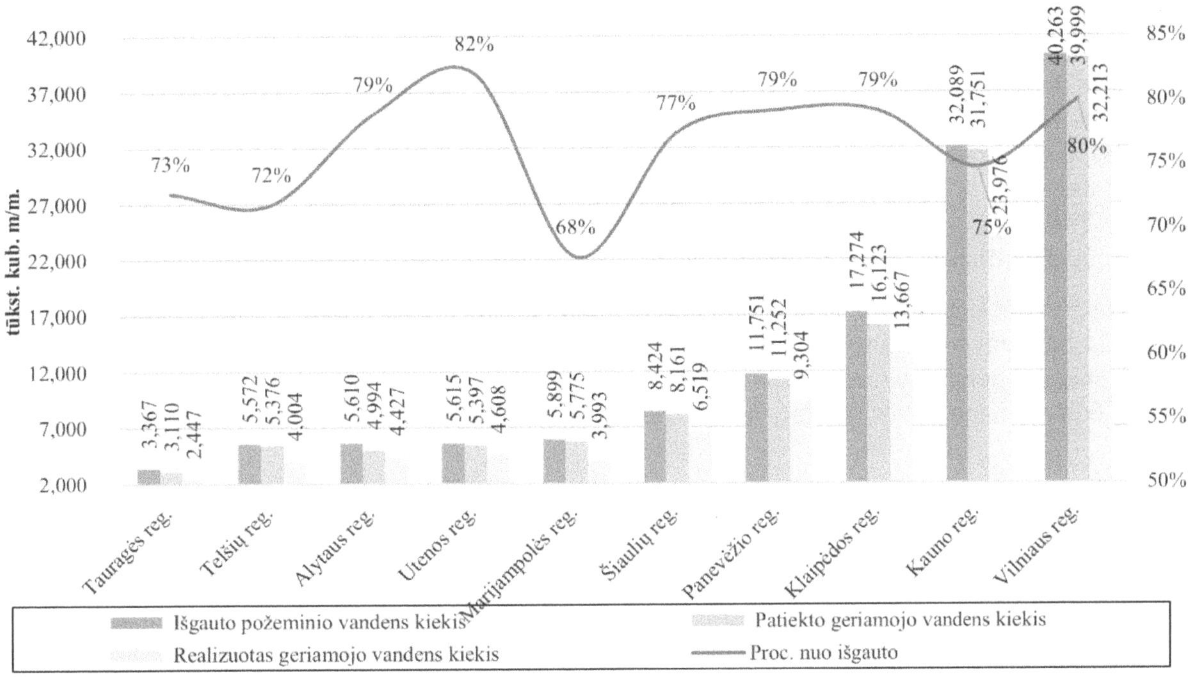

Source: Ministry of Environment of Lithuania
Translation: Amount of extracted groundwater; Amount of drinking water sold; Amount of drinking water supplied; Proc. from extracted.

According to available data, in 2018, licensed drinking water supply and wastewater treatment management companies experienced an average of 26 percent losses of drinking water (see figure below). The company's largest drinking water loss experienced for distributional networks. Regional performance varies from 20% (Panevėžys region), up to 37% (Marijampolė region).

Figure 1.9. Drinking water losses

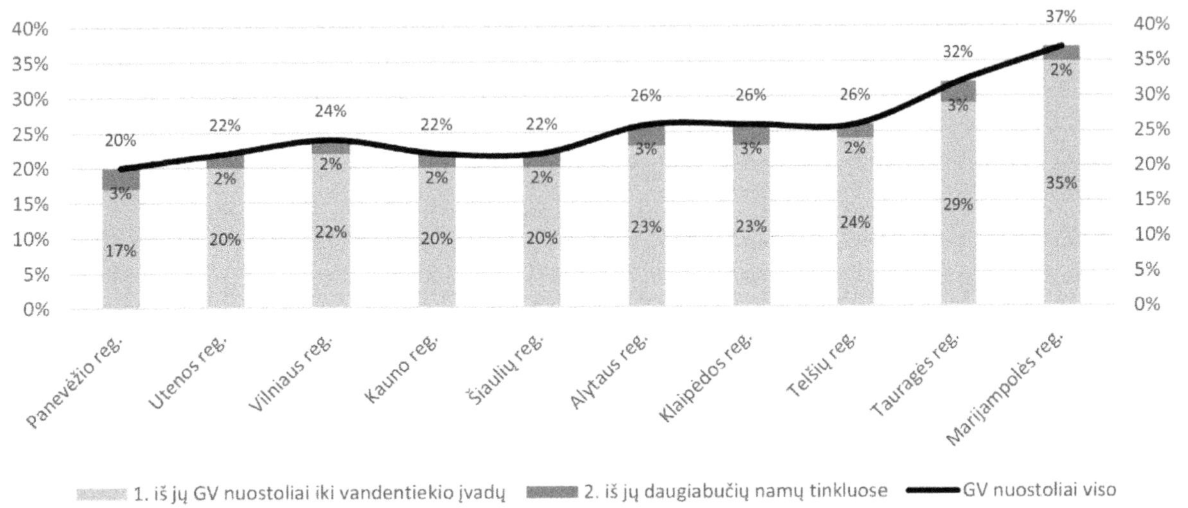

Source: Ministry of Environment of Lithuania
Translation: of which drinking water losses in distributional networks; of which in apartment house networks; total drinking water loss.

1.4.3. Regional disparities in water consumption and wastewater production

Drinking water consumption by municipality and consumption per consumer in selected municipalities for 2018 are shown below. The largest consumption of drinking water is in Vilnius (40 million m3), Kaunas (31.6 million m3) and Klaipėda (16.1 million m3) regions. The lowest consumption of drinking water is in the Taurage region (3.1 million m3). Comparing the population share and the amount of drinking water consumed, the Tauragė region stands out - although the consumption is 2.4 per cent of the total drinking water but the share of the population in this region is twice as high - 5 percent of the entire population of Lithuania. The share of drinking water consumed in Šiauliai region is also significantly lower than the share of the population (drinking water consumption - 6.2%, and the share of the population - 9%).

A high share of drinking water consumption is in the Kaunas region - the share of consumed drinking water reaches 24 percent, and the share of the population - 20 percent from the entire population of Lithuania. Also, the share of drinking water consumed is significantly higher than the share of population in the Vilnius region (1.3 percentage points difference) and the Klaipėda region (1.2 percentage points).

Figure 1.10. Drinking water consumption by municipality

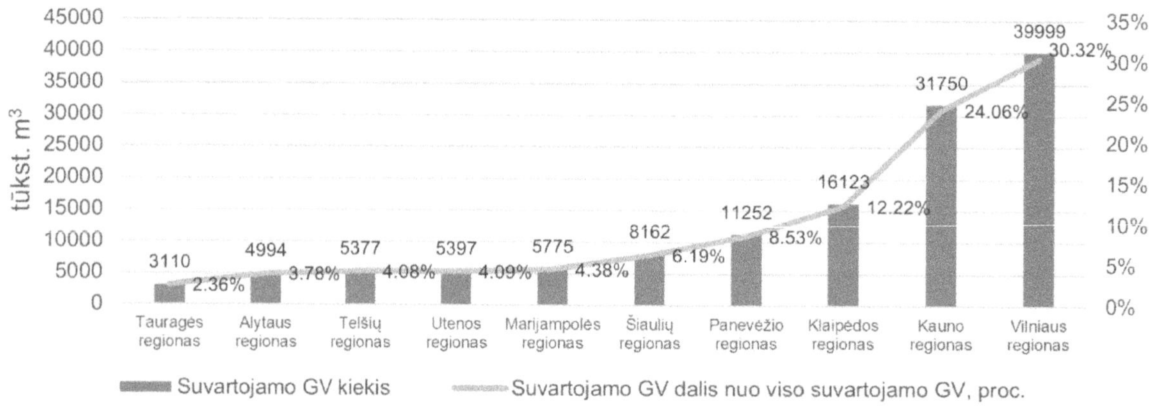

Source: Ministry of Environment of Lithuania
Translation: Drinking water consumption; the share of drinking water consumed in total drinking water consumption

Figure 1.11. Drinking water consumption per consumer in selected municipalities

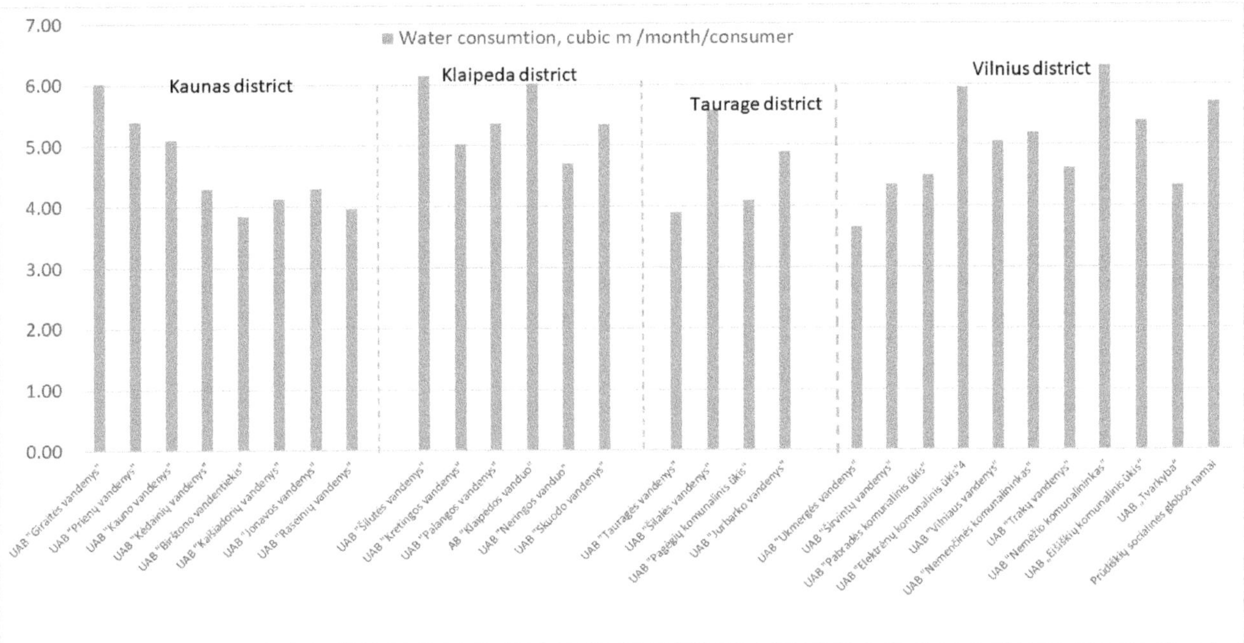

Source: Ministry of Environment of Lithuania
Note: Water companies' names are provided in Lithuanian.

The total amount of wastewater generated is 23.7 percent higher than the amount of drinking water consumed. This difference, partly, could be explained by rainwater collected. Only major towns have large separate rainwater systems in Lithuania. Smaller cities have all public sewer systems. No investments have been made in the rainwater systems since the 1990s. To date, more than 30% of rainwater systems are too small and over 70% in unsatisfactory condition. The largest amounts of wastewater are generated in Vilnius (45 million m3), Kaunas (35.9 million m3) and Klaipėda (16.1 million m3) regions. The lowest amount of wastewater is generated in Taurage region (3.9 million m3).

Figure 1.12. Wastewater generated by regions

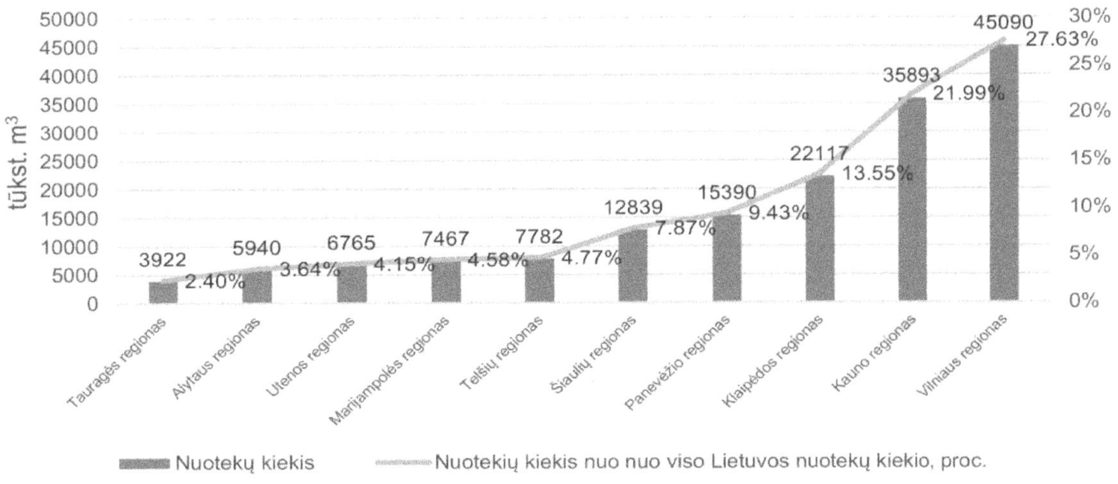

Source: Ministry of Environment of Lithuania
Translation: amount of wastewater; the amount of wastewater from the total amount of wastewater in Lithuania

1.4.4. Financial performance of water companies

According to the 2018 reporting data of drinking water supply and wastewater treatment companies, about half of the companies operate profitably[1] and the costs of their drinking water supply and wastewater treatment activities are covered by revenues from the provision of drinking water supply and wastewater treatment services.

These companies include all the largest drinking water supply and wastewater treatment companies (9 out of 10 regional centers). An overall financial performance of the companies is also positive: in 2018 more than EUR 8.9 million profit generated (difference between drinking water supply and wastewater treatment income and drinking water supply and wastewater treatment costs). However, considering the data of the last 3 years, this amount is decreasing (in 2016 it amounted to EUR 10.3 million, and in 2017 - EUR 10.2 million).

Analysing the absolute values of the indicators of 2018, 7 regions of the country were assessed positively according to the accumulated profit of the companies operating in them, only the total financial result of Marijampolė, Alytus and Šiauliai regions was negative (companies in these regions generated EUR 51 thousand and a loss of EUR 337 thousand).

However, the assessment of the average profitability of companies in each region shows a significantly worse situation.

Figure 1.13. Average hypothetical profitability of companies in individual regions

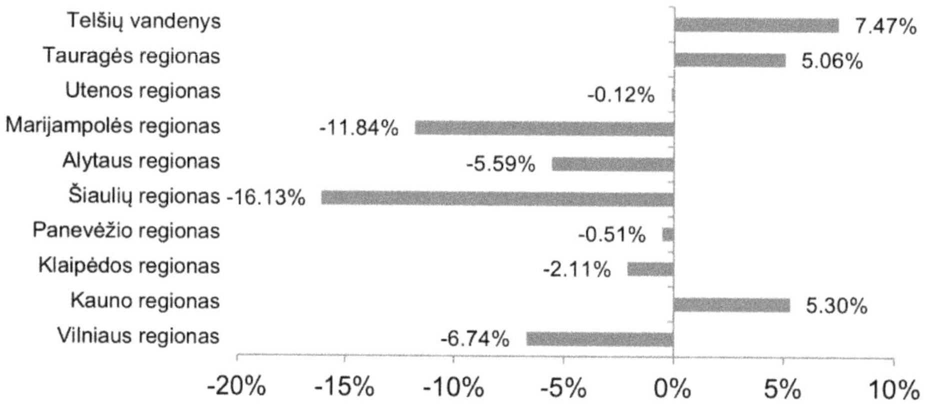

Source: Ministry of Environment of Lithuania

According to the assessment of the hypothetical[2] profitability of an average company, in contrast to the assessment of absolute profit, only 3 regions (Telšiai, Kaunas and Tauragė) have a positive value of the indicator, while the average profitability of companies in other 7 regions is negative, i.e. there are more loss-making enterprises than profitable ones in the region and / or their loss is higher than the profitability of profitable enterprises. The worst average profitability is demonstrated by the companies of Šiauliai (-16.1%), Marijampolė (-11.8%), Vilnius (-6.7%) and Alytus (-5.6%) regions. Thus, large metropolitan companies often operate in regions without inefficient and financially unsustainable drinking water supply and wastewater treatment facilities.

It should be noted that, despite the total profit of the drinking water supply and wastewater treatment sector and relatively high hypothetical profitability, the income of drinking water supply and wastewater treatment activities of the majority of companies (39 out of 70 or 52.9%) does not cover the costs of services provision. This structure is accompanied by a deteriorating trend in overall indicators (overall hypothetical profitability of the sector and a gradual decline in hypothetical profits) and clear concentrations of loss-making companies among the largest players in the drinking water supply and wastewater sector on a regional basis.

Assessing the direct and indirect subsidization of the price of drinking water supply and wastewater treatment by municipalities, it is noticed that only 3 municipalities directly subsidize the price of drinking water supply and wastewater treatment - Kelmė district, Neringa and Vilnius district municipalities.

1.4.5. Regional disparities in WSS costs

Tariffs for WSS services vary across and within regions. The most uneven drinking water supply prices per m3 are in Panevėžys, Marijampolė and Klaipėda regions, and the most even in Tauragė regions.

The largest absolute difference (in euros) between the highest and lowest drinking water supply prices per m3 is observed in Klaipėda region. The maximum price applied in the region is twice as high as the highest price applied in Tauragė region (see the figure below). However, when analyzing the relative difference, the biggest difference between the prices is in the Panevėžys region - here the minimum price is 3 times lower than the maximum one. The smallest relative and absolute differences are in the Tauragė region - the minimum and maximum price differ by only a quarter.

Figure 1.14. Difference (in EUR) between the highest and lowest water prices per m3

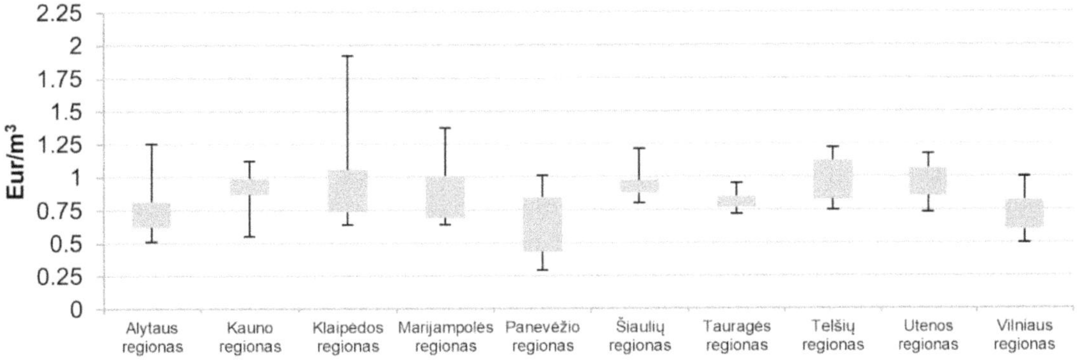

Source: Ministry of Environment of Lithuania

Wastewater treatment prices per m3 in the region differ the most between companies providing services in Utena, Alytus and Panevėžys regions, and the smallest price differences between companies in the region - in Marijampolė and Tauragė regions. The lowest wastewater treatment price per m3 (0.47 Eur / m3, excluding VAT) applies to companies operating in Panevėžys, and the highest - to companies operating in the Utena region (2.18 Eur / m3, excluding VAT) (figure below).

Figure 1.15. Difference between the highest and lowest wastewater prices per m3

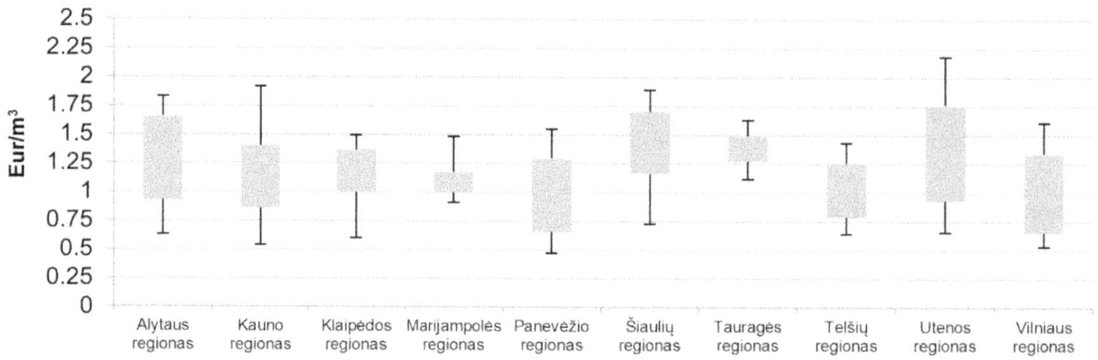

Source: Ministry of Environment of Lithuania

The price of drinking water supply per m3 applied by different companies to consumers and subscribers is 0.29 - 1.92 Eur without VAT. The most even drinking water supply prices (excluding the highest and lowest prices) are applied by companies operating in the region in Tauragė (0.75 - 0.89 EUR without VAT), and the most unequal - in Panevėžys regions (0.29 - 0.92 EUR without VAT).

Assessing the price of drinking water supply and wastewater treatment and the ratio of the average wage (gross) in regions and municipalities, the price of drinking water supply and wastewater treatment is highest in Šiauliai region (EUR 2.51) and Tauragė region (EUR 2.45), while the average labor salary (gross) in these regions is one of the lowest - in Šiauliai region (EUR 772.80), Tauragė region (EUR 731). The lowest price for drinking water supply and wastewater treatment is in the Vilnius region (EUR 1.25), while the average wage (gross) in this region is one of the highest (EUR 1034.60). This shows that residents from smaller municipalities (such as Kelmė district municipality, Pakruojis district municipality, etc.), where a lower average wage (gross) prevails, pay more for drinking water supply and wastewater treatment than those residents, whose average wage (gross) is higher (eg, Vilnius city municipality, Vilnius district municipality, etc.) (see the figure below).

Figure 1.16. Cost of WSS services and the ratio of the average wage (gross) in municipalities

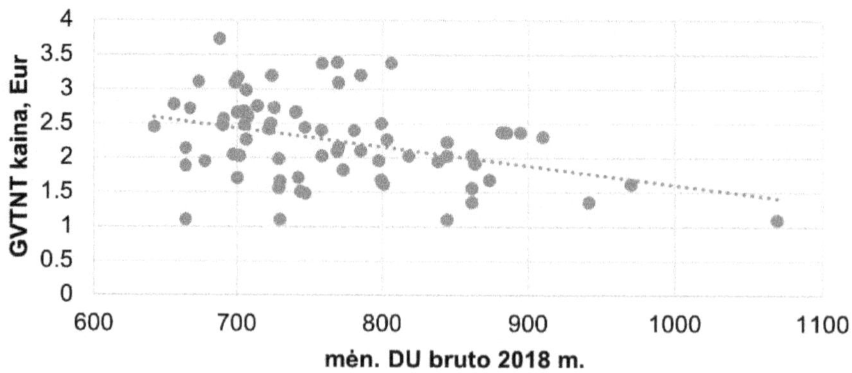

Translation: cost of drinking water supply and wastewater treatment; eur/month; Gross monthly salary in 2018
Source: Ministry of Environment of Lithuania

The price of drinking water supply and wastewater treatment is indirectly subsidized by 38 municipalities. In most municipalities, social compensation is provided to cover the costs of drinking water supply and wastewater treatment for indigent citizens. It should be noted that as the price of these services increases, it is likely that there will be more municipalities that will have to provide subsidies to cover prices.

1.4.6. WSS strategic policy making and financing water supply and sanitation

A National Progress Plan is the main forward-looking strategic document for the water management sector. The sixth goal of the Strategic Plan is to ensure good quality of the environment and sustainability of the use of natural resources, to protect biological diversity, to mitigate Lithuania's impact on climate change and to increase resilience to its impact. In order to achieve this goal, it is planned to improve the status of water bodies (Baltic Sea, surface and groundwater) - in particular to reduce diffuse pollution from the agricultural sector, ensure compliance with agri-environmental requirements, reduce point source pollution, and, most relevant for this project, ensure adequate quality of wastewater treatment. It is also planned to develop centralized drinking water supply and wastewater treatment systems, thus increasing the availability and safety of services and creating conditions for reducing environmental pollution and for the rational use of water resources.

A National Environmental Protection Strategy is also part of the strategic framework for the sector.

The Water Management Program 2017–2023, approved by the Government of the Republic of Lithuania in 2017 is a medium-term strategic document contributing to the National Environmental Protection Strategy approved by the Seimas of the Republic of Lithuania in 2015.The purpose of the program is to determine the goals, objectives and desired results of the Lithuanian water sector until 2023, which would be in line with other related policies based on the country's traditions, European Union (EU) legal norms, international conventions, resolutions, agreements and programs.

The program covers several areas of water management, one of which is drinking water supply and sanitation. The program identifies drinking water supply and wastewater services as services of general interest that determine the quality of life of citizens and the environment. These services must meet established safety and quality requirements, be affordable and implement the basic principles of cost recovery and polluter pays for the sector. Part of the EU funds for the period 2014–2020 is allocated to the development and renovation of drinking water supply and wastewater treatment infrastructure. In order to use these funds efficiently for the development of the drinking water supply and wastewater treatment farm, the development directions, goals and objectives of this sector have been established.

The Program consists of a description of the current situation (the state of river basins, the marine environment, floods, drinking water supply and wastewater management), objectives, tasks, evaluation criteria and their values.

The main objectives of the Program are to:

- to improve the status of surface and groundwater bodies;
- to achieve and / or maintain a good state of the Baltic Sea environment;
- to reduce the risk of floods and their consequences throughout the country;
- to provide the population of the country with high-quality public drinking water supply and wastewater treatment services and to reduce environmental pollution with wastewater;
- more effective implementation of water protection and use requirements.

The Program is implemented in accordance with a 7-year action plan, which includes measures for the implementation of all the objectives and tasks of the Program. The Action plan was approved in 2017, by an Order of the Minister of Environment of the Republic of Lithuania, Minister of Agriculture of the Republic of Lithuania. For each measure, a responsible executor is appointed and the time of its implementation is specified. The Minister of the Environment also approves water protection objectives, which define the target values for good status for each surface water body.

1.4.7. Investment needs, now and in the future

Over the last decades, investment in WSS infrastructure and household connection has been largely financed with EU support. Infrastructure development was essentially financed through international support (70% of funds came through the EU Cohesion and Structural funds or grants). New financing capacities are required to operate and maintain existing assets, adapting services to changing needs, driven by more stringent environment and health regulations, or a changing climate.

During the EU funding period 2007-2013, the national and EU subsidies for water companies amounted to a maximum of 95% of the total cost of the projects. In the period 2014-2020, subsidies for water companies have been somewhat reduced, and they can range from 50-80% of the total cost of a project, depending on the size of the enterprise's service area. In the case of water companies with a service area between 200-2000 inhabitants, the support rate for projects is up to 80%, and for larger service areas (more than 2,000 inhabitants), water companies can receive support up to 50% of the total value of the investment. Water companies operating in service areas with the population of less than 200, do not qualify for support.

In the event that water tariffs do not cover the enterprise's actual costs or the water company's efficiency is low, water companies can also receive subsidies from local governments. As water companies in Lithuania are national monopolies, subsidies granted to them are not considered state aid.

Local authorities are drawing up and confirming plans for developing drinking water and wastewater infrastructure. These plans, among other things, determine which areas should be covered by the public water supply and in which areas the service must be provided by local authorities (so-called 95% consumer coverage).

At the beginning of 2020, the Ministry of Environment collected information from municipalities and drinking water supply and wastewater treatment companies on the current need for funds. The survey showed that the need for municipal funds for various activities in the water management sector in this sector amounts to EUR 127.17 million. An Investment Plan for the Lithuanian Water Management Sector is currently being prepared, which aims to more accurately assess the financial needs of the water management sector.

Table 1.6. Levels of investments for WSS (2017-2019)

Capital Investment in WSS (million EUR)	2017	2018	2019
National budget (or government organizations)	0.7	1	0.9
IFIs, EU and donors	15.4	30.8	42.5

In 2019, EUR 103.4 million was invested in drinking water supply and wastewater treatment infrastructure, of which 40 percent was allocated from the EU Structural Funds. Investments were made to develop services, increase quality of services, security of supply, etc.

During the financial periods 2007-2013 and 2014-2020, municipalities were able to benefit from European Union investments. In order to solve the problem of connecting the population to centralized wastewater management systems, the Ministry of Environment in 2017–2018 allocated EUR 2.35 million a grant to municipalities from the Environmental Protection Support Program and 2018–2019. EUR 4.2 million from the Lithuanian Environmental Investment Fund (hereinafter - LEIF) to finance the construction of sewage networks up to the dwellings of the population. The Water Management Fund (hereinafter - VF), financed from the Cohesion Fund, was established in 2018. VF provides soft loans together with a repayment subsidy to water management companies for the development of wastewater collection networks in agglomerations > 2000 p.e. (population equivalent). It is planned that fund will continue to provide loans for public service providers.

1.4.8. WSS pricing

Lithuanian water companies can make a profit, but prices for services are regulated and based on the principle that all costs must be covered by water tariffs. The reasonable profitability of water companies is calculated in Lithuania, applying the reasonable cost of capital on regulatory asset base (RAB), when the reasonable cost of capital equals the weighted average cost of capital (WACC). As stated earlier, the necessary costs, depreciation, and profits are taken into account when determining water tariffs. Despite the inclusion of depreciation costs, it is not possible to take into account at today's water tariff the depreciation costs of assets financed by EU funds. The calculation of the corresponding depreciation costs would increase the average price of drinking water and sewage by 18%.

In Lithuania, the water price is calculated using the nationally approved pricing methodology approved by the European Commission. The Water Law states that water tariffs must be based on two principles: "polluter pays" and "full coverage of costs by water tariffs." The Lithuanian National Regulatory Commission will ensure that these principles are taken into account when setting the water tariff.

In Lithuania, a water company is not allowed to differentiate the price based on the location of the consumer. However, it is possible to set different prices by customer segments.

1.4.9. Social consequences of water tariffs

Affordability of water tariffs is monitored. According to the Law of the Republic of Lithuania on Drinking Water Supply and Wastewater Management, after setting new prices, the amount paid by consumers each month for drinking water supply and / or wastewater treatment services should not exceed 4 percent of the average monthly family income. The State Energy Regulatory Council when adjusting the base prices of drinking water supply and sanitation services, recalculates the base prices of drinking water supply and sanitation services annually, assesses whether the monthly price paid by consumers will exceed 4 percent monthly family income. In cases where price for service exceeds 4 percent of the average monthly family income the SERC may require the submit a plan setting out specific actions how the costs of services should be reduced that the amount paid by consumers for its drinking water supply and sanitation services does not exceed 4 percent of the average monthly family income.

In Lithuania, drinking and wastewater costs account for 1.7% of the average household member's net income (varying from 1.24% to 5% for different segments of the population). If the water price exceeds 4% of the net income of the household, the water company must submit to the Commission a plan on how to get the price of the water under 4%.

1.4.10. Lessons from previous attempts with agglomeration of utilities

In Lithuania, there are no mandatory requirements for the development of regional water companies. At the same time, the Union of Lithuanian Water Companies points out that the merging of water companies would help keep water tariffs at the current level or even lower.

The goals set by the state are to reduce the differences in the prices of centrally provided drinking water supply and wastewater treatment services in municipalities, to ensure the implementation of national and EU obligations (to provide quality drinking water supply and wastewater treatment services to the population) and to achieve greater efficiency (reduce operating costs, change cost structure, implement the principle of cost recovery) and to enhance sustainability of the sector.

The Ministry of Environment, implementing the Program of the Government of the Republic of Lithuania approved in 2017 and Objective 4 of the Water Development Program for 2017–2023 - "to increase the efficiency of drinking water supply and wastewater treatment companies, improve the quality of services provided" - developed a model aimed at consolidation of water utilities to achieve operational efficiency (reduce operating costs), change the cost structure, fully implement the principle of cost recovery, reduce inequalities in service prices in municipalities, improve the quality and accessibility of services and the implementation of the environmental requirements and goals set by the state. The model was prepared in accordance with the report "Lithuanian Drinking Water Supply and Wastewater Management Company Management Improvement Plan".

The key objectives pursued of WSS consolidation in Lithuania are:

- to enhance sustainability of WSS services in the country;
- to ensure higher operational efficiency;
- to reduce the disparity in prices for WSS services.

Three pairs of municipalities are considering consolidation of their water utilities. In all cases, these are neighbouring, contiguous municipalities; each pair consists of a stronger company (regional leader) and a weaker one. Reorganization by consolidation would reorganize municipality-owned companies that are financially weak (failing to meet national and EU obligations, failing to achieve efficiency criteria, incurring losses in drinking water supply and wastewater treatment activities) by merging them with financially strong companies. It is planned to reorganize companies that have voluntarily submitted applications to participate in the reorganization process. Such companies would be eligible for funding from the Water Fund, from which companies could receive loans and grants at a very favourable rate. It is planned to amend the Law on Water Supply and Wastewater Management.

In essence, a larger, more capable company joins a small company, takes over its responsibilities and rights, serves the existing customers of that company, invests, expands the infrastructure and services throughout the territory served by the consolidated companies.

To date, the law provides for the possibility for municipalities to voluntarily merge (consolidate) water companies. Experience shows that such a consolidation is practically non-existent, only Klaipeda city and district companies have joined. At the moment, AB "Klaipėdos vanduo" provides services in the city and district municipalities. That voluntary consolidation of Klaipeda city and Klaipėda district water management companies provides a useful reference. After the reorganisation, the tariff of services for urban residents slightly increased, while for the district, the tariff decreased by almost 50%. Currently, the company is financially sustainable and invests in the district. UAB "Vilniaus vandenys" is the largest water utility in Lithuania. It is owned by four municipalities, where it operates.

With the introduction of a more favourable EU funding mechanism, more municipalities are interested in consolidating water management companies.

A reform of the water sector is currently being proposed, which will encourage the consolidation of companies, monitor their performance more closely and take timely action if companies fail to meet their obligations to ensure high-quality and uninterrupted provision of essential drinking water and wastewater services. It is planned to promote the consolidation of water management companies through the Water Management Fund (for companies that will carry out consolidation actions, to apply an attractive ratio of preferential loans to repayable subsidies).

Another effective means of ensuring the quality of water management services and promoting operational efficiency is the licensing of companies. Therefore, it is planned to amend the Law on Water Supply and Wastewater Management by establishing:

- additional licensing criteria - number of users, service development (to perform a certain percentage of development within a certain period of time), infrastructure renewal (to allocate a certain percentage of the company's turnover for renewal), financial licensing criteria;
- a new mechanism of the guarantee water supplier, i.e. instead of the currently guaranteed drinking water supplier (director of the municipal administration), if the company's operating license were suspended or revoked, the functions of the guaranteed drinking water supplier would be performed by the strongest company operating in the region;

- pricing measures for transitional period, i.e. the price of the consolidated companies would not be equalized immediately, but after a certain period, for example after 3 years; efficiency measures would be implemented in the weaker company during that time. A higher return on investment was set for the regional company to meet the increased investment needs. Separate pricing for subscribers (consolidated companies) should be considered, so that during the reorganization of consolidated companies, industrial enterprises would not have a financial incentive to disconnect from centralised infrastructure and supply water, treat wastewater individually.

The main challenges associated with implementation of WSS consolidation in Lithuania are the lack of motivation and willingness to implement the proposed reform (consolidation of water management companies).

Municipalities consider that they will have less influence in the management of consolidated water company as the decisions will have to be coordinated among at least two municipalities. Also there are fears that part of employees will have to leave consolidated water utility. The fact that tariff will likely increase for the consumers of the stronger water utility is politically sensitive. Also the strong water utility will bear additional financial burdens for implementation of necessary actions in the territory of former financially weak water utility.

1.5. Suggestions for further work

Background information on the state of play and preliminary understanding of concerns about its sustainability and pending issues help characterise a list of topics that deserve further attention, as they can support reforms that effectively encourage agglomeration of water utilities and put water supply and sanitation services in Lithuania on a sustainable basis.

The proposed topics for further investigation are listed below. This list is destined to ignite a discussion with Lithuanian authorities and stakeholders. A fine-tuned programme of work in the context of this project will unfold, in line with the detailed project description and with the experience and ambition of Lithuanian counterparts.

A preliminary list of topics for further analysis includes:

- Make the case for change. Explain that business as usual is not an option and the national and local governments and water users will be affected by the unsustainable management and operation of WSS services.
- Consider a range of options for agglomeration, which are flexible and can adjust to local contexts. They are not based on geographical scale only. They may vary according to functions (planning; programming expenditure; technical skills; relationship with users; billing and tariff collection).
- Address practical issues to expedite consolidation, using an example of 1-2 pilot regions (to be selected in consultations with the Ministry of Environment)
- Further strengthen the role and capacities of the economic regulator. This would cover WSS tariff setting as a policy instrument to drive investment and utilities' performance; benchmarking the performance of utilities on multiple relevant dimensions. The strengthening would explore options regarding the status, skills and governance of the economic regulator.
- Clarify and address other regulatory and legal issues related to asset ownership. Explore options to transfer ownership to entities operating at larger geographical scales, or to combine local ownership with operation at larger geographical scales.

Annex 1.A. Operational and financial performance of WSS operators (2019)

Annex Table 1.A.1. Indicators of operation and financial performance

Municipality	Water Company/ Operator	Cost Coverage Ratio 3	Total Debt (short term +long term liabilities) / Revenues	Non- Revenue Water 4	CAPEX / Total Costs 5
Kauno c. mun.	Kauno vandenys	92,22%	21,85%	26,37%	60,47%
Klaipėda c. mun.	Klaipėdos vanduo	94,96%	52,16%	16,08%	78,04%
Vilnius c. mun.	Vilniaus vandenys	100,73%	45,37%	16,34%	86,33%
Alytus c. mun.	Dzūkijos vandenys	125,61%	58,13%	19,65%	63,84%
Marijampolė mun.	Sūduvos vandenys	86,98%	34,90%	35,39%	69,40%
Panevėžys c. mun.	Aukštaitijos vandenys	92,65%	53,68%	15,94%	14,46%
Šiauliai c. sav.	Šiaulių vandenys	117,78%	104,17%	15,03%	108,13%
Mažeikiai c. mun.	Mažeikių vandenys	92,57%	53,61%	29,95%	51,88%
Utena c. mun.	Utenos vandenys	105,48%	51,12%	7,31%	76,06%
Druskininkai sav.	Druskininkų vandenys	98,13%	51,73%	15,21%	113,50%
Kėdainiai d.mun.	Kėdainių vandenys	99,59%	68,39%	28,40%	33,92%
Palanga c. mun.	Palangos vandenys	104,28%	12,38%	22,27%	12,80%
Pasvalys c. mun.	Pasvalio vandenys	97,64%	78,25%	31,58%	112,41%
Kaišiadorys c. mun.	Kaišiadorių vandenys	93,42%	70,47%	26,43%	-40,01%
Rokiškis c. mun.	Rokiškio vandenys	118,29%	99,79%	18,88%	97,64%
Šilutė c. mun.	Šilutės vandenys	102,95%	106,89%	20,97%	36,79%
Ukmergė c. mun.	Ukmergės vandenys	95,50%	18,79%	23,34%	27,05%
Telšiai d. sav.	Telšių vandenys	95,70%	95,34%	22,83%	112,57%
Jonava c. mun.	Jonavos vandenys	99,91%	70,88%	19,51%	129,79%
Kaunas c. mun.	Giraitės vandenys	99,70%	76,62%	25,08%	205,01%
Plungė c. mun.	Plungės vandenys	87,40%	56,90%	22,20%	64,18%
Tauragė c. mun.	Tauragės vandenys	94,67%	63,51%	22,45%	-35,30%
Jurbarkas c. mun.	Jurbarko vandenys	97,70%	13,43%	21,24%	-10,58%
Kretinga c. mun.	Kretingos vandenys	93,28%	45,24%	37,57%	11,90%
Radviliškis c. mun.	Radviliškio vanduo	99,95%	30,13%	23,54%	-36,34%
Raseiniai c. mun.	Raseinių vandenys	91,69%	57,71%	34,73%	137,45%
Šakiai c. mun.	Šakių vandenys	108,12%	49,70%	32,73%	-63,19%
Trakai c. mun.	Trakų vandenys	109,55%	76,77%	41,60%	7,35%
Varėna c. mun.	Varėnos vandenys	109,67%	134,09%	27,34%	41,47%
Vilkaviškis c. mun.	Vilkaviškio vandenys	139,58%	40,81%	23,95%	7,66%
Prienai c. mun.	Prienų vandenys	102,36%	29,42%	21,77%	79,86%

Anykščiai c. mun.	Anykščių vandenys	124,13%	65,23%	20,36%	27,98%
Birštonas sav.	Birštono vandentiekis	86,83%	13,39%	20,32%	23,29%
Šilalė c. mun.	Šilalės vandenys	105,89%	87,61%	22,21%	144,58%
Joniškis c. mun.	Joniškio vandenys	103,29%	78,36%	28,36%	97,88%
Kupiškis c. mun.	Kupiškio vandenys	114,11%	56,95%	51,75%	18,42%
Molėtai c. mun.	Molėtų vanduo	105,41%	125,12%	19,31%	36,46%
Neringa mun.	Neringos vanduo	96,49%	9,70%	20,26%	-8,72%
Pakruojis c. mun.	Pakruojo vandentiekis	93,33%	105,61%	16,05%	123,82%
Širvintos c. mun.	Širvintų vandenys	96,56%	74,03%	15,42%	14,77%
Skuodas c. mun.	Skuodo vandenys	105,77%	117,95%	40,94%	-18,83%
Zarasai c. mun.	Zarasų vandenys	98,46%	59,12%	20,46%	51,06%
Ignalina c. mun.	Ignalinos vanduo	105,61%	43,74%	42,99%	3,60%
Biržai c. mun.	Biržų vandenys	107,60%	8,85%	37,49%	-74,13%
Akmenė c. mun.	Akmenės vandenys	99,30%	41,38%	10,99%	-3,41%
Kelmė c. mun.	Kelmės vanduo	99,48%	1081,72%	29,74%	82,55%
Šiauliai disc. mun.	Kuršėnų vandenys	129,39%	73,38%	43,40%	34,73%
Lazdijai c. mun.	Lazdijų vanduo	100,44%	94,43%	29,63%	450,93%

Annex 1.B. Population forecast by region

Annex Table 1.B.1. Population forecast by 2028 and 2050

Region	Municipality	Population 2018 year	Population 2028 year	Change, per cent,. 2028 year	Population 2050 year	Change, per cent,. 2028 year
Alytus reg.	Alytus c. mun.	51534	39897	-23	17130	-67
	Alytus disc. mun.	26077	23279	-11	20791	-20
	Druskininkai mun.	19605	16635	-15	12164	-38
	Lazdijai disc. mun.	19115	14686	-23	5508	-71
	Varėna disc. mun.	21764	16700	-23	6555	-70
Kaunas reg.	Birštonas mun.	4168	3621	-13	2929	-30
	Jonava disc. mun.	42052	35487	-16	26248	-38
	Kaišiadorys disc. mun.	30257	25176	-17	17066	-44
	Kaunas c. mun.	288363	250514	-13	204600	-29
	Kaunas disc. mun.	92644	101649	10	151938	64
	Kėdainiai disc. mun.	46626	36250	-22	16187	-65
	Prienai disc. mun.	26492	21908	-17	14188	-46
	Raseiniai disc. mun.	32510	25764	-21	12880	-60
Klaipėda reg.	Klaipėda c. mun.	148908	131140	-12	111341	-25
	Klaipėda disc. mun.	56131	61992	10	94633	69
	Kretinga disc. mun.	37945	33214	-12	27705	-27
	Neringa mun.	3224	4136	28	7660	138
	Palanga c. mun.	15381	15073	-2	17790	16
	Šilutė disc. mun.	38749	30169	-22	13264	-66
	Skuodas disc. mun.	16914	11700	-31	194	-99
Marijampolė reg.	Kalvarija mun.	10776	9077	-16	6305	-41
	Kazlų Rūda mun.	11764	9931	-16	6973	-41
	Marijampolė mun.	54600	45380	-17	30180	-45
	Šakiai disc. mun.	28039	21972	-22	9987	-64
	Vilkaviškis disc. mun.	36108	27443	-24	9233	-74
Panevėžys reg.	Biržai disc. mun.	23778	17780	-25	5097	-79
	Kupiškis disc. mun.	17097	12748	-25	3573	-79
	Panevėžys c. mun.	88678	74375	-16	50081	-44
	Panevėžys disc. mun.	35734	31311	-12	26434	-26
	Pasvalys disc. mun.	23967	17992	-25	5404	-77
	Rokiškis disc. mun.	29472	22059	-25	6472	-78
Šiauliai reg.	Akmenė disc. mun.	19606	14377	-27	3385	-83
	Joniškis disc. mun.	21583	15240	-29	1167	-95
	Kelmė disc. mun.	26778	18815	-30	1138	-96

	Pakruojis disc. mun.	19546	13767	-30	956	-95
	Radviliškis disc. mun.	36170	27389	-24	9703	-73
	Šiauliai c. mun.	100575	87485	-13	72956	-27
	Šiauliai disc. mun.	41209	36367	-12	32812	-20
Tauragė reg.	Jurbarkas disc. mun.	26043	20320	-22	9016	-65
	Pagėgiai mun.	7793	5433	-30	61	-99
	Šilalė disc. mun.	23060	18577	-19	10122	-56
	Tauragė disc. mun.	38921	32306	-17	21235	-45
Telšiai reg.	Mažeikiai disc. mun.	52208	44222	-15	31717	-39
	Plungė disc. mun.	33707	27932	-17	17866	-47
	Rietavas mun.	7542	5936	-21	2866	-62
	Telšiai disc. mun.	40682	32071	-21	15291	-62
Utena reg.	Anykščiai disc. mun.	24149	17942	-26	4786	-80
	Ignalina disc. mun.	15366	11089	-28	1896	-88
	Molėtai disc. mun.	17856	13928	-22	6195	-65
	Utena disc. mun.	37914	30561	-19	17278	-54
	Visaginas mun.	18686	13052	-30	1033	-94
	Zarasai disc. mun.	15668	11934	-24	4284	-73
Vilnius reg.	Elektrėnai mun.	23724	21778	-8	21880	-8
	Šalčininkai disc. mun.	31265	26472	-15	19575	-37
	Širvintos disc. mun.	15570	12639	-19	7769	-50
	Švenčionys disc. mun.	23881	18193	-24	6781	-72
	Trakai disc. mun.	32492	29596	-9	28698	-12
	Ukmergė disc. mun.	34376	26295	-24	10378	-70
	Vilnius c. mun.	547484	566590	3	750683	37
	Vilnius disc. mun.	96575	97366	1	123703	28

Annex 1.C. Questionnaire for data collection on the state of play

Legislation, institutional and regulatory framework

1. Please briefly describe the key pieces of legislation (e.g. water law/code, acts defining WSS assets ownership) and the regulatory framework (e.g. water quality standards, permitting/licensing) for WSS services provision.

2. Is the WSS services consolidation envisaged in the legal or regulatory frameworks? If yes, is it a mandatory or voluntary process, please describe the mandatory provisions and the legal forms that consolidation may take place.

3. Which institutions are in charge of setting WSS policies, development planning?

4. Characterise the main priorities (access in cities; access in rural areas; health or environmental standards; quality of service; adaptation to climate change; energy efficiency; connection to existing infrastructures; else).

5. Characterise the main drivers for change
   - Demographic trends since 2000; projections to 2030, or 2050; regional disparities; urban/rural; trends in size of households, ageing;
   - GDP growth since 2000; projections for the next 5 years.

The organisation of service provision

6. Which institution is accountable for service provision (central government; municipalities; other)? Has the WSS assets ownership been transferred from the central governments to municipalities? When? To what extent?

7. How is service provided?
   - Please describe WSS services provision at local level. Please describe modalities of inter-municipal cooperation for WSS provision (e.g. agreements on cooperation between municipalities) if it takes place.
   - Role and status of utilities, public or private (e.g. what legal forms (delegation, lease, management contracts) it can take between municipalities and water companies). In case of municipal public utility for WSS - are revenues from water supply and sanitation service earmarked for water-related expenditure only? Or any share of revenues accrue to other types of expenditures at local level?

8. How many municipalities exist in Lithuania? Changes since 2010 (any trend towards consolidation)?
   - Please provide a map of municipalities in Lithuania
   - Population by municipality.

9. How many entities/utilities provide services for water supply? For sanitation? Changes since 2010 (any trend towards consolidation)? Are there any municipalities with 2 or more WSS utilities?

The performance of service providers

10. Who sets objectives for service quality (e.g. continuity)?

11. How is performance measured (key indicators) and monitored

12. Has the oversight of utility performance been a responsibility of central or local governments (municipalities)? Report any major change in the devolution of responsibility over the last 5-10 years/ or planned reforms in this area. Is an independent regulator involved in setting targets, monitoring performance, benchmarking service providers?

Tariff setting

13. Have a specific/dedicated tariff regulation for WSS services (or WSS and other communal services) been adopted in Lithuania? When? By which part of the government?

14. Please describe the WSS tariff regulation process.

15. Have professional regulatory bodies regulating tariffs for WSS services (or WSS and other communal services) been established? When? What is their status vis-à-vis the government?

16. Please describe the access (if any) to water utility data, potential gaps in monitoring water utilities performance.

17. Are public budget subsidies envisaged to compensate water utilities for difference between tariff and cost?

18. Has an affordability check become a part of the tariff setting procedure for WSS? Please provide the information on the recent affordability ratio for different municipalities (if available).

19. How do water users participate in tariff revision (public hearings, consultations)?

20. How is information collected and shared, on the performance of service providers, and tariffs for services?

Inter-agency co-ordination and cooperation for WSS service provision

Please briefly describe and provide information on the following items.

21. Institutions in charge of designing and implementing policies that affect water supply and wastewater management (departments in charge of Health; Environment; Urban development; Infrastructure; Investment and finance; else).

22. Arrangements in place for co-ordination and co-operation among the institutions listed above.

23. Arrangements in place for ensuring effective multilevel governance (co-ordination and co-operation among different levels of government) involved in policies that affect drinking water supply and wastewater management (authorities at national, local or other sub-national levels, such as catchments or river basins).

Mapping WS service coverage and recent trends in service provision

24. Volume of drinking water produced and wastewater collected, treated (by municipality).

25. Share of the population with access to safe water and sanitation by municipality? Please describe distinction between urban/rural areas.

26. Age of assets and main periods for the construction of existing networks for water supply? For sanitation?

27. Rate of water losses and recent trends.

28. Please provide information on regional and social differences or disparities in WSS services provision:

- regional disparities: e.g. access, challenges, state of the infrastructure, performance
- social disparities: e.g. access, affordability; lack of access to water supply and sanitation services, wastewater and rainwater collection and treatment.

WSS strategic policy making and financing water supply and sanitation

29. Please describe roles and responsibilities for WSS strategic development and investment programming in Lithuania.

30. Please indicate and summarise strategic planning documents (e.g. national financing strategies) for the WSS sector in Lithuania. Are these plans backed by financing strategies? If yes, please characterise these financing plans:

- Investment needs, now and in the future
- Projected sources of finance (share of revenues from water tariffs; domestic public funds; EU financial support; else).
- Please describe public budget allocations to the WSS sector (if any). Are budget transfers from national governments earmarked for water supply and sanitation services?

31. If inter-municipal cooperation/aggregation of WSS services was considered in these documents, please describe key recommendations or planned actions. Is the WSS consolidation incentivized? If yes, please explain how?

32. Please characterise past (factual) WSS financing since 2000, and provide more specific information for the last 3 years:

- Levels of investment

Annex Table 1.C.1. Capital Investment in WSS

Capital Investment in WSS (million EUR)	2017	2018	2019
Total investment			
Total investment in fixed assets for WSS			
as % of GDP			
Total investment in fixed assets for water supply			
Total investment in fixed assets for sanitation			
Sources of finance			
Public budget, total			
National budget (or government organizations)			
Regional budget			
Municipal budget			
IFIs, EU and donors6			
Water utilities own funds			
Private sources, total (incl. private operators)			

- Operation and maintenance costs (total)
- Any dedicated mechanism (such as a national water/environment/climate fund) in place or considered?

Experience with consolidation of municipalities and/or service providers

33. What are the key objectives pursued of WSS consolidation in Lithuania (e.g. improvement of service provision, financial sustainability, economic efficiency, capacity, environmental benefits; else)?

34. Has consolidation/aggregation of municipalities already been considered for implementation of the EU Water Directives? If yes, how did it influence service provision, investment and WSS tariffs in those municipalities?

35. What are the key drivers and objectives pursued by WSS consolidation in Lithuania, e.g. improvement of service provision, financial sustainability, economic efficiency, capacity, and environmental benefits?

36. Please describe key dimensions of consolidation under consideration, or already taking place:
    - Geographical scale (administrative, watershed or regional boundaries)
    - Functional scale (investment and service coverage; operation and maintenance; administration & customer relationships)
    - Scope of service provision (provision of raw water; water supply; wastewater collection; wastewater treatment; pluvial and storm water collection; else)

37. Please describe:
    - The potential for WSS consolidation in Lithuania
    - Possible scenarios (from a legal, financial, technical, social or political perspectives)
    - The main challenges associated with implementation of WSS consolidation in Lithuania.

Operational and financial performance of WSS operators

Please provide information by municipality/service provider (2019 or most recent year).

Annex Table 1.C.2. Indicators of operational and financial performance

Municipality	Water Company/ Operator	Cost Coverage Ratio[7]	Total Debt (short term +long term liabilities) / Revenues	Non- Revenue Water[8]	CAPEX/ Total Costs
XX	...	%	%	%	%
...					

Please provide information on WSS tariffs rates, revenues from user charges and affordability ratio (2019 or most recent year).

Annex Table 1.C.3. WSS tariffs, revenues and affordability ratio

Municipality	Water Company/ Operator	Household WSS tariff, applied by water operator	WSS tariff for other consumer (EUR/m3 on average)	WSS tariff collection rate for households	Revenue from user charges (households) EUR	Revenue from user chargers (other	Affordability9 for households (if estimated)

		(EUR/m3, on average)				consumers) EUR	
XX	…			%			%
…							

In 2017-2020 what was the level of public operational subsidies* to the utilities providing WSS services? (if relevant)

Annex Table 1.C.4. Public budget subsidies

WSS, EUR	2017	2018	2019
Public operational subsidies to water utilities*			

Notes

[1] Note that this assessment does not reflect the amortisation of investments that was covered by EU funding, which is a predominant share of the total capital expenditure of the sector in Lithuania. See below.

[2] Evaluated during the study carried out by economists (Lithuanian Drinking Water Supply and Wastewater Management Company Management Improvement Plan)

[3] Cost coverage ratio: visos sąnaudos / visos pajamos;

[4] Unaccounted for water: (amount of groundwater extracted - amount of drinking water sold - amount of water consumed through hydrants for firefighting) / amount of groundwater extracted * 100;

[5] The Council does not collect CAPEX data for the performance of its functions, the indicators are calculated according to the formula: ((residual value of fixed assets in 2019 - residual value of fixed assets in 2018 + depreciation of fixed assets in 2019) / total costs), estimating preliminary data provided by enterprises.

[6] Please specify if development finance is channelled through public budgets, to avoid double counting

[7] Defined as the share of total costs covered by revenues

[8] Defined as the share of water that is losses through leakages + bills that are not recovered

[9] Defined as a share of disposal income

2 Summary of the kick-off meeting

A kick-off meeting was convened, to inform stakeholders about the dialogue, its ambition and the working method. The agenda was designed to build a momentum and appetite for next steps.

2.1. General Overview

The Ministry of the Environment of Lithuania, jointly with other governmental authorities and stakeholders, the European Commission DG Reform, and the OECD are partnering to enhance the sustainability of water supply and sanitation services in Lithuania.

The kick-off meeting was co-convened by Lithuanian authorities and the OECD Secretariat, on 18 February 2021, as a virtual meeting. The aim was to discuss the findings of the background report (Chapter 1) and the priorities for the remainder of the project. It was structured around four Agenda items (see Annex A).

The meeting was chaired by Mr Vitalijus Auglys from the Ministry of Environment of Lithuania. It gathered more than 150 delegates from national and local authorities, water utilities, the Lithuanian water utility association, and international participants from the EC (DG Reform) and the OECD Secretariat (see Annex B for List of Participants).

This note captures the main messages of the meeting on the state of play of the water supply and sanitation (WSS) sector reform, OECD analysis and official and expert opinions expressed at the meeting.

2.2. Agenda Item 1: Opening and Welcoming Remarks

Mr. Darius Kvedaravičius, vice Minister of Environment of Lithuania, welcomed participants. He provided a brief overview of the most recent experience with the water policy reform in Lithuania and emphasised the importance of WSS consolidation as one of the mechanisms to enhance sustainability of the sector. The approach still needs to be tested in pilot regions to explore potential benefits of consolidation. Such an analysis will facilitate the policy discussion in the coming months.

Mr. Kaspar Richter, Head of Unit, DG Reform, welcomed participants of the meeting. Mr Richter underlined the value of cooperation programmes in different environment related areas and mentioned other ongoing DG Reform initiatives for Lithuania on climate neutrality and digitalisation.

2.3. Agenda Item 2: The state of play in the WSS sector of Lithuania

Mr. Xavier Leflaive, OECD, presented the project purpose, the importance of and mechanisms for collaboration with national experts and stakeholders in the course of project implementation, and key project milestones and timeline.

Ms. Indrė Musviciene, State Energy Regulatory Council, shared the experience with application of the WSS tariff methodology and the accompanying approval procedure. The presentation highlighted the role of utility performance monitoring and mid-term investment planning to encourage optimal technical solutions.

Ms. Agnė Kniežaitė-Gofmanė, Ministry of Environment, shared the vision for the sector development, including aspects related to:

- compliance with the EU legislation in long term
- tariff policy and related affordability concerns
- the role of licencing and monitoring of utility performance
- stepwise voluntary consolidation of WSS service provision.

Mr. Bronius Miežutavičius, Water Utility Association, signalled the need to reflect proper amortisation costs in the tariff formula, taking into consideration that the purchasing power in Lithuania is low. Mr.

Miežutavičius suggested that the difference in water prices across the country (from 2.2 EUR/m3 to 4 EUR/m3) called for further strengthening of tariff regulation to enhance cost-efficiency.

Mr. Ričardas Leckas, UAB Elektrėnų komunalinis ūkis, commented on the need to strengthen costs management of utilities. It is topical to support the sector modernisation. Also in the context of the requirements to introduce new wastewater treatment technologies, there might be a need to consider stepwise approach to minimise the risk of environmental taxes in case of non-compliance.

A representative from the Kauno rajono savivaldybes administracija signalled that consolidation is a complex issue, which requires a careful analysis of every cost item, to make sure the expected benefits materialise.

2.4. Agenda Item 3: Towards sustainable WSS in Lithuania: policy issues

Ms. Tatiana Efimova, OECD, shared the key findings of the Background report. The presentation is appended.

The discussion highlighted:

- A massive investment programme implemented to comply with the EU Water Directives in Lithuania. However, financing challenges remain, associated with further needs to build new or rebuild existing assets
- Performance monitoring is critical to evaluate sector policies and programmes. Performance is not systematically benchmarked across utilities in Lithuania, though some elements are in place, in relation to licensing and tariff regulation
- The cost of replacing decaying assets is not properly reflected in the tariff-setting process. Most utilities are unable to generate the revenues to renew and upgrade existing infrastructure financed by EU funds
- Ms. Indrė Musvicienė, State Energy Regulatory Council, confirmed the need to develop an optimal methodology to calculate depreciation. Along the same line, Mr. Bronius Miežutavičius, Water Utility Association, confirmed that the prevailing methodology for WSS tariff setting does not provide revenues for the modernisation and maintenance of existing assets, affecting the financial sustainability of water companies.

Issues related to incentives for consolidation of service providers were discussed. Representative of regional operators confirmed the benefits of consolidation for rural areas to secure WSS service. Local authorities recognised the need to systematically explore opportunities for inter-municipal cooperation but noted a general lack of trust, which prevents a bigger cooperation.

Participants took note and endorsed the suggestions for further work under the project:

a) *Zoom-in on the issues* affecting sustainability of WSS services in Lithuania

b) *Address practical issues to expedite consolidation, using an example of 1-2 pilot regions*

c) *Advance the role for the economic regulator for WSS:* i) set and enforce performance targets; ii) assess the opportunity and efficiency of expenditure programmes; and iii) set tariffs as policy instruments to reap economies of scale, drive investment and performance.

2.5. Agenda Item 4: Next steps and priorities for the coming period

Mr. Darius Kvedaravičius, vice Minister of Environment of Lithuania, summarised the priorities for the next steps, including assessment of potential risks associated with consolidation, and possible solutions. He also stressed the need to work towards a bigger trust and cooperation between municipalities to ensure effective service provision. Mr. Kvedaravičius expressed the hope that the following project activities will help to identify the steps to accelerate WSS consolidation and develop necessary policy recommendations.

Mr, Vitalijus Auglys, the Ministry of Environment, thanked participants for their participation, and closed the meeting.

Annex 2.A. Agenda

Kick-off Meeting

Thursday 18 February 2021 (14:00h-16:30h, Vilnius time) via ZOOM

The meeting will be chaired by Vitalijus Auglys, Ministry of Environment of Lithuania

14:00 ~ 14:15

Item 1. Welcome and Adoption of the Agenda

- Welcome by the vice Minister of Environment of Lithuania (Mr Darius Kvedaravičius)
- Welcome by DG REFORM (Mr. Kaspar RICHTER, Head of Unit, DG REFORM)
- Adoption of the Agenda

14:15 ~ 14:45

Item 2. The state of play in the WSS sector of Lithuania (led by the Ministry of Environment)

- Brief overview of the project (OECD)
- Brief overview of the WSS sector performance in Lithuania (State Energy Regulatory Council)
- Consolidation strategy of the WSS sector of Lithuania. (Agnė Kniežaitė-Gofmanė, Ministry of Environment of Lithuania)

Short interventions from representatives of municipal authorities and regional WSS operators.

Questions for clarification

14:45 ~ 16:15

Item 3. Towards sustainable WSS in Lithuania. Policy issues (led by OECD)

- Focused discussions on selected policy issues
    - Financial sustainability of utilities (financing needs and capacities, now and in the future; potential sources of finance)
    - Cost-effectiveness and performance of the sector (now and in the future)
    - Social issues (access; affordability of water bills)
- Options to expedite agglomeration of water utilities
- Selection a pilot region(s): ambition, criteria for selection. Short interventions of municipalities expressed the interest.
- Suggestions on further work under the project: milestones and key outputs

Discussion

16 :15 ~ 16:30

Item 4. Next steps and priorities for the coming period

Conclusions and a wrap up of the meeting

3 Issues paper

The issues paper builds on the background report compiled by Lithuanian authorities and discussions at the kick-off meeting. It lists key issues to be addressed in the roadmap implementation and the action plan for the consolidation of water utilities active in the pilot regions and nationally.

3.1. Background and objectives of the project

In Lithuania, the Law on Drinking Water Supply and Wastewater Treatment Services (2006, amended in 2014[1]) introduced the reform of the WSS sector and the concept of consolidation of water utilities on a voluntary basis. By 2019, it resulted in the creation of a regional water operator for the Klaipėda region and a reduced number of operating water companies (one company for one municipality). Reluctance of municipalities to consolidate their water companies remains one of the main obstacles for implementation of this reform.

The Government of Republic of Lithuania is working towards the enhanced sustainability of WSS services in the country. The Implementation Plan of the Government Programme[2] includes activities for the consolidation of the drinking water supply and wastewater treatment sector, to ensure higher operational efficiency and to reduce the disparity in prices for WSS services. A roadmap for consolidation of water companies was recently elaborated by the Government (2019). Modalities of the reform implementation, including options for consolidation of the water utility sector, have to be further considered and included into the proposal to the Government.

This Project will support the development of detailed recommendations for implementation of the roadmap for the consolidation of water utilities of Lithuania[3] including recommendations on financial and governance incentives to facilitate a broader water sector reform in the country. The expected impact of the Project will be a sustained capacity of consolidated utilities to finance needed investments to comply with EU acquis and deliver better services to the population, including segments who currently do not have access.

The main outcome will be enhanced self-financing capacity of water utilities and increased social equity in access to and prices for WSS services in Lithuania, through consolidation of service providers, robust tariff policy and adequate accompanying measures.

The issues paper builds on previous project outputs, namely the background report characterising the state of play[4], and the kick-off meeting[5], where the Government officially launched and announced the project and main stakeholders voiced their support and priorities. Its purpose is to focus further the discussions between the OECD Secretariat and Lithuanian stakeholders.

The paper lists key issues to be addressed in the recommendations for the roadmap implementation and the action plan for the consolidation of water utilities active in the pilot region. It builds on the following activities:

- A first round of interviews with stakeholders in Lithuania. The OECD Secretariat collects information on the main issues to be covered, and stakeholders' vision/perspectives;
- Selection of a pilot region or regions in consultation with the beneficiary. Interviews with the key players of the WSS sector in the pilot region(s) will be arranged at a later stage;
- Review of international experience with similar reforms. Further analyses are under way, to characterise lessons learned from these countries. Main lessons will be shared at an international workshop before the summer 2021.

3.2. Issues to be covered by the project

The list of issues below derives from the background report, which was endorsed by Lithuanian authorities. It resonates with the preliminary list of issues that feature in the Detailed Project Description, with adjustments that reflect information collected in the early stages of the project.

3.2.1. Make the case for change

Business as usual is not an option and national and local governments and water users will be affected by the unsustainable management and operation of WSS services in Lithuania. The background report provides ample evidence on:

- Additional work needed to secure access to safe water supply and safely managed sanitation services in Lithuania
- Additional drivers that affect future costs and revenues for WSS service provision (including climate change and demographics)
- Significant investment needs, to renew the massive assets that were built during the last few decades, often with EU financial support
- Limited financial capacities of service providers, which are too small to generate the revenues needed to operate and maintain existing assets
- Shortcomings in the tariff setting process and guidance, which inappropriately reflect amortisation (in particular of granted assets) and which are too low to generate the revenues needed to cover the operating costs of service providers
- Room for manoeuvre to bolster the operational efficiency of service providers and the economic effectiveness of development plans and expenditure programmes, considering opportunities for economies of scale and scope.

The rest of the project will build on this characterisation of the state of play to reiterate that the situation is not sustainable, and that consolidation is an appropriate option, when it helps to address some of the issues noted above, including opportunities for economies of scale and scope, options to enhance the efficiency and financial sustainability of service providers, now and in the future. The project will also claim that consolidation will only deliver if accompanied by a range of measures to address related issues, such as revising the tariff formula, and strengthening economic regulation of the sector.

3.2.2. Consider a range of options for agglomeration, which are flexible and can adjust to local contexts

At the moment, the vision of consolidation considered by Lithuanian authorities consists in a larger, more capable company joining one or several small companies, taking over responsibilities and rights, serving the existing customers of these companies, investing and expanding the infrastructure and services throughout the territory served by the consolidated companies.

Two pairs of municipalities are currently considering consolidation of their water utilities. In both cases, these are neighbouring, contiguous municipalities; each pair consists of a stronger company (regional leader) and a weaker one. Consolidation would reorganise municipality-owned companies that are financially weak (failing to meet national and EU obligations, failing to achieve efficiency criteria, incurring losses in drinking water supply and wastewater treatment activities) by merging them with financially strong companies.

The main incentives being considered to trigger voluntary consolidation is preferred access to cheap public finance. It is planned to reorganise companies that have voluntarily submitted applications to participate in the reorganization process. Such companies would be eligible for funding from the Water Fund, from which companies could receive loans and grants at a very favourable rate.

Such a vision is robust, but has proven ineffective to drive change. It could be enriched by:

- Considering a menu of options for consolidation: options do not need to be based on geographical scale only. They may vary according to functions (planning; programming expenditure; technical skills and maintenance; relationship with users; billing and tariff collection) and location (urban / rural).

- Exploring a range of incentives, in line with the priorities and concerns of municipalities and service providers in Lithuania.

This section sketches different options, which can inspire the consolidation process in Lithuania. Subsequent analyses and work in the context of this project will explore which options are best able to support and expedite consolidation of WSS services in Lithuania.

Scenarios for agglomeration of water services

Many OECD countries have aggregated (or are considering aggregating) small utilities to generate economies of scale and scope, and make the best use of central, piped infrastructures. Heavy investment costs and the phasing out of government subsidies have prompted local utilities to concentrate part or all of the tasks related to the provision and delivery of WSS services at upper levels of government (OECD, 2013a; see also Chapter 1 for selected illustrations).

In New Zealand, the amalgamation of several councils gave the Auckland Council the necessary scale to tackle issues that were previously beyond the capacity of individual councils. Since amalgamation, the Council has been able to accelerate the modernisation of the region's antiquated wastewater treatment systems, substantially upgrade its two key wastewater treatment plants and progress the NZL 950 million (New Zealand dollar) "central interceptor" project that will reduce overflows from the combined waste and stormwater system of the Auckland isthmus. In Korea, cities in the Gyeongnam province achieved cost efficiency by amalgamating urban water services (see Appendix).

Amalgamation eventually results in combining different services at different scales. France's Ile-de-France region has a three-tier management system: street sewers are municipal, interceptors and storm sewers are run by the counties (four departments) and sewage treatment is operated by a joint-county (almost regional-level) board.

Several countries have separated water or treated wastewater production and the delivery of the service to customers:

- In Boston, a metropolitan authority consolidates water production and sewage treatment, leaving member municipalities in charge of system management.
- In Portugal, the government created a national water company in 1994. Municipalities in the same area were offered the opportunity to manage treatment plants jointly, while communes kept responsibility for operating water and sewer mains.
- In Australia, the 1994 reform planned by the Council of Australian Governments mandated the unbundling of former urban water monopolies, with bulk water production and sewage treatment organised at the regional level (by one public company) and retail water services at a more local level (by several water distribution companies). This choice paved the way for alternative water supply technologies (e.g. recycling and desalination).

Rural sanitation offers yet a range of options[6]. For instance, localised wastewater management systems serve individual or small groups of properties. They can recover nutrients and energy, and can also be connected to local water supply and reuse technologies. They require less upfront investment than larger-scale, centrally piped infrastructures and are more effective at coping with the need to expand services. Various commentators suggest that they have a role to play in urban water management, even in major developed cities.

Localised WSS can be used to serve populations not connected to public systems. In Europe, the proportion of households not connected to sewers is higher in low-density or low-revenue countries or regions – e.g. Portugal and Spain, southern Italy and Greece, eastern European and Nordic countries,

Ireland and even some German Länder. In these areas, populations are not yet fully connected to public water systems. Ireland has officially kept a large number of grouped water schemes, providing water to 8% of the population at small community scales. Localised sanitation systems are not merely a remedy to the limited number of centrally piped systems. They are increasingly used in countries such as the United States, where on-site sanitation now comprises some 40% of all new developments. Sustainable neighbourhoods in cities are partly – or fully – replacing traditional public systems with decentralised technologies. Paradoxically, these innovations take place in the richer and higher-density European Union (EU) Member States.

The performance of localised systems can compare with that of centrally piped infrastructures. For instance, an evaluation of localised systems in Ireland shows that despite difficulties in meeting the standards now imposed at the European level, such schemes sometimes operate better than public water systems, and the population they serve is largely committed to keeping them. Innovation can contribute to improved performance of localised systems. Research is ongoing to provide communities reliant on individual and community systems with robust and simplified treatment systems, equipped with real-time information and communication technologies (ICTs, such as remote sensors), to help set up community services operated from distant centres.

These developments explain the renewed interest for localised, on-site sanitation. The Australian Academy of Technological Sciences and Engineering (ATSE), for example, recommends that Australian governments encourage investment and uptake of such systems.

An interesting development regards the scale at which localised, decentralised systems are best managed. The concept of a public service operating non-networked systems is a promising avenue. In France, the 5 million septic tanks currently in operation are now considered technologies that should be kept and upgraded. The implementation of the Urban Wastewater Directive led to a zoning of networked and non-networked areas, the latter being served (or at least controlled) by public services for decentralised sewerage (SPANC). Indeed, the collective management of decentralised technologies creates business opportunities for (public and private) utilities.

The scenarios above open a range of options for Lithuania to consider agglomeration. They suggest that mere agglomeration at higher geographical scales is one option; but others could be considered as well:

- Considering different scales for different functions of WSS services (water supply, wastewater collection and treatment; investment planning, operation and maintenance of services)
- Managing localised services (including individual sanitation) at a larger level. Several options could be considered, from merging, to coordinating local service provision through a public service; such a public service can cover a wide and diverse territory, focusing on localised sanitation only.

The different options can be assessed on multiple criteria, including:

- Opportunities to minimise cost (investment needs in infrastructure; operation and maintenance costs) and enhance financial sustainability of WSS
- Opportunities to mutualise skills (technical skills to operate and maintain assets; commercial skills to interact with users, including through billing)
- Opportunities to optimise performance (quality of service to users), now and in the future (sustainable service provision)
- Opportunities to strengthen monitoring and supervision (assessing development plans and expenditure programmes; monitoring performance of service providers).

Some of the options can work in combination, or in sequence, providing for a staged approach. Lessons learned at one stage can inform further developments on the road to agglomeration of WSS to the appropriate scale in Lithuania.

Incentives for local authorities to ignite change

Mobilising local authorities requires a clear case for the costs and benefits of the consolidation process. It also requires that a set of technical issues be tackled in pragmatic ways (see the next section). Intense consultation is a must, with multiple opportunities for local governments to voice their concern – and support – and comment on the roadmap, the incentives being considered and the responses to their queries. This project is designed to offer such opportunities.

As is currently the case in Lithuania, financial incentives mater. They are likely to be even more effective when:

- local authorities have a clear understanding of emerging issues related to WSS in the country, and their responsibility in cases of failure to deliver WSS services in the context of emerging challenges (see the previous section on Making the case),
- service providers understand that their operation is at risk if they cannot perform at the expected level (see the section below on the potential for economic regulation); and
- finance is scarce (in a context where EU funds for WSS will be gradually phased out).

The points above suggest that, in addition to financial incentives, national authorities can consider more diverse incentives to ignite change: setting performance targets for service provision, and monitoring compliance with rewards and sanctions based on performance; the licencing process can also drive change, if licence renewal is conditional on achieving set levels of performance or other criteria.

Additional support can take the form of practical guidance to facilitate agglomeration on the ground. This may include the following accompanying measures:

- Strengthening the role of county associations of municipalities, to support the creation of regional utilities
- Support to contractual arrangements between such associations and the regional utilities. Performance-based management contracts, whereby the revenues of the service provider are conditional to achieving set levels of investment or service, could be promoted
- Water Operators Partnerships (WOP) consisting of reputable operators. If regional utilities are large enough, operators could engaged in performance-based management contracts with the boards of the regional utilities for a transition period (possibly 2 years). Under such arrangements, the management of a regional utility would be temporarily delegated to the operator under the association's supervision. Partnerships with experienced operators is critical to develop and strengthen the newly formed organisations. The key objectives of the WOPs (or management contracts) would be to:
    - Support the organisation of regional utilities' management, through the identification, hiring and training of professionals and specialists for the central and support services
    - Strengthen the regional utilities' operational local branches through the introduction of common procedures
    - Help regional utilities implement the tariff policy.

At the end of the transition period, the regional utilities would be expected to manage the company efficiently, under the associations' supervision and according to the terms of the contracts.

Address practical issues to expedite consolidation, using an example of 1-2 pilot regions

The limited track-record of Lithuania with agglomeration of service providers for WSS suggests that a number of practical reasons can explain why a good idea does not necessarily materialise. These reasons can block initiatives towards consolidation, whatever, the intention of stakeholders and the incentives in place.

The Ministry of Environment selected two regions (Kaunas and Marijampolė) to pilot recommended actions towards consolidation.

Several issues relate to the transition period, when regional entities are set up:

- Acknowledging that in Lithuania, WSS tariffs vary across regions, which tariff should apply and should tariffs converge for all water users served by that entity? In Klaipeda - the region where a regional WSS operator was created - the tariff of services for urban residents slightly increased after the reorganisation, while for the district, the tariff decreased by almost 50%[7].
- In practice, reorganisation raises issues that relate to asset ownership. Acknowledging that, in Lithuania, the water utility owns the asset, what type of arrangement is required between a regional utility and local authorities, to either operate assets owned by local utilities (which will not directly operate these assets anymore) or transfer asset ownership to the regional utility? What kind of governance structure is then required, to ensure that local authorities keep some control over decisions related to the asset on which service delivery depends?

These issues can only be addressed through practical recommendations, which reflect the political sensitivities in Lithuania and comply with the existing legal and regulatory framework. Further work will inventory pending issues and will consider how they can be addressed in the context of the legal and regulatory framework in Lithuania. In-depth analysis of the two pilot regions will provide the empirical evidence and background for that work.

Other options may require amendments to prevailing legal and regulatory frameworks. Policy discussions will clarify the level of ambition for the reform.

3.2.3. Further strengthen the role and capacities of the economic regulator

The OECD argues economic regulation can play a significant role to enhance the performance of WSS service providers and driving a dynamics towards consolidation. In particular, economic regulation can contribute to:

- Setting WSS tariff as a policy instrument to drive investment and utilities' performance. The background report indicated that in Lithuania, WSS tariffs are very different from region to region[8]. This is considered an issue if differences reflect more than differences in the capital and operating costs of the service. Moreover, tariffs need to balance the need to raise additional revenues (in particular where population and water demand is decreasing) to ensure the financial sustainability of the service provider, and concerns for the affordability of water bills, in particular for poor households.
- Benchmarking the performance of utilities. In Lithuania, Water utilities' performance is measured and monitored by licenses. The licencing process provides some guidance on minimal requirement and capacities to operate water services; it identifies fours principles with which utilities must comply (security, reliability, efficiency, non-discrimination).

OECD work on the governance of economic regulators also indicates that there are different ways to discharge economic regulatory functions. The project will explore options regarding the status, skills and governance of the economic regulator for WSS in Lithuania.

Figure 3.1. The functions of economic regulation for WSS

Source: Authors.

Issue with tariff setting and depreciation of granted assets

The tariff methodology is a key part of economic regulation. In simple terms, independent economic regulation of WSS aims to ensure that customers receive the appropriate water service for the right price. *Appropriate* here refers to the combination of various objectives: economic (robust allocation of water and discouraging wastage), environmental (conservation of the resource), social (addressing affordability concerns) and financial (ensuring utilities' capacity to finance the operation of the service, now and in the future). The figure below illustrates the potential tensions across these objectives.

Typically, economic sustainability requires that tariff levels reflect the opportunity cost of using water and discourage wastage; such a policy can raise social issues (affordability); it can also generate fluctuation in tariff levels (the opportunity cost is lower when water is abundant), potentially affecting the financial sustainability of service provision. Similarly, financial sustainability may benefit from higher tariffs, potentially triggering affordability issues for poor households. Better reflection of environmental costs in service provision can also drive tariffs up and have harmful social consequences on selected communities. These tensions can only be addressed through a policy process that balances the different objectives, and lead to tariff levels and tariff structured tailored to reflect the preferred balance. OECD work on the issue insists that affordability issues are best addressed outside of the water bill, through targeted social measures.

Figure 3.2. Tensions between policy objectives for water tariffs

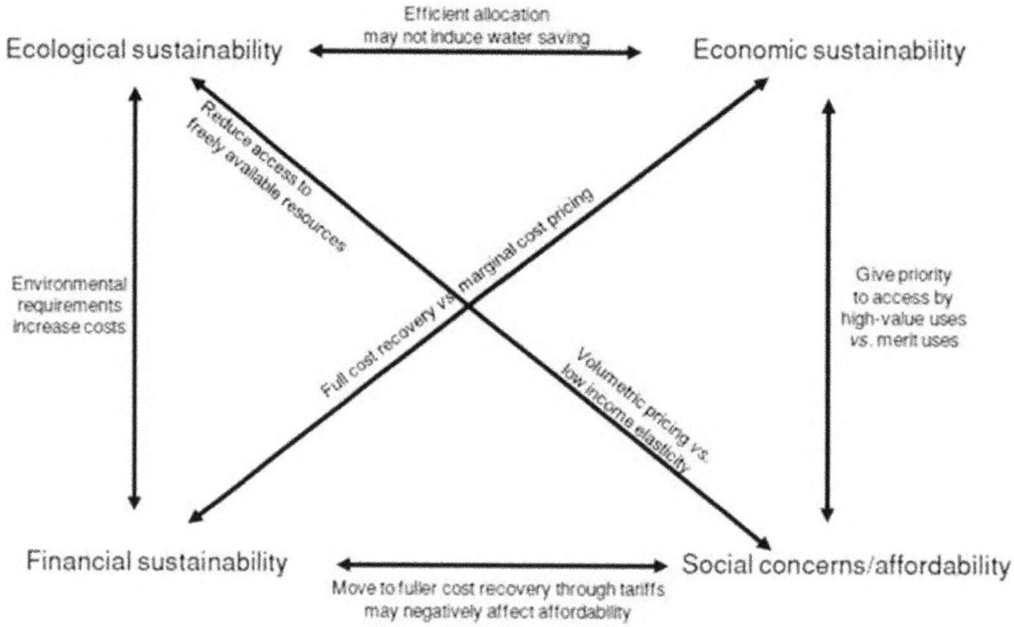

Source: OECD (2010), *Pricing Water Resources and Water and Sanitation Services*, OECD Publishing, Paris

The main issue with the tariff policy in Lithuania is exclusion of granted assets from the base over which the return on assets and eligible depreciation expenses is calculated. A consequence is that the method does not properly reflect the cost of maintaining and renewing existing assets. Then, water tariffs cannot generate the revenues water companies need to finance a sustainable provision of water services, now and in the future. In the absence of subsidies, this financing model cannot be sustained, after the rapid extension of water infrastructures in Lithuania.

One solution to this dilemma may be to set tariffs for a multi-year period (possibly with options for in-between revisions), as is the case in France. Another option might be to allow for *infrastructure renewal charges*, such as in England and Wales, Scotland or Kosovo: such charges consider as eligible expenses the actual costs to maintain the asset base rather than the depreciation charge.

Driving water companies' performance

Incentives to enhance the performance of water companies can be a key driver for change. Clear performance targets, supported by robust monitoring, adequate rewards (or sanctions) can set a common ambition, signal deficiencies and urge water companies to take action.

Two sets of issues deserve attention. First, the regulator does not set targets for quality of service or performance of service delivery, beyond the quality and safety of water supplied and treated wastewater. It is not clear how other features of service quality are considered (e.g. energy efficiency, efficiency of networks, responsiveness in cases of breach or failure). Moreover, it is not clear how the review of development plans considers long term performance of service provision and cost-efficiency of expenditure programmes. Setting standards or targets on such features would drive investment and expenditure plans and dictate requirements for technical skills and capacities in the future. This is missed opportunity to set common levels of ambition (beyond compliance with EU standards) and drive performance enhancement.

The second set of issue relates to setting, monitoring, and rewarding performance. Lithuania has limited experience with benchmarking the performance of water companies. Addressing these deficiencies would require:

- Explicit and agreed-upon objectives as regards the quality of service and the performance of service providers;
- A tailored set of criteria, aligned with objectives
- A systematic review of performance on a regular basis, with clear responsibilities from the economic regulator (with adequate resources and skills)
- An incentive regime (including reward to achievements and sanctions for non-performance) that can enhance value for money and potentially drive change towards more effective and cost-efficient water industry in Lithuania.

Investment and expenditure planning

In Lithuania, economic regulation is based on the principle of full cost recovery. The State Energy Regulatory Council of Lithuania is responsible for monitoring eligible costs reflected in tariffs. But this institution needs strengthening to assess the opportunity of expenditure programmes and appropriate eligible costs to be reflected in tariffs. This is an issue, in particular as water and sanitation services are capital intensive: risks of duplication are costly, in particular in the long term, when the need to maintain and renew existing assets is factored in. The demographic trends can only increase such unnecessary costs.

Several options can be considered, to address this issue. A National Water Strategy, backed by a thorough and realistic financing strategy, could be envisaged, to set the overall level of ambition and provide a reference to draft investment and expenditure plans and assess the opportunity of projected investment, and possibly encourage local governments to join forces. The objective of the proposed strategy would be, for each municipality, to:

- Identify long-term needs (based on population and economic development forecast) and source of water supply; impacts of climate change (and risks of flooding or scarcity) should be factored in, as appropriate
- Identify investment needs for rehabilitation, replacement or extension of the water and sewerage facilities (including granted assets, which will need to be renewed even though they were financed without domestic finance) and their costs
- Explore options for mutual investment and joint action with neighbouring communities. The proposed options could be prioritised when they align with the national water strategy and financial strategy.

This work would help to update and review the needs defined in local investment and expenditure plans, and conduct a proper consolidation of investment needs at the national level in cooperation with the economic regulator and the Ministry of Finance.

Table 3.1. Wrapping up

ISSUES	OPTIONS TO BE CONSIDERED
Consider a range of options for agglomeration	
Scenarios for agglomeration of water services	geographical; functional; urban/rural
Incentives for local authorities to ignite change	Options for financial incentives (privileged access to public funds, possibly through the Environmental Fund), preferred treatment (e.g. authorisation programmes, licencing)
Address practical issues to expedite consolidation, using an example of 1-2 pilot regions	
Tariff-setting for the transition period	Separate tariffs for distinct territories, or convergence towards a unified tariff for regional operator
Consolidation and management of assets	Modalities for delegation of assets management
Further strengthen the role and capacities of the economic regulator	
Issue with tariff setting and depreciation of granted assets	Options for tariff structure, targeted social measures (to address affordability issues), provision for renewal of granted assets
Driving water companies' performance	Options to set performance targets, indicators to monitor utilities' performance, a benchmarking process, rewards/sanctions for performance achievements
Investment and expenditure planning	Incentives to consider opportunities to draft investment and expenditure plans at an aggregate level; role of a national strategy

Annex 3.A. Interviews

Annex Table 3.A.1. List of people interviewed in Lithuania

Member of the working group	Institution	Thematic focus
Agnė Kniežaitė-Gofmanė	Ministry of Environment of the Republic of Lithuania	Strategizing of WSS consolidation reform in Lithuania; Economic and financial incentives; Compliance with EU Directives; investment planning
Irmantas Valūnas	Ministry of Environment of the Republic of Lithuania	Strategizing of WSS consolidation reform in Lithuania; Economic and financial incentives; Compliance with EU Directives; investment planning
Monika Sakalauskaitė	Ministry of Environment of the Republic of Lithuania	Strategizing of WSS consolidation reform in Lithuania; Economic and financial incentives; Compliance with EU Directives; investment planning
Inesis Kiškis	Ministry of Environment of the Republic of Lithuania	Strategizing of WSS consolidation reform in Lithuania; Economic and financial incentives; Compliance with EU Directives; investment planning
Vilma Slavinskienė	Ministry of Environment of the Republic of Lithuania	Strategizing of WSS consolidation reform in Lithuania; Economic and financial incentives; Compliance with EU Directives; investment planning
Raimonda Juknaitė	Ministry of Environment of the Republic of Lithuania	Strategizing of WSS consolidation reform in Lithuania; Economic and financial incentives; Compliance with EU Directives; investment planning
Kastytis Tuminas	Environmental Project Management Agency of the Ministry of Environment of the Republic of Lithuania	Strategizing of WSS consolidation reform in Lithuania; Economic and financial incentives; Compliance with EU Directives; investment planning
Donatas Jasas	State Energy Regulatory Council	Scenarios for WSS consolidation reform in Lithuania; issues related to investment planning and tariff regulation. Needs for better monitoring of utility performance. Legal and regulatory reforms.
Dalius Krinickas	State Energy Regulatory Council	Scenarios for WSS consolidation reform in Lithuania; issues related to investment planning and tariff regulation. Needs for better monitoring of utility performance. Legal and regulatory reforms.
Indrė Musvicienė	State Energy Regulatory Council	Scenarios for WSS consolidation reform in Lithuania; issues related to investment planning and tariff regulation. Needs for better monitoring of utility performance. Legal and regulatory reforms.
Rasa Valatkevičienė	State Energy Regulatory Council	Scenarios for WSS consolidation reform in Lithuania; issues related to investment planning and tariff regulation. Needs for better monitoring of utility performance. Legal and regulatory reforms.
Irma Vasarytė	State Energy Regulatory Council	Scenarios for WSS consolidation reform in Lithuania; issues related to investment planning and tariff regulation. Needs for better monitoring of utility performance. Legal and regulatory reforms.
Aleksandra Čepukėnienė	State Energy Regulatory Council	Scenarios for WSS consolidation reform in Lithuania; issues related to investment planning and tariff regulation. Needs for better monitoring of utility performance. Legal and regulatory reforms.

Annex 3.B. Preliminary characterisation of lessons learned from international experience with consolidation of WSS

The case studies are sketched here. Additional information and analyses on the objectives, process and accompanying measures will be available at the time of the international workshop. They can inspire reforms and action plans in Lithuania.

Austria - Successful voluntary aggregations in rural context

In Austria, there are several examples of association of small rural service providers with similar characteristics that successfully grouped together. Austria provides concrete examples to explain why (purpose) and how (scale, scope, governance) these small utilities grouped together.

Chile – Benchmarking the performance of water utilities

Chile is well regarded both for its water sector performance and its well-designed social services. Water sector reform started in the 1970s, leading to regionalisation and gradual tariff increases.

A highlight of this process was establishment of an independent economic regulator Superintendencia de Servicios Sanitarios (SSIS). In addition, four principles of tariff setting were set: non-discrimination, cost recovery, economic efficiency and encouraging conservation. The small SSIS developed a model company against which the 14 utilities operating in Chile could be compared. When setting the tariffs, the future efficiency improvement measures of the utilities were factored in. Under SSIS, leakage levels and cost recovery improved. Still, investment remained too small. SSIS initially failed to have leverage on some of the larger inefficient utilities.

These issues were resolved by:

- granting SSIS more power and independence, including funding through a levy on water utilities
- attracting finance for infrastructure through equity sales, concession contracts and involving the private sector, raising USD 1 bln that was subsequently wholly invested in infrastructure.

Among its main activities, SSIS monitors performance of both the sector and concession contracts.

Chile has a lot to share as regards options to cope with lack of affordability of water tariffs. From a social perspective, having no access to water is more costly than access at cost recovery tariff levels. Social measures have concentrated on funding extension or financing the costs of increased access, half of which went to the poor.

All consumers are billed the same full rate for the metered amount of water consumed. Means- tested poor customers, however, can bring bills to the municipality. The municipality pays part of the bill, provided the beneficiary pays the other part. In this way, municipalities cover on average 6% of turnover of water utilities.

There can be little debate about the success of Chile in water sector reform. It is not clear, however, to what extent others can achieve the same results. Chile has a long tradition of effective administration and an acceptance of a contractual approach in public sector management. As a result, it has been able to provide targeted support to the poor and raise capital, mostly for wastewater treatment investment. The case of Chile illustrates that economic regulation needs periodic recalibration with policy targets, which is a task for the government at large.

Croatia - Overlooking context and purpose is associated with higher risk of failure

The context in which aggregation takes place is characterized by the enabling environment in the country and in the sector, as well as by the physical environment in which utilities operate. The purpose of the aggregation can be manifold as the reform can target economic efficiency, performance improvement, professionalisation, environmental benefits and/or solidarity. The context should be taken into account and the purpose has to be clarified when designing aggregation. Disconnecting the former from the latter can lead to failure.

Moreover engaging with all stakeholders throughout the entire aggregation process is key to foster success. Whether mandated or not, systematic consultations between national and local stakeholders should be organized early in the process to ensure they can inform the process and to confirm alignment of interests between the national and local levels. Such an early engagement helps build stakeholder ownership of the reform. It allows implementers to tackle potential problems or resistance, and diffuse their potential impacts, thus improving conditions for success.

In 2012, the Croatian government initiated a series of utility sector reforms that, in addition to establishing a proper water sector regulatory framework and benchmarking system, have included a proposed merger of utility service providers into about 20 regional utilities. The main drivers of this aggregation effort were the need to efficiently absorb EU funds and to cross-subsidise the operation of water and wastewater systems in smaller settlements, which would find compliance with the new EU standards prohibitively expensive and unaffordable.

In early 2015, aggregation design was completed along with the required legislative framework. However, owing to the sensitivity of the political situation at that moment (2015 was an election year) and potential backlash from local authorities, it first was delayed and then lost political support following the change in the central government. The reform had been driven largely by technocrats within the line ministry, who failed to acknowledge that they lacked the political champion and national government power to impose the reform process over the concerns of local stakeholders.

Flanders – on social water tariffs

The Flanders region of Belgium has a most advanced system of setting (social) water tariffs. First, there is only a small fixed fee for costs related to customers such as metering and billing. Overall, it is less than 10% of the bill. The volumetric part of the bill is charged either as "normal" or as "social". The normal tariff structure is a straightforward Increasing Block Tariff (IBT), but based on the household size rather than on fixed brackets (blocks). In this way, larger households pay a similar price per cubic metre as small households, provided they are in the same tariff group and have a similar per capita consumption.

The social tariff is zero for the first 15 m3 per person per year or 41 liter per consumer per day (lcd). Above that threshold, the social tariff is lower than the normal tariff. Figures below illustrate the concept. The built-in cross subsidy between smaller and larger units of consumption ensures the marginal price of water is the most expensive for rich and poor alike. In this way, there is an incentive to reduce consumption.

Annex Figure 3.B.1. Composition of annual water costs for various household sizes and consumption levels, 2017

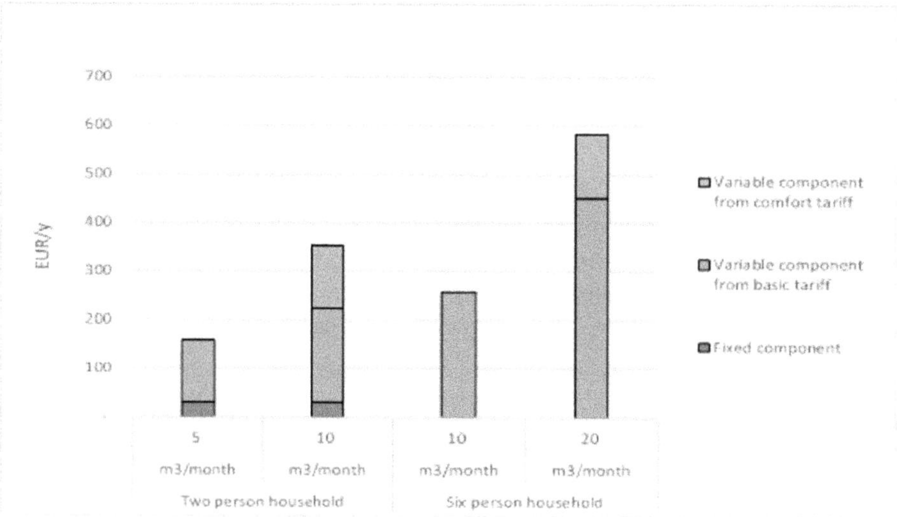

Source: https://www.farys.be/nl/watertarieven .

Annex Figure 3.B.2. City of Ghent: total household bill equivalent costs per m3 for different household sizes (2018)

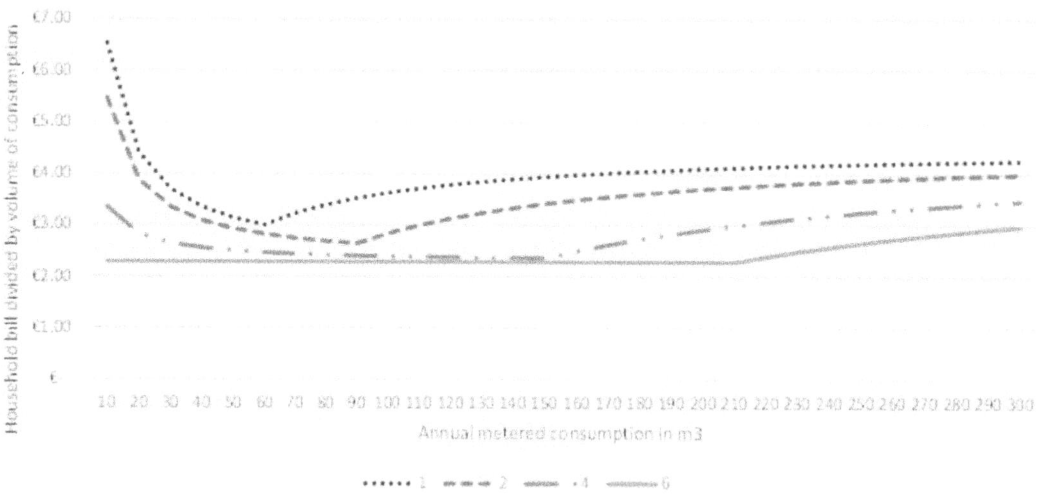

Source: https://www.farys.be/nl/watertarieven

The concept is appealing. It combines social, environmental and financial benefits.

Flanders illustrates an advanced social system carried out through the tariff. The regulator exercises a strong influence on social policy, stipulating the thresholds for the IBT and the relative tariff differential. There are two blocs (below and above 30 m3 per household member per year). The tariff in the first bloc shall be half that of the second one. The regulator also stipulates the size and conditions of the social tariffs, presently at one-fifth of the normal fixed and variable tariff elements.

The dual block tariff, however, puts an administrative burden on the utilities. To charge appropriately, utilities have to maintain records on inhabitants per household. Expenditure for WSS is in the order of 1-

2% of household income i.e. quite affordable by international standards. It is difficult to assess how well the system maintains affordability for the poor. The per capita delineation of the tariff blocs addresses the most pressing argument against IBTs. But little is known on how well the blocs and tariffs perform in maintaining affordability in relation to, for instance, single volumetric tariffs. Brackets are not adjusted in light of updated, more recent poverty statistics.

This type of redistribution can only take place within the service area. Small consumers and social cases are subsidised by other customers within the service area. Three factors are necessary for this type of social measure to function optimally:

- The average tariffs should be similar among the service areas in the region
- The distribution of income within the service areas should be similar.
- Per capita income across the service areas should be similar.

Deviations on these conditions bring regional distortions to distribution of benefits that are difficult to quantify. Assuming the conditions have been sufficiently met in Flanders, one can still ask whether the social benefit of increased affordability of services outweighs the costs of the increased administrative burden for utilities.

France - A reform targeting economic efficiency and solidarity, facing long-lasting resistance

The NOTRe Act has mandated the progressive transfer of water and sanitation services competence from municipalities to integrated intercommunalities. Some key features, which will be explored in more details:

- Context of aggregation: top-down, mandated with a progressive implementation schedule
- Purpose of aggregation: economic efficiency (through economies of scale and scope), solidarity (through economies of scope)
- Scale and scope of aggregation: vertical and horizontal consolidation of utilities embedded in the reform
- Example of governance arrangement for aggregated utilities: institutional elements (legal form and organization; shareholder rights and power distribution; oversight and coordination of tariff and performance; exit and entry clauses); financing, assets, and liabilities (cost- and revenue-sharing agreements; asset ownership, transfer, development, and management)
- Risk of failure: political resistance which has postponed initial reform deadlines from 2019 to 2026.

Korea - Amalgamated water services – Gyeongnam Province

Many Korean municipalities are having a hard time managing their own waterworks: the lack of revenue from low water tariffs leads to financial constraints on renewing existing water infrastructures. Ageing water infrastructures, particularly ageing water mains, are the predominant cause of water leakage, driving production costs and water tariffs up.

To solve these issues, the central government supports and encourages municipalities to amalgamate water supply services and assign amalgamated services to specialised water agencies. Four local governments in southwest Gyeongnam Province amalgamated their water supply systems and assigned their operation to K-water. Each local government retains ownership of its water supply system and remains responsible for providing the service and setting its tariffs, as well as for planning and extending water mains in order to increase access to tap water. The tasks devolved to K-water include water abstraction and treatment, distributing treated water to customers, and notifying and collecting water tariffs.

K-water has installed an integrated remote-control centre to monitor and control each municipality's water sources, treatment plants and reservoirs. Most facilities, except those located far from city centres, have no staff. Operators of the integrated remote-control centre monitor water pressure and manage facilities 24 hours a day, 7 days a week. They are available at all times to respond immediately to calls from a facility. If the systems are out of order, engineers working for a local service centre are expected to be able to reach the facility within 30 minutes through a network of emergency contacts.

In order to enhance operational efficiency, K-water covers the upfront capital costs of renewing and upgrading ageing infrastructures. It charges each local government on a monthly basis for the operating expenses, including investment recovery. The contract specifies the amount to be paid by the municipalities, providing them with the ability to plan expenditures in advance.

The project has received positive reviews from the central government and municipalities involved. It is expected to cut costs by KRW 24 billion (Korean won) (EUR 19 million) over the contract duration (between 20 and 30 years), compared with business as usual. The volume of water accounted for has increased between 17.1% and 41.3% in the new system.

The Netherlands – achieving economies of scale and scope

In the mid-1970s, the Netherlands considered that its municipal water works lacked economies of scale and scope to deliver efficient services in the future. The 1975 Water Law kicked-started a regionalisation process that resulted in the ten current suppliers of drinking water. They are incorporated public entities that are 100% owned by municipalities and provinces.

Wastewater collection has remained a municipal responsibility. It is financed through a special municipal tax. Responsibility for wastewater treatment and water management rests with the democratically elected water boards. Water boards are legal entities, the first one of which was established in 1255. The 23 water boards operate on a regional scale.

Historically, the rationale behind regionalisation has been the need for efficient operations. Regionalisation, however, has supported affordability for the less densely populated areas

If all agglomerations up to 1 000 population equivalent (PE) charged based on cost recovery, then tariff rates in rural areas would need to be three times higher than those in large urban conglomerations. Income of rural households is typically smaller. Regionalisation of operations and harmonisation of tariffs across each expanded service helped share this burden. High-income/low WSS unit cost consumers cross-subsidise the lower-income/high WSS costs rural population through the harmonised tariff.

Municipalities collect the following:

- The wastewater collection charge to cover municipal sewerage costs. The charge can be based on drinking water consumed, property value or the number of inhabitants.
- The wastewater treatment charges and pollution charges on behalf of the water boards. The charge is not based on metered water consumption, but on three categories: single person households, two person households and households with three or more persons.
- The water system charges on buildings and land, also on behalf of the water boards, for water resource management. It is charged on the main occupant of the house or apartment (or land), as a fraction of property value (or as fee per habitant).

These charges mostly provide a fixed component to the WSS- related expenditure and may be seen as regressive.

Municipalities in the Netherlands provide for a WSS-related social measure through a partial or full exemption of (exclusively) their poorer citizens. Exemption of only fixed elements of the WSS-related bills leaves intact the incentives to save drinking water.

The Dutch system of WSS provision is complex and appears fragmented. Because of the long tradition and a strong culture of coordination among authorities, it does provide for a high level of service and reliability. The regionalisation of services has enabled an automatic cross-subsidy mechanism that would otherwise have been impossible to set up. In addition, a decentralised targeted WSS-related social assistance is in place through the exemption of fixed charges on poor citizens.

Romania - A top-down mandatory and financially incentivised aggregation process

A comprehensive water sector aggregation reform was designed in 2005–2007 and implemented during the five following years. This regionalization consisted of a top-down mandatory process incentivized by EU investment grants—Sectoral Operational Program Environmental (SOP E) funds - which were allocated only to projects led by a regional operator.

Regionalization was based on three key institutional elements: the Intercommunity Development Association (IDA), the Regional Operating Company (ROC), and the Contract of Delegation of Services' Management.

Achievement/finding:

- From low cost-low performance to high cost-high performance (aggregation path).
- Introduction of performance indicators (as such, aggregation introduced better knowledge about utilities' operation with a view to improving it over time).
- Gradual implementation strategy allowed by the subsidiary principle of the aggregation reform (allowing flexibility in implementation ensures local stakeholders can own the aggregation process and adapt it to their local context).

Lessons learned:

- Risk of cherry-picking practices, as service providers naturally preferred to extend services to wealthy populations for cost recovery reasons, and to easy-to-reach areas where infrastructure already existed. By doing so, they selected solvent customers for good revenue collection and seek to avoid sunk investment costs and associated OPEX increases. Hence binding rules must be put in place to safeguard the principle of solidarity and overcome cherry-picking practices.
- Transaction costs can hamper aggregation success as staff transfer generally translates into labour cost increases that can jeopardize the financial sustainability of aggregated entities.
- Risk of withdrawal (importance of entry and exit clauses).

Notes

[1] available here https://e-seimas.lrs.lt/portal/legalAct/lt/TAD/TAIS.280587/asr .

[2] available here https://e-seimas.lrs.lt/portal/legalAct/lt/TAD/4824cba0315d11e79f4996496b137f39/asr.

[3] available here : https://am.lrv.lt/uploads/am/documents/files/2020%2001%2020%20galutin%C4%97%20ataskaita%20(su formatuota)_final(1).pdf.

[4] See Chapter 1, based on responses to a questionnaire drafted by the OECD Secretariat.

[5] Convened remotely on 18 February 2021; see Chapter 2.

[6] This development builds on OECD (2015), *Water and Cities: Ensuring Sustainable Futures*, OECD Studies on Water, OECD Publishing, Paris, https://doi.org/10.1787/9789264230149-en. See the publication for references.

[7] Of note: in Lithuania, a water company is not allowed to differentiate the price based on the location of the consumer. However, it is possible to set different prices by customer segments. It remains to be seen how this principle is compatible with agglomeration in practice.

[8] At the kick-off meeting, a delegate from the Water Utilities Association mentioned that water prices across the country range from 2.2 EUR/m3 to 4 EUR/m3. He suggested that such a difference called for further strengthening of tariff regulation to enhance cost-efficiency of service providers.

4 Report with recommendations on financial and governance incentives

Financial and governance incentives matter to accelerate the consolidation of water services in Lithuania. The chapter explores options to address the specific concerns of small municipalities and well-managed utilities, who believe they might be worse off after consolidation. Practical options inspired from international good practices confirm this does not need to be the case.

4.1. Introduction

Chapter 4 highlights why financial and governance incentives matter to accelerate the consolidation of water services in Lithuania. Experience over the last few years suggests that reorganisation of water services in Lithuania raises issues that relate to the governance of water utilities. Two sets of issues have emerged. The first one is political. On the one hand, small municipalities are reluctant to merge utilities with larger ones as they fear their voices would not be heard in the larger context. The Chapter claims this can be addressed by flexible governance arrangements, which acknowledge the rights of all municipalities. On the other hand, well managed (usually larger) utilities are reluctant to consolidate with smaller ones, as they project that they would need to raise tariffs to compensate the lack of efficiency and the investment needs of less performing ones. The Chapter argues that this concern can be addressed through tariff policy.

A second set of issues relate to more technical considerations, such as the ownership of assets n a merged entity, or the possibility of withdrawing from consolidated entities. The Chapter shares some models in place in European countries, which can help address these issues.

As explained in Chapter 3, progress towards some form of consolidation requires that types of arrangement are clarified between a regional utility and local authorities, to either operate assets owned by local utilities (which will not directly operate these assets anymore) or transfer asset ownership to the regional utility. Progress also requires that governance structures are available, which ensure that local authorities keep some control over decisions related to the asset on which service delivery depends.

The Chapter should be read in combination with others. In particular, Chapter 7 explores financial incentives in the context of the tariff setting process, in particular through accelerated depreciation of granted assets under certain conditions, which could include development plans that seriously consider options for efficiency gains through consolidation of assets and services.

Of note: the issues mentioned above essentially emerge in the context of merger of utilities. More flexible consolidation arrangements discussed in other Chapters, in particular in Chapter 6 on scenarios for two pilot regions, make these considerations less pressing, or offer more time to address them.

4.2. The governance of utilities. Practical options to facilitate consolidation

As mentioned above, two sets of governance issues need to be addressed to overcome practical resistance to consider consolidation of water utilities in Lithuania. The first one relates to the organisation if the governance structure, to reflect the interest of the different constituencies; it relates to power and political considerations. The second one – more technical in nature – refers to the status of assets and other managerial issues. A third type of incentive is discussed in this section, as it is being considered by the Ministry: the revocation of licences to operate water and sanitation services.

As illustrated in Chapter 5, "lighter" organizational arrangements would address potential concerns related to the governance of consolidated entities, as they allow for the consolidation of the sector while maintaining existing water companies, although with different levels of responsibility and independence. These arrangements include: (i) cooperation agreements between providers with a well-defined scope; and (ii) delegated contracts signed between the jurisdiction level in charge of service delivery and an operator, transferring all or most of operational responsibilities. See Chapter 5 for a more detailed discussion.

4.2.1. Organising power relations in consolidated entities

The concern expressed by smaller entities that their capacity to make decisions and reflect the interest of the customers would be diluted in cases of consolidation is valid. It needs to be considered and addressed. The international workshop on lessons learned from European experience with consolidation of water utilities provides a range of options, which can be adjusted in the Lithuanian context. They reflect a range of decision-making arrangements and voting rights allocation. In most cases, the power sharing arrangement is done in such a way that it does not provide exclusive power to the largest city as a single shareholder, to ensure a balance of power and create incentives for consensus-building (see the Table below).

Table 4.1. Comparative advantages of alternative methods for allocating voting rights

Method for allocating voting rights	Potential advantages	Potential drawbacks	Examples
According to the number of customers, the number of connections, or the value of the assets	Sound economic basis	Varies from year to year	Águas do Ribatejo (Portugal)
One entity = one seat	Simplest rule	Can be unacceptable for larger entities	SDEA and SEDIF (France)
Specific powers for the dominating entity, if there is one	Necessary to gain confidence of the larger entity	Small entities have limited influence	This rule was used to a certain extent in Raja Constanta utility (Romania)
Mixture of the two solutions above	More democratic rule, with a minimal representation for small communities	May deter the more powerful municipalities from joining	Nîmes Metropole (France)

Source: The World Bank (2005)

One institutional arrangement deserves particular attention, as it illustrates how flexibility can guarantee access to decisions (see also Chapter 5, where this case is presented as well). In France, *Syndicat des Eaux et de l'Assainissement Alsace-Moselle* (SDEA) is an aggregation of water utilities, triggered by a national regulation. The NOTRe Act mandated the progressive transfer of water and sanitation services competence from municipalities to integrated intercommunalities, with the purpose to achieve economic efficiency (through economies of scale), and solidarity (through economies of scope).

The SDEA is a public establishment of cooperation specialized in the water field and federates different municipalities/group of municipalities/Strasbourg EuroMetropol and the Bas-Rhin department. The idea from this federation is to have one establishment that manages drinking water production, river streams, reservoirs, and wastewater collection and treatment for all members of the federation. It comprises 737 municipalities and is administrated by local elected officials from different municipalities. The SDEA comprise three levels of governance, and namely:

- Global scale: bodies at the local scale include a General Assembly, a Board of Directors, a Permanent Commission, Thematic Commissions and Tender Commissions. This level is in charge of overall policy and economies of scale, adaptation of the common tool to the challenges, grouped purchases and pooling of financing capacities;
- Territorial scale: bodies at the territorial scale include Territorial councils and Contracts Commissions. This level is in charge of synergies, common projects, consultations across territories, pooling of local investments and sharing of best practices;
- Local scale: this level is administered by Local Commissions. It is in charge of proximity management, analytical financial management, definition of tariffs and financing, investment programs, awarding of work contracts and follow-up of local affairs.

The role of each constituency is adjusted at each level, according to different criteria, to ensure each municipality (and their dwellers) has some capacity to participate in decisions that affect it. Also, each municipality can opt for various levels of consolidation, staring by sharing information, and some functions, towards more coordinated planning and integrated management. This flexible arrangement provides for progressive consolidation, leaving time to build trust in to the consolidated entity.

Such a flexible and dynamic model could be considered in Lithuania, to address the inherently political resistance of small municipalities towards consolidation.

4.2.2. Managerial issues in consolidated utilities[1]

Entry and exit clauses

Entry and exit rules set out the technical and financial conditions under which a service can join or withdraw from the consolidated entity. These conditions commonly include an asset inventory as most exit clauses foresee the repayment of depreciation costs when investments have been made. In addition, these rules also include governance arrangements that apply to newcomers.

Entry by new members can reinforce economies of scale and increase the demand and revenue base for the consolidated utility. Before allowing a new member to enter the aggregation, it is recommended to conduct a thorough analysis of the impact of such incorporation on the existing consolidated utility and to ensure that the following conditions hold:

- the new member accepts the general conditions of the grouping without too many changes
- the inclusion of the new member does not significantly change the aggregated structure's financial viability.

Once the new entry is accepted, the financial impact of this incorporation should be carefully evaluated to determine the value of the assets that may be brought in by the new entity, any potential financial compensation for such assets upon entry, and the number of shares or voting rights to be allocated to the new member.

Most aggregated structures make it difficult or costly for an existing member to leave. This is to discourage such exit because it can have a serious impact on the consolidated entity. For these reasons, the articles of association of the aggregated structure should include a section about exit rules which should establish rather severe conditions, such as:

- a minimum time between the time when the request to leave the grouping is formulated and the implementation of this separation (at least one year).
- the leaving entity should support transaction costs, as well as the costs of replacing shared facilities and infrastructure.

The articles of association may prescribe that:

- upon termination of membership the contribution is not refunded (although the member shall be paid the share of the assets it would receive if the association were dissolved)
- a member of an association shall pay reasonable compensation to the association upon leaving the association if exit son causes significant damage to the association.

Upon withdrawal from the association, return of the assets to the original holder should be carried through as prescribed in the articles of association or in the members' agreement. A solution upon withdrawal from the association may be as follows:

- the member may (re)acquire any WSS assets it has transferred to the association and/or any assets created by the association that are located in the territory of the member municipality (or in the previous service area of a water undertaking);
- as a general rule, the leaving member may (re)acquire such assets free of charge (except as set out below);
- if the association has outstanding loan obligations connected to the creation of such assets, the leaving member shall compensate the association any such outstanding amounts;
- if such WSS asset is used to provide services to several members, the leaving member shall compensate the association the potential loss or damage resulting from such asset being removed from the possession of the association;
- any other reasonable technical or financial conditions upon (re)acquiring the assets (e.g. if the assets are created using financial aid, the conditions of the financier must be met).

4.2.3. Asset ownership, transfer, and management

Aggregation case studies exhibit a diversity of situations with regard to asset ownership, transfer and management. In most cases, asset remains under the ownership of local jurisdictions while its operation is handed over to an intermunicipal structure or directly to the aggregated utility through some form of concession contract. Inventories are then carried out to value the infrastructure and establish a depreciation schedule for future years.

When local jurisdictions transfer their WSS asset to the aggregated utility, this transfer can happen either for free, or according to one of the three following compensation methods; each of them bearing potential advantages and drawbacks (see Table below):

- through the granting of shares in the new entity
- through direct reimbursement by other members
- or through the payment of a lease fee.

Table 4.2. Potential advantages and drawbacks of alternative compensation solutions

Compensation solution	Potential advantages	Potential drawbacks
Shares in the new entity	Nobody has anything to pay	The entity bringing more assets has more voting rights, even if it is small
Direct reimbursement	All debts are cleared at the agreement signature	This solution could absorb most of the cash available for some entities, limiting their capacity to invest in new facilities development
Lease fee	A good formula for assets that cannot be sold (for example, water rights)	Potential difficulties arise if the leaseholder wants to leave

Source: The World Bank (2005)

Liabilities

Service providers that are aggregating may hold liabilities with regard to staff, suppliers and financiers, or claims on customers. These liabilities can represent significant transaction costs for aggregating utilities. As such, they have to be covered, either during the aggregation by the aggregated utility or separately from the aggregation by the local government budget. In most cases, the second option is favoured.

Harmonization of processes and practices

During the aggregation process, employment issues can be very sensitive. It is therefore important to consider issues of staff transfer very carefully. The transfer of the entire staff from the individual entities to the new aggregated structure is often not necessary, nor even desirable. Therefore, in most of cases, the consolidation process includes transferring some key staff to the new entity, often on a voluntary basis.

Transfer of staff from municipal structures into the aggregated utility must be planned and documented in quantitative and financial terms, including possible pension liabilities.

As labour cost is generally among the top budget items for a utility and the one where most optimization potential exists through consolidation, it is crucial to allow for the economies of scale to materialise. Indeed, staff transfer from former municipal structures into the newly aggregated utility generally creates heavy transaction costs, which translate into labour cost increases and can hamper the financial sustainability of aggregated entities.

Similarly, the harmonization of IT systems and administrative practices can generate transaction costs that can limit or delay the materialization of aggregation benefits. As such, they should be carefully dealt with. The aggregation agreement should include clear costing and strategy with regard to IT systems harmonization and integration, and database management.

When the scope of aggregation includes consolidation of functions, harmonization of administrative practices across consolidating utilities is necessary. This harmonisation strategy - which encompasses tasks such as procurement, accounting, quality control - has to be set up ahead of the aggregation implementation. In the best-case scenario, this harmonization leads to levelling standards up to those of best practices. However, under less favourable circumstances, harmonisation may lead to levelling costs up, thus hampering the success of aggregation.

4.2.4. The role of and process for licence revocation

The fact that Ministry is making the threat of licence revocation in the future does have quite a big effect on the context within which any arrangements would be applied, such as those discussed in Chapters 7 (on water tariffs) and 8 (on the performance of water utilities).

The Ministry of Environment's planned WSS sector reforms include the development of new criteria – including service quality requirements - for licensed activities, operating a mechanism that applies when a licence is revoked, and strengthening the role of the regulator. This section considers the Ministry's proposal with respect to licence revocation. It also sets out why there looks to be a strong case for the Ministry to adopt and ongoing coordination and tracking role with respect to the achievement of environmental policy objectives and obligations.

In regulated sectors, licence revocation would typically be viewed as a fairly extreme intervention, and one that reflected the conclusion that other available options within the licensing framework were unlikely to provide a sufficient response. Those options can potentially be quite varied and will in some jurisdictions include scope for significant financial penalties to be applied where a company can be shown to have been operating in breach of its licence obligations.

That said, the explicit consideration of licence revocation in the Ministry of Environment's planned reforms looks to be well-judged, and to reflect and important and legitimate concern over how the WSS sector in Lithuania might evolve. That is, Ministry is clearly identifying the 'opening' position as not a sustainable one, such that it expects material changes to the structure and operation of the sector to be necessary feature of addressing adequately the challenges that are faced. The Ministry is looking to facilitate the transition of the sector through the enhancements to the framework that it is developing, but the risk remains that some companies may not respond in ways that provide for a level of progress that is viewed sufficient. Licence revocation is being explicitly pointed to as a potential 'backstop' measure, which could be used if such circumstances arise.

The scope for licence revocation to occur can be understood as having important incentive properties. In an obvious sense, the force of the licence – and the conditions it provides for – can be viewed as closely related to the scope for revocation, with this providing the ultimate sanction in the face of non-compliance. Also, however, the possibility of revocation can affect the likely significance of ratchet effects of the kind discussed in Chapter 7. In particular, while ratchet effects can tend to dampen incentives to bring forward efficiency improvements (because they may be used by the regulator to impose a tougher control going forward), scope for licence revocation can be understood as putting companies on notice that sufficient efficiency improvements will need to be implemented within an overall period – say 10 years. It can therefore provide a desirable source of counter-pressure, in a context where there may otherwise be significant inertia and/or incentives to defer the kind of actions that might be required to deliver improvements.

An important question arises, however, as to the extent to which the prospect of revocation is likely to be viewed as credible. That is: to what extent would companies and municipalities consider it likely that the process of licence revocation would actually materialise? A critical issue here typically concerns the extent to which a clear process has been identified in terms of how licence compliance risks are managed within the regulatory framework, and then the extent to which that process is actually used in practice. This is important, because the severity of licence revocation as a regulatory response is such that one would expect it to have been preceded by a range of other less severe actions that can be shown to have been insufficiently effective. Where that is not the case, there may be significant risks of a revocation decision being challenged (legally and/or more broadly) as being disproportionate, premature and/or as otherwise unfair.

Regulators often seek to manage these kinds of enforcement risks through developing and publishing (and then demonstrably applying) an enforcement policy, setting out how they will go about responding to identified risks concerning licence compliance. A critical feature of such a policy is typically setting out an approach to escalation: that is, setting out the steps of increasing severity that the regulator might expect to adopt where compliance risks have been identified. This escalation process can then provide a guide that the regulator can use when tackling a specific issue, or set of issues, and where its actions do not appear to be generating an appropriate regulatory response in terms of behavioural change and outcome improvement. Ofwat's enforcement policy illustrates how its regulatory approach would be expected to move from one where largely informal, ad hoc communications may be viewed sufficient, through a process of more formal reviews and sanctions, before a special administration process would be invoked.

4.3. Financial incentives to facilitate consolidation of water utilities

Stakeholders met in the kick-off meeting, in consultation meetings and in regional meetings argue that financial incentives are required to make consolidation attractive. In the recent past, such incentives have been the main drivers for utilities to consider consolidation. However, opportunities for financial incentives have decreased drastically as a combination of two factors: the gradual phasing out of EU funding for investment in water supply and sanitation in Lithuania, and the scarce domestic public financial resources.

Still, several options exist that provide financial incentives for the consolidation of water supply and sanitation services in Lithuania. The first one consists in revoking a financial disincentive. The second one is embedded in proposed revision of the tariff policy: it consists in rewarding best-performing utilities, in particular the ones that consider some form of consolidation in their development plans.

4.3.1. Addressing issues related to the convergence of water tariffs after consolidation

As noted above, larger utilities are concerned that their customer based would be affected in vases of consolidation, if consolidation leads to an increase in water tariffs. While it is likely that consolidation leads to an increase in tariffs of best managed entities, this concern can be addressed in three ways.

First, it can be argued that the impact on water bills for the better managed (often larger) utility would be minor, as the customer base on that company is larger than the one of the smaller – less efficient – one. In Klaipeda - the region where a regional WSS operator was created - the tariff of services for urban residents slightly increased after the reorganisation, while for the district, the tariff decreased by almost 50%[2].

Second, it is likely that customers of the larger utility can afford a higher tariff, as they would usually be better off (assuming they live in urban settlements, with access to labour and other services).

Finally, and most importantly in terms of policy, consolidation does not necessarily require convergence of water tariffs. While convergence certainly makes sense, it can be managed over an extended period, smoothing the transition and avoiding political resistance. Actually, as mentioned in the comments on the draft water law (Chapter 5), convergence of water tariffs in cases of consolidation raises some potential problems in terms on consolidation, and would seem to merit careful attention. This is particularly so as Article 34(6) appears to limit the scope for price differences within a newly consolidated regional supply area to 3 years. Such a requirement could be viewed as generating a significant disincentive to consolidation for those customers whose initial prices are lower, and who would effectively be asked to pay more to cross-subsidise other customers. A more flexible approach could be considered, where the long-term objective of price convergence could be maintained without that translating into a necessary price increase for those customers in the low-cost area in the short-term.

4.3.2. Embedding incentives in the tariff policy

Tariff policy provides an opportunity to incentive performance through some form of consolidation. The instrument to be considered relates to the depreciation of assets, more specifically of granted assets (i.e. assets financed through EU funding). Chapter 7 explains how the policy options for asset depreciation contribute to several - at times conflicting – policy objectives or priorities: putting pressure on utilities towards efficiency, keeping tariffs low to address social issues, and generating financing capacities for future development and the maintenance of existing assets. The prevailing method in Lithuania favours the first two priorities above. Utilities have an interest in the third one, which would require an extension of the regulated asset base, meaning the allowance to depreciate granted assets.

Chapter 7 argues that, while the prevailing method should be maintained in the Lithuanian context, it could be amended to allow accelerated depreciation under specific conditions. Accelerated depreciation benefits utilities as it triggers a raise in tariff, generating additional revenues from water bills to finance future expenditures. The conditions under which accelerated depreciation could be granted are to be set by the Ministry, in coordination with the regulator. They could include some form of consolidation. As discussed in more depth in Chapter 6 (on scenarios for two pilot regions), these forms are not limited to full merger. They could include the lighter arrangements mentioned above, such as sharing of functions. A most demanding coordination, such as coordinated development plans, would be particularly rewarded.

Similarly, as discussed in some depth in Chapter 8 (on benchmarking the performance of water utilities), the allowed return on equity could vary depending on the level of ambition shown in a company's price submission or development plan, where ambition here refers to the exploration of options to trigger efficiency gains through some form of consolidation, most appropriately, through coordinated development plans.

Notes

[1] This section builds on a review of European experience with consolidation of water utilities, by Maria Salvetti.

[2] Of note: in Lithuania, a water company is not allowed to differentiate the price based on the location of the consumer. However, it is possible to set different prices by customer segments. It remains to be seen how this principle is compatible with agglomeration in practice.

5 Comments on the draft Law on Drinking Water Supply and Wastewater Water Management

While the project was being implemented, Lithuanian authorities developed a draft law to set the scene for future organisation and performance of water service provision in the country. This chapter captures comments by the OECD Secretariat and one international expert on the draft law.

5.1. Introduction

The OECD team was invited to comment on the draft Law circulated by the Lithuanian government to the Parliament. Written comments are destined to support a discussion between the OECD team and the Ministry of Environment. They provide some substance to consider adjustments of the draft Law so that it fits with the ambition of the Ministry. Comments may also provide responses to objections that may be raised in the parliamentary process.

A general comment relates to the level of specificity and detail in some parts of the Draft Law and the potential benefits of a clear delineation between primary legislation (the Law) and secondary legislation (that specifies technical issues in relation to the Law). Indeed, at places, the level of details of technical provisions seems surprising and may be worth consideration. Such level of details triggers risks of unduly inflexible positions being hard-wired into the legislative arrangements and difficult to adjust in the face of new conditions. For example, parts of what is included in **Article 9** [figure in 9(21)] or **Article 15** [in particular, references to specific figures in 15(11)] may be better suited to a subsidiary document that could be given explicit force in the legislation, where relevant principles could be set out. Also, there are a range of time limits for response and decision at various points in the Draft Law, some of which may be better addressed in a subsidiary document, allowing some greater flexibility.

In the note, comments are clustered in three broad categories. The first relates to explicit reference to the ambition of the Law and the leading role of the Ministry of Environment, which sets the tone for other agencies to discharge their duties. The second signals opportunities to refer to and incentivise performance enhancement – and consolidation as an option to promote efficient and sustainable service delivery. The third category refers to the practicalities of core principles in service provision, which should be considered thoroughly to avoid tensions with the emphasis on efficiency and sustainability of service provision.

One caveat applies: comments were provided on the basis of automated translation of the draft Law. While the readability of the English draft was generally good, some misunderstandings may derive from the limitations of such a device. Some ambiguities or apparent inconsistencies may result from automated translation. For instance it is not clear whether entities that transport wastewater or sludge should be licensed or not (apparent discrepancy between **Articles 21** & **24**), or whether shutting individual users who did not pay for the service is allowed or not[1] [**Articles 16(28)**, **20(3)** & **22(2)**].

5.2. Clarifying the ambition of the Law and the leadership from the Ministry of Environment

Section 1 states general provisions as regards the purpose of the Law. **Section 2** goes into quite some depth in the allocation of tasks and responsibilities of several institutions as regards the regulation of the provision of water supply and sanitation services. Sections 1 & 2 could be more closely knitted together if Section 1 stated the ambition of the new law more explicitly and Section 2 insisted on i) the leadership of the Ministry in setting the policy objective and ii) providing other institutions – in particular the economic regulator – with guidance on how they can help achieve that ambition. As regards the level of ambition a more explicit reference to efficiency – and thereby sustainability - of service delivery would make a strong case for the new law and set the scene for the role of the various institutions that contribute to the governance of service provision. Such a reference would justify subsequent incentives to reconsider the way service provision is organised on the ground and explore such alternative options as functional or geographical consolidation.

5.2.1. An explicit reference to efficiency in service delivery

It may be helpful for the 'Purpose of the Law' - as set out in **Articles 1&2** – to include an explicit statement in relation to the efficiency objectives that the introduction of the new law is intended to help achieve. That is, it could be said that there are already general requirements associated with the provision of the relevant services in line with what is described in Article 1, and governing relevant relationships in line with what is described in Article 2.

It would seem helpful to explicitly state the purpose of the new law is to facilitate the more efficient meeting of the general requirements currently set out in Article 1. This could be presented as sitting within a broader policy objective of seeking to ensure that service provision and related environmental requirements can continue to be met over time in an affordable and financially sustainable manner. Whether addressed here and/or later (see below), it would seem helpful to make some more explicit reference to the relevance of efficiency considerations.

In line with the emphasis on performance, it is noteworthy that the criteria to become a guarantee supplier [see **Article 15(11&14)**] only refer to financial performance and size, and do not factor other dimensions of the operational performance of the service provider. Some minimal level of performance or reference to a benchmarking process would seem in line with the overall ambition of the Law.

Related to the above point, is a question of whether it might be helpful to include some provisions that adopt a more dynamic perspective in **Section 2**. As it is, **Articles 4 – 11** seem to be focused primarily on describing the boundaries of the competencies of the different institutions with regulatory responsibilities. Section 2 can be read in a static way and would benefit from setting the scene for a dynamic interpretation and evolution of governance arrangements. For instance, while **Article 10** sets the competences of municipal authorities in governing water supply and sanitation services, reference could be made to the potential for cooperation across municipalities, in pursuance of economies of scale and scope for service provision.

Moreover, the success of the planned reforms may depend to a significant extent on how different institutions - and most importantly the State Energy Regulatory Council (SERC, as economic regulator) – interpret their duties, and seek to apply the powers and responsibilities they have been given.

This would seem to raise two different sorts of issues which are commented on further in the next few points below, and which relate to questions of whether it would be helpful for the new law to include:

- More in relation to some of the boundary issues that might be expected to arise (as below, the role of the economic regulator in reviewing/assessing 'operation plans' may be one particularly important issue).
- Further scope for the Ministry to influence how duties are being interpreted and applied.

5.2.2. Stipulating the role of the economic regulator

The first point above seems relevant because economic regulators can seek to interpret the scope of their powers in different ways. A critical issue concerns the extent to which the regulator seeks to engage with service delivery issues in the short and longer term. That is, while economic regulators are typically primarily given responsibilities related to charging matters, this has often led regulators to engage extensively with questions concerned with what utilities are delivering in return for being able to levy those charge levels. This follows from the fact that in order to address the question of how reasonable or otherwise a given potential charge level is, it is necessary to consider what is actually being paid for and delivered: what level of service quality is being provided, and how well prepared and resilient are the service provision arrangements to future developments?

An important point here in the context of WSS in Lithuania is that the efficiency of future service provision arrangements may heavily depend on the efficiency of the 'operation plans' that underpin charging proposals (and indeed the efficiency of the infrastructure plans that underpin the operation plans).

This suggests that – in line with experience in some other jurisdictions - it may be appropriate for the economic regulator to have some form of active role in challenging the robustness of operation plans it is being asked to approve funding for, and in particular testing the extent to which alternative options (including different forms of consolidation options) were considered in the development of those plans. In the absence of this, considerable reliance would seem to be being put on the **Article 15** provisions, without there being such a clearly regulatory role in relation to ongoing incentives, and the operation of the price control process.

Under such an approach, while municipalities would retain clear responsibility for the development of such plans, the fact that a plan had been approved at the municipality level would not necessarily mean that the costs identified by the utility as associated with delivering on that plan (even if viewed as reasonable from a narrow perspective) would be allowed by the economic regulator to be included in charges.

To some extent – and in particular in relation to affordability - the Draft Law already explicitly recognises that this kind of tension might arise, and that the regulator may push back on a utility's plan looking for a lower cost alternative. There is a question, though, of whether it would be helpful in **Section 2** of the Draft Law to more explicitly recognise this broader role of the economic regulator in terms of considering service quality and the efficiency of capital plans and their delivery when assessing pricing proposals.

It should be noted that incentives to explore lower cost options should not be limited to "cheap" alternatives: they should invite to explore the potential economies of scope and scale that can derive from different modes of consolidation (sharing of functions, or merging at larger geographical scales). Therefore, explicitly emphasising the role of the economic regulator to pursue cost-efficiency would actively encourage consolidation on an ad hoc basis, in accordance to the bottom-up approach favoured by the government.

5.2.3. Acknowledging the leadership of the Ministry of Environment

The second point above is intended to reflect the risk that various institutions may end interpreting the provisions of the new law in unduly and undesirably limited ways. This could create a context where the Ministry considers that the new law provides a framework that would and should be capable of being used in order to better achieve desired policy objectives, but that is not in practice used that way.

There are a range of reasons why this situation might arise. One concerns legal risks that could arise if new, more progressive approaches were to be adopted, such that institutions –in particular, the economic regulator - may end up having a preference for adopting a more conservative and low risk approach over time. This may be particularly likely if a range of other parties challenge the legitimacy of the economic regulator adopting a more expansive role, and the new law itself provides limited basis for support.

A related issue here is that decisions associated with WSS developments can give rise to material trade-offs that are difficult for regulatory authorities to weigh up, such that their judgements may raise different kinds of legitimacy concerns.

Both of these types of risk could potentially be addressed by including a more dynamic and ongoing role for the Ministry in providing occasional guidance to the economic regulator on factors it should be taking into account when undertaking its duties, and including a requirement for the economic regulator to have regard to such guidance. This approach has been widely used over a number of years in the UK through the provision of social and environmental guidance to regulators from the relevant government department. This is something that could be included in **Section 2** if considered appropriate.

5.3. Alignment with the need to incentivise performance in service delivery

The draft law provides guidance on three sets of issues, which can contribute to - or hinder - cost-efficiency and sustainability of service provision.

5.3.1. Convergence of water tariffs in cases of consolidation

The non-discrimination principle presented under **Article 26** raises some potential incentive problems in terms on consolidation, and would seem to merit careful attention. This is particularly so as **Article 34(6)** appears to limit the scope for price differences within a newly consolidated regional supply area to 3 years. The broader point here is that while aligning prices within a region may be straightforward and have only limited impact on any individual customers in some circumstances, there seems to be a reasonable prospect that this will not always be the case, particularly given the extent of price disparities at present. Given this, a requirement for prices to rapidly converge after consolidation has taken place could be viewed as generating a significant disincentive to consolidation for those customers whose initial prices are lower, and who would effectively be asked to pay more (than they otherwise would) and cross-subsidise other customers as a result of the consolidation going ahead.

The potential adverse incentive effects of this look to merit careful attention. Consideration could be given to adopting a more flexible approach, where the long-term objective of price convergence could be reflected without that translating into a necessary price increase for those customers in the low-cost area in the short-term. Again, more room for manoeuvre would be provided if such considerations were not stated in the Law, but left for further discussion in the context of secondary legislation.

5.3.2. Assessment of costs of service provision

Section 8 provides detailed guidance on the definition of costs of service provision and urges service providers to ensure efficient and reasonable costs (**Article 33**). While this inclination is welcome, it misses the opportunity to look for cost-efficiency beyond the fence of individual service providers. As discussed in previous occasions, the role of SERC, as economic regulator, is to challenge performance of individual utilities and encourage the exploration of performance enhancement through different modes of consolidation, to reap economies of scale.

Performance benchmarking can contribute to this, as it can point at rooms for improvement of development plans and operational performance. Article 33(2&3) could refer to performance benchmarking and performance standards (which would be further defined in secondary legislation), in particular when discussing efficient and reasonable costs.

Similarly, lack of fund and achievement of a "reasonable return on investment" should not necessarily translate into tariff increases, as suggested in Article 33(1). Opportunities to deliver services cost-efficiently and to generate a reasonable return on investment may derive from coordination across service providers and some form of consolidation. Here, consolidation can be an alternative to tariff increases, which would be socially preferable. **Article 33** could be rephrased to suggest that tariff increases could be considered by SERC, after other options to enhance operational efficiency – possibly beyond individual service providers – have been explored. Similarly, **Article 34(15)** could refer to some form of consolidation, as an option to reduce costs

From that perspective, the provision in **Article 34(7)**, which sets a minimal requirement for the volume of investment of merged utilities, may be missing the point. Attention should be paid to the level of service and to service performance, not to the volume of investment per se. Actually, if connection triggers economies of scale, the appropriate level of service provision and performance could be achieved with less investment (economies of scale).

5.3.3. Duration of development plans and tariff reviews

Article 34(4) provides that development plans be set for 3 years (minimum). **Article 34(13)** also requires that tariffs be reviewed on a yearly basis.

There would be multiple benefits to provide for longer development plans and extend the period for which tariffs are set. Longer development plans allow service providers to invest and reap the benefits of their investment, in terms of service provision and efficiency of service delivery.

An extended period for tariff setting would not result in tariffs being set for that duration. The review could provide for a stable mechanism to adjust tariffs, for instance based on consumer price index, labour costs or the cost of energy. The Law could actually provide that best performing utilities or regional service providers could benefit from relaxed supervision and control, and extended periods for tariff setting. This would constitute a further incentive for performance enhancement and for consolidation.

5.3.4. Acknowledging consolidation as an option to enhance efficiency and sustainability of service delivery

While the preference of the Lithuanian government for a bottom-up approach to service consolidation remains, the draft Law could be used as an opportunity to set the scene for more explicit guidance and awareness raising. In addition to comments above on Articles 33&34, the current draft provides multiple opportunities to move into that direction:

- As mentioned above, **Article 10** could include a reference to intermunicipal cooperation as a desirable option to promote efficiency in service provision
- Similarly, **Article 13(1)** could consider the opportunity to devolve responsibility to intermunicipal or regional authorities, where they exist and when appropriate
- **Article 21(6)** could provide more flexibility is to where sewerage sludge should be transported for treatment. Treatment capacity and performance of facilities nearby (but not necessarily n the same municipality) could be factored in
- The definition of effectiveness in **Article 26(3)** could make reference to cost-efficiency rather than to the amount of costs (which in itself is not an indication of efficiency)
- The conditions for granting licences [**Article 27(4)**] or for revoking them could also make explicit reference to operational efficiency and performance standards (which could be defined in the context of secondary legislation).

For the same reason, the requirement to modify licence when the area of operation of a service provider changes can operate as a barrier to change. In principle, if licences are granted on the basis of the capacity of a utility to deliver and reach performance standards, it could be assumed that that level of performance would be achieved in other areas. Licences could then be revoked ex post, in cases where this assumption was proved wrong. Such a principle would provide more flexibility for licenced operators to consider opportunities to operate in other areas and jurisdictions.

More generally, the capacity of the SERC to incentive consolidation could be acknowledged and clearly stated, in particular in reference to the review of development plans, proposed tariffs and expenditure programmes.

5.4. Considering practicalities in relation to core principles for service provision

The Law makes duly reference to core principles for the organisation and financing of water supply and sanitation services, namely cost recovery and Polluter Pays principle. However, it does so in ways that may prevent sound implementation of these principles in the Lithuanian context today. A more flexible or staged approach may contribute to robust progress towards efficient service delivery and robust financing strategies.

As regards cost-recovery, **Article 18(1)** states that costs 'must cover the necessary costs for... the long-term operation, renovation and development...' etc. As in our earlier briefing note, while this can be expected to be a sensible longer objective for charge levels, there may be undesirable consequences from treating this an appropriate basis for determining the level at which charges should be set in the short- to medium-term. In particular, such an ambition may conflict with incentives for efficiency improvements that the regulator would be otherwise seeking to generate.

Similarly, it may be worth considering whether the presentation of the Polluter Pays principle in **Article 18(2)** presents the responsibility of water sector somewhat too starkly. That is, water sector environmental programmes can often be viewed as addressing broader environmental issues (including those associated with agricultural run-off), and it may be undesirable to present things in such a clear-cut manner. In particular, one desirable water sector response in other sectors has been for companies to try to find ways of targeting other sources of pollution in order to lessen the extent to which broader environmental problems (such as those associated with phosphorus concentrations) are treated as (only) wastewater treatment plant problems.

Note

[1] Note that several EU countries consider shut-off as inappropriate (and indeed unlawful in some jurisdictions) and prefer other options to make users pay. Flow restriction is one option. Note that it is not clear how wastewater collection and treatment can be discontinued in practice when users do not pay their bill.

6 An Action Plan for the consolidation of water utilities in the pilot regions

The chapter reviews the state of play in two pilot regions – one with a strong urban centre and one more rural – and reports on engagement with regional stakeholders to figure out practical modes of consolidation of water utilities. The consultations provided valuable feedback to inform recommendations at national level.

6.1. Introduction

6.1.1. The context: background and objectives of the OECD collaboration with Lithuania

In Lithuania, the Law on Drinking Water Supply and Wastewater Treatment Services (2006, amended in 2014) introduced the reform of the Water Supply and Sanitation (WSS) sector and the concept of consolidation of water utilities on a voluntary basis A new version of the law is currently being discussed in the parliament. It is expected that the new (improved) version of the law will be adopted by the end of the year.

By 2019, it resulted in the creation of a regional water operator for the Klaipėda region and a reduced number of operating water companies (one company per municipality). Reluctance of municipalities to consolidate their water companies remains one of the main obstacles for implementation of this reform.

The Government of the Republic of Lithuania is working towards the enhanced sustainability of WSS services in the country. The Implementation Plan of the Government Programme includes activities for the consolidation of the drinking water supply and wastewater treatment sector, to ensure higher operational efficiency and to reduce the disparity in prices for WSS services. A roadmap for consolidation of water companies was recently elaborated by the Government (2019). Modalities of the reform implementation, including options for consolidation of the water utility sector, have to be further considered and included into the proposal to the Government.

The OECD supports the Ministry of Environment of the Republic of Lithuania in operationalising the national strategy to enhance the sustainability of the WSS sector and compliance with the EU acquis in this area. The collaboration entails a focus on two pilot regions and derives lessons for the reform implementation. Lithuania selected Kaunas and Marijampole as pilot regions.

This Project supports the development of detailed recommendations for implementation of the roadmap for the consolidation of water utilities of Lithuania, including recommendations on financial and governance incentives to facilitate a broader water sector reform in the country. The expected impact of the Project will be a sustained capacity of consolidated utilities to finance needed investments to comply with EU acquis and deliver better services to the population, including segments who currently do not have access.

The main outcome will be enhanced self-financing capacity of water utilities and increased social equity in access to and prices for WSS services in Lithuania, through consolidation of service providers, robust tariff policy and adequate accompanying measures.

Output 6 is an important step of the OECD collaboration with the Ministry of Environment of the Republic of Lithuania. It builds on previous project outputs, and namely:

- Chapter 1 - Background report characterising the state of play;
- Kick-off meeting , where the Government officially launched and announced the project and main stakeholders voiced their support and priorities;
- Chapter 3 – Issues paper, where the need for reform and current issues for consolidation are investigated. Following this report, two pilot regions – Kaunas and Marijampole – were identified for investigating scenarios for consolidation and the development of a roadmap for implementation. The OECD Secretariat convened one workshop in each region in October 2021, focusing on the main issues related to WSS in each region and preliminary reactions to the Ministry's intention to accelerate agglomeration of water services as a means to enhance operational efficiency and financial sustainability of the sector; and
- Marijampoles and Kaunas County Analysis, two reports providing detailed data and information on the water sector in the two pilot regions.

Chapter 6 also informs other chapters, on pricing, performance monitoring, and accompanying amendments of the legal framework.

6.1.2. Chapter 6: objectives and main steps

The objectives of Chapter 6 report are to:

- Develop scenarios for the consolidation of water utilities in the Kaunas and Marijampole regions; and
- Provide practical recommendations for implementing consolidation of water utilities in the two regions.

After reviewing previous project outputs, additional case studies were reviewed to inspire potential consolidation arrangements in Lithuania; similarly, the most inspiring examples among the case studies identified in Chapter 3 report were identified. This allowed for a preliminary identification of preliminary scenarios, and practical steps towards consolidation, to be discussed and evaluated with representatives of water utilities and municipalities in the two regions.

To this end, in June 2022 the OECD Secretariat convened a second workshop in each of the two regions to discuss, refine and evaluate the proposed scenarios and practical steps towards consolidation.

The outcomes of the two workshops were presented and discussed with Irmantas Valunas and Monika Sakalauskaitė of the Ministry of Environment of the Republic of Lithuania.

6.1.3. This report

Chapter 6 presents the results of the process illustrated above, and includes:

- Why is reform needed? A synthesis of the previous phases of the OECD project;
- Options for consolidation: possible practical arrangements and sharing of functions;
- Preferred options for consolidation in the two pilot regions; and
- The way forward: practical steps towards consolidation in the two pilot regions and beyond.

6.2. Why is consolidation needed?

6.2.1. Country overview

Lithuania is characterized by abundant freshwater supply, mainly from groundwater sources. The country has undertaken significant investments, in the last two decades, to reach the EU water *acquis* on WSS. The massive investments focused on building new infrastructures to connect most of the population to WSS. However, the goal of 95% of the population having access to drinking water supply and sanitation services is not yet achieved. Only 9 municipalities (2018) were able to achieve the goal.

A part of the population is not yet connected to the water supply nor to the wastewater treatment networks. For that, the country needs further investments to reach the objective. Originally, the infrastructure development was financed through EU funding – more than 1 billion euros came through EU Cohesion policy or other grants. 3.5 billion euros of investments are still needed to reach full compliance with the EU and national water supply and wastewater treatment regulation. However, water utilities are not able to attract new investors due to low financial viability and long payback period of the projects. The new financing capacities are needed to operate and maintain water assets, adapt services to changing needs, driven by more stringent environment and health regulations, or a changing climate.

Furthermore, there is a need to properly operate and maintain the recently constructed infrastructure to ensure lasting service provision and performance and avoid cost related to premature decay of existing infrastructure. To do so, the water companies should ensure sustainable financing for the operation and maintenance of the water utilities. Nevertheless, companies operating the water utilities are already facing financial difficulties to maintain the proper investment levels to operate the water utilities. This means that the current infrastructure might be at risk.

In Lithuania, the water utilities are owned by the municipalities and local governments (62 water utilities in 2020). They bear most of the cost of providing water supply and sanitation services and operating and maintaining existing systems. They face severe challenges, be it on the financial level such as a) lack of professional staff to run the water utility that could further increase operational cost and b) low population density – which makes it difficult for the water utility to connect all population; or on technical level such as losses in drinking water supply – on average 26% (2020).

In addition, there are significant disparities in water prices and quality service across the country. It is unclear how revenues from tariffs for WSS can cover the projected costs. Water utilities, operating in small municipalities and rural areas are not able to provide adequate service and proper access to WSS services. Water tariffs are usually higher in small municipalities where investment needs are higher. Higher-income urban population pays less for WSS services than the population of small municipalities, where incomes are significantly lower, thus contributing to social inequality (see Figure 6.1 below).

Figure 6.1. Cost of WSS services and the ratio of the average wage in municipalities

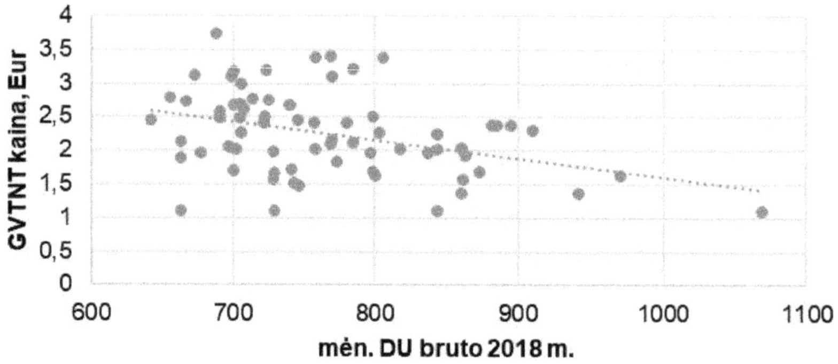

Translation: Y axis: cost of drinking water supply and wastewater treatment; eur/month; X axis: Gross monthly salary in 2018
Source: Ministry of Environment of Lithuania

Furthermore, a proper maintenance and operation of the WSS system would require a further increase of WSS tariffs, going beyond an affordability threshold and reaching 4% for low-income households. This situation is not financially sustainable. It puts sector reforms at risk as Lithuania lacks a sustainable funding strategy for the long-term operation and maintenance of WSS services.

This project focuses on two pilot regions in Lithuania, the Kaunas and Marijampole regions. For what concerns water management challenges and practices, these two regions present similarities among them and to the national context. At the same time, they also present some differences, and in particular:

- In the Kaunas region, 65% of the population is concentrated in the Kaunas city, the second largest city in Lithuania. Overall, population density is higher than in Lithuania as a whole, although still significantly lower than the EU average. These two aspects make it easier for water companies to connect the population to the network, as shown by the higher connection rate to WSS services – and, to some extent, also to carry out operation and maintenance. Another effect is that population is projected to decrease less dramatically (-9%) than in the Marijampole region;

- The Marijampole region is mostly rural. Marijampole city is in fact only the seventh largest city in Lithuania, and it hosts 46% of total population in the region. As a result, population density is significantly lower than the national average. This exacerbates the challenges faced by WSS operators in connecting the population to the network, as shown by a lower-than-average connection rate, and also in operating and maintaining the system. Being mostly rural, the region is projected to experience a massive population decrease (-50%) by 2050, and this can represent a major challenge when it comes to investment in new WSS infrastructures or the maintenance of the existing ones: it means that the customer base of water utilities are also projected to decrease by 50%, resulting in half of the revenues from WSS tariffs – a vital funding source for the sector.

The table below illustrates the key figures with respect to water management in Lithuania and the two pilot regions.

Table 6.1. Key figures on water management in the Kaunas and Marijampole regions

Key figures in relation to water management	Lithuania – national level	Kaunas region	Marijampole region
Population (inhabitants)	2.8 million	445 185	127 002
Of which: living in urban areas	65% (19% in Vilnius)	65% (Kaunas city)	46% (Marijampole city)
Living in rural areas	35%	35%	54%
Expected population growth by 2050	Not available	-9%	-50%
Population density (inhabitants/km²) *EU average: 109*	44.6	55	28.4
Connection rate to WSS services	82% drinking water, 74% sanitation	86.6%	80%
Average losses in drinking water supply	26%	24%	29%

The differences highlighted above also emerged in the discussions with water operators and municipalities in the two regions, as shown in chapter 3. The following sections provide more detailed data on WSS in the two pilot regions, highlighting the challenges currently faced by the water sector.

6.3. Challenges faced by the WSS sector in the Kaunas region

6.3.1. Key challenge 1. Disparities in connection rates across municipalities

Kaunas region is the second largest region in Lithuania, and it includes five municipalities. The distribution of the population across municipalities is shown in the figure below.

Figure 6.2. Distribution of population in the different municipalities of Kaunas region

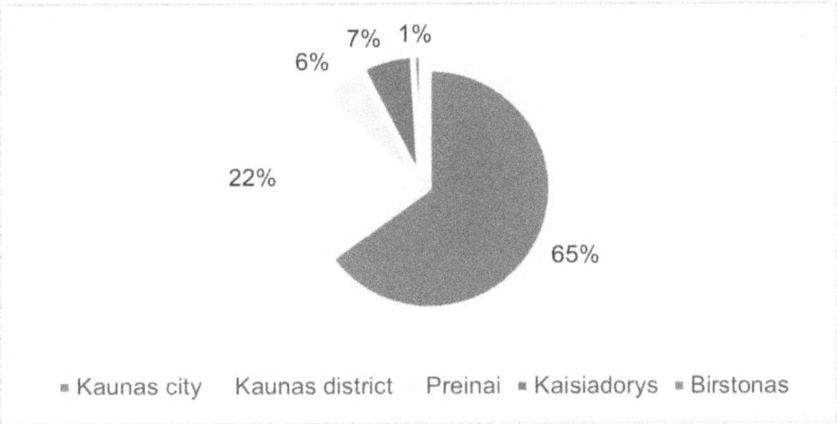

Most of the population is connected to drinking water and sanitation services (86.63% of the overall population – 2020) (Figure 6.3). The connection to water services differs from one municipality to the other, with disparity in connection rates being related to the importance of population living in (less-populated) rural areas.

Figure 6.3. Part of the population connected to the water services - Kaunas region

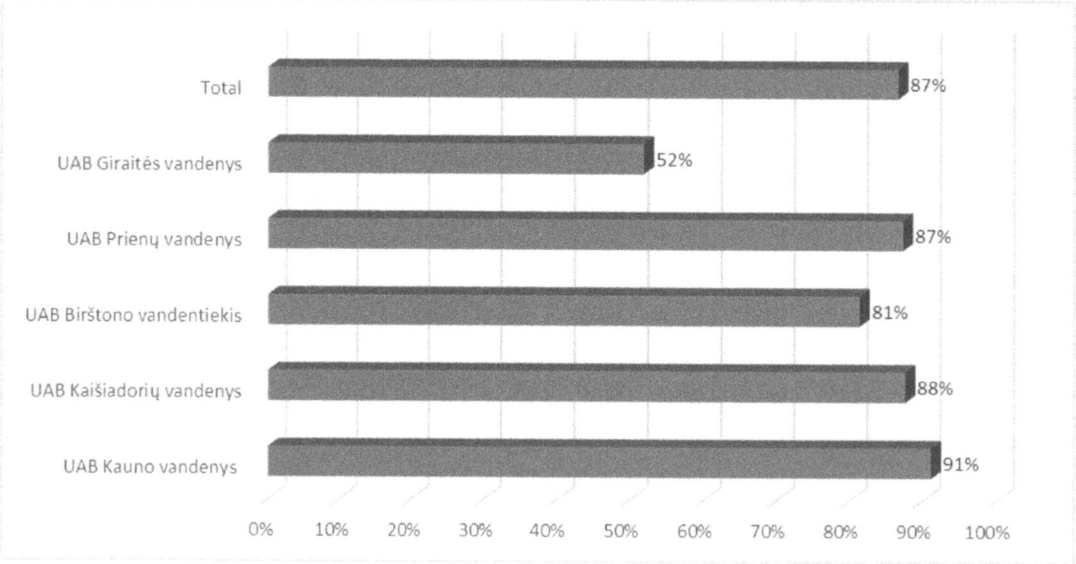

The majority of the population is connected to both drinking water supply and sanitation services (91% of the population) (see Figure 6.4), with the remaining receiving either sewage treatment service or drinking water services.

Figure 6.4. Different services provided for consumers - Kaunas region

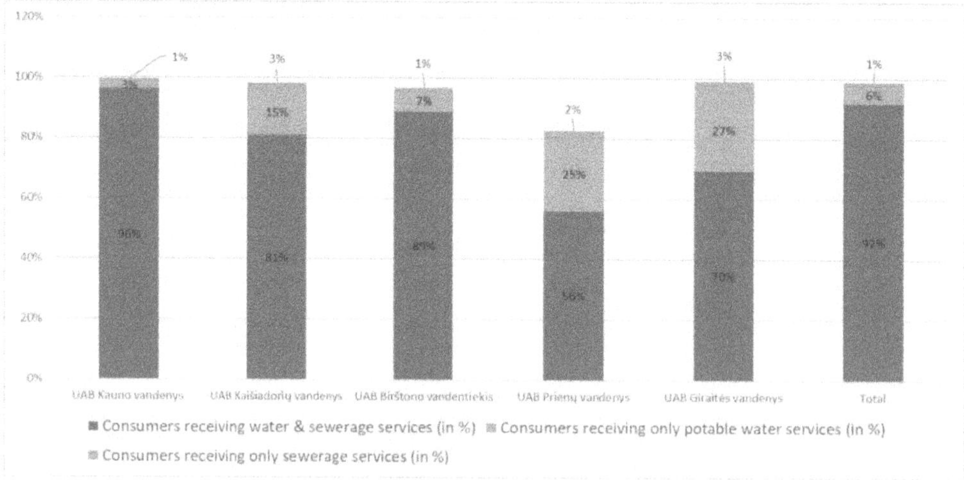

Key challenge 2. Losses in water supply service

In 2020, the volume of water extracted and distributed by the five companies was 27 858 thousand cubic meters. However, the companies managed to sell only 20 905 cubic meters (76% of the overall volume). This indicates a loss of (approximately) 24% in the distribution networks, with the majority of these losses

(84%) being attributed to the drinking water supply network, 12% to losses in house/apartment pipe system and the remaining 3% being technological losses (see Figure 6.5).

Figure 6.5. Losses in water supply service - Kaunas region

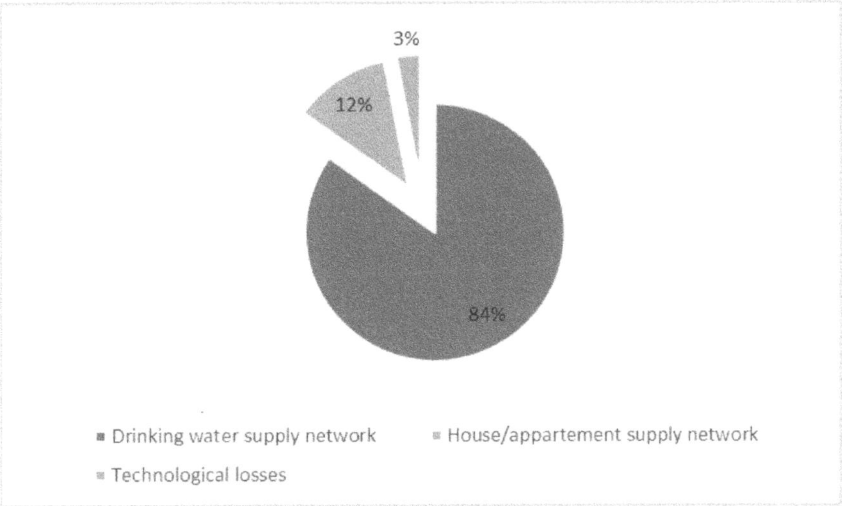

Key challenge 3. Unknown level of wastewater treatment in the region

In relation to sewage treatment, data that have been collected in the frame of the present study only shows the total volume of wastewater collected from households, (approximately) 30 751 thousand cubic meters (2020). However, there is no evidence found on the current level of treatment as well as on the number of treatment plants per municipality. Such data would help better understand whether the environmental norms set by the different European directives (e.g. Water Framework Directive, Urban Wastewater Directive) are currently complied with or not.

The discussions with water operators and municipalities revealed the presence of three WWTPs in the Kaisadory district. One of the three WWTPs has been renovated and is working efficiently and respecting the environmental norms. The other two plants are old and need to be renovated, with steps currently taken for the renovation of a second plant. The operator and municipalities are currently identifying sources of (European) funding that could be mobilised for carrying out the renovation of the plants

Key challenge 4. Price disparities across urban and rural municipalities

Large water tariff disparities exist across municipalities (see Figure 6.6), in line with the general situation at the national level. The lowest water tariffs are recorded in Kaunas, the largest municipality (in terms of population), an urban area with higher income levels, whereas the highest water tariffs are recorded in the smallest municipality, a rural area with lower income levels that might face more significant affordability challenges.

Figure 6.6. Water prices - Kaunas region

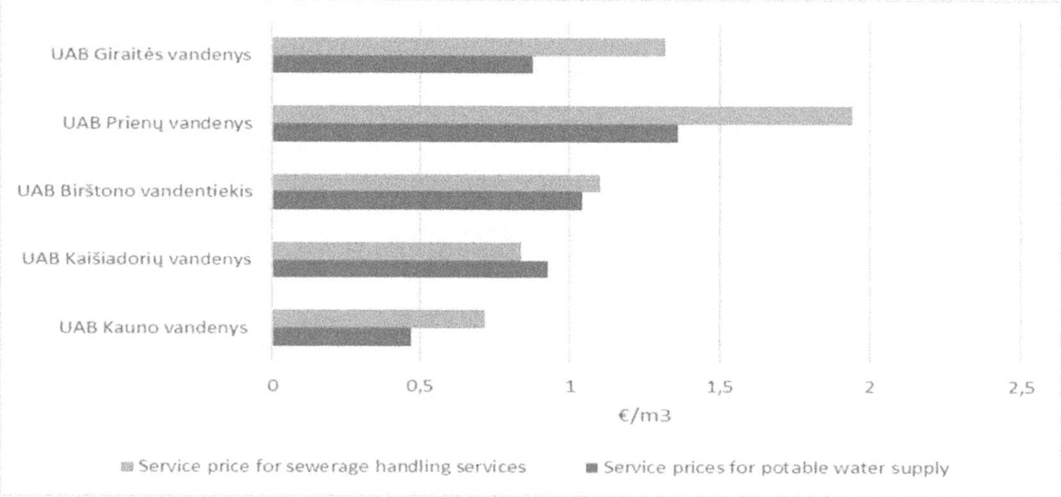

Key challenge 5. Importance of different cost categories and impact of rising energy prices

The five companies of the Kaunas region spent 29 million euros in 2020. The analysis of the different cost components (see Figure 6.7) stresses the importance of labour costs (32% of the total costs) and of asset amortization (22% of the total costs). Energy costs represented 12% of total costs; these costs experiencing currently a significant increase as a result of the worldwide energy crisis.

The discussions with water operators highlighted that current increase in energy prices is making it difficult for water operators to distribute water without increasing WSS prices. Two solutions are being adopted in Kaunas to overcome the continuous increase in energy prices. The first one is regulatory solution. The water operators will be allowed to apply for compensation from the government when energy prices increase by 30%. The water companies in Kaunas are currently preparing to apply for this compensation. It is noteworthy that this process creates a backlog as the delay in tariff adjustment urges utilities to postpone needed maintenance. The second one is the installation of solar power panels that allow to decrease the electricity bill for the operator.

Figure 6.7. Cost categories for water operators - Kaunas region

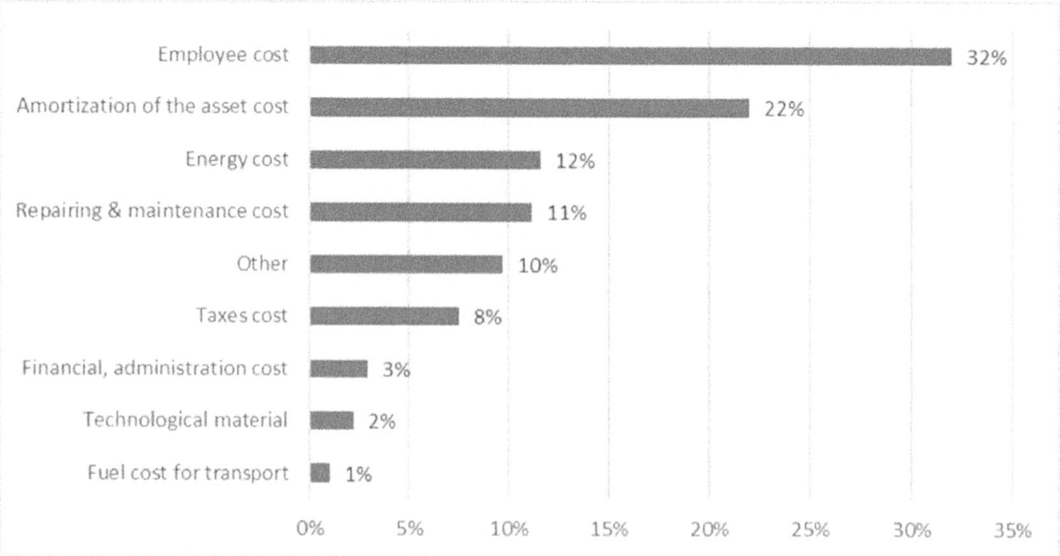

Key challenge 5. Diverse cost-recovery levels across municipalities

Only two out of five companies are managing to recover all their costs with revenues from water tariffs (see Figure 6.8). However, when the costs and revenues for all companies are aggregated, the total cost-recovery ratio is above 100%.

Figure 6.8. Financial performance of water companies in Kaunas region

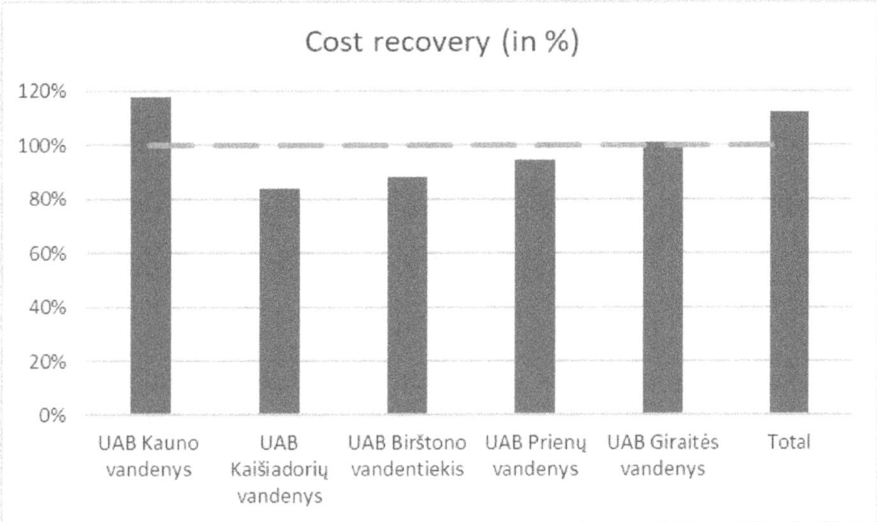

6.4. Challenges faced by the WSS sector in the Marijampole region

6.4.1. Key challenge 1. Disparities in connection rates across municipalities

The Marijampole region covers 6.8% of the area of Lithuania and is composed of four municipalities. Except for Marijampole city, it is a mostly rural region. The distribution of the population across municipalities is shown in the figure below.

Figure 6.9. Distribution of population in the different municipalities of Marijampole region

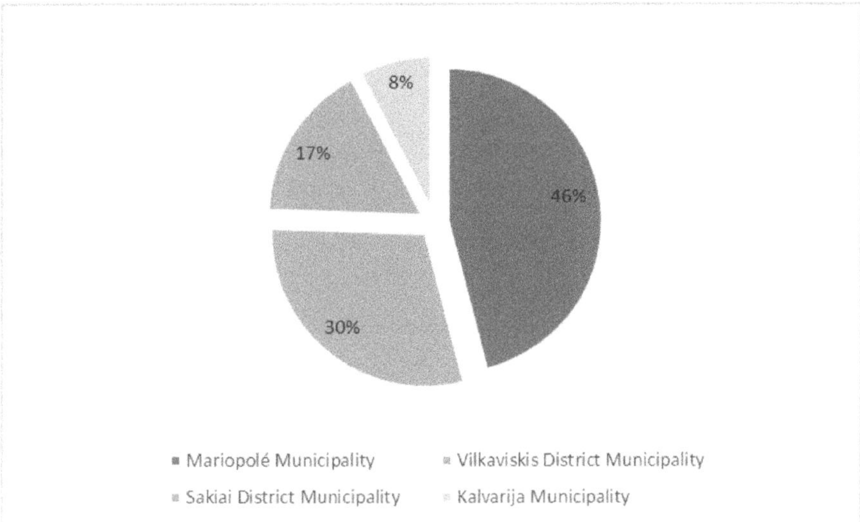

Most of the population is connected to both drinking water and sanitation services (80% of the overall population – 2020), with significant differences among municipalities translating the relative importance of rural areas (see Figure 6.10) with scattered population.

Figure 6.10. Part of the population connected to the water services – Marijampole region

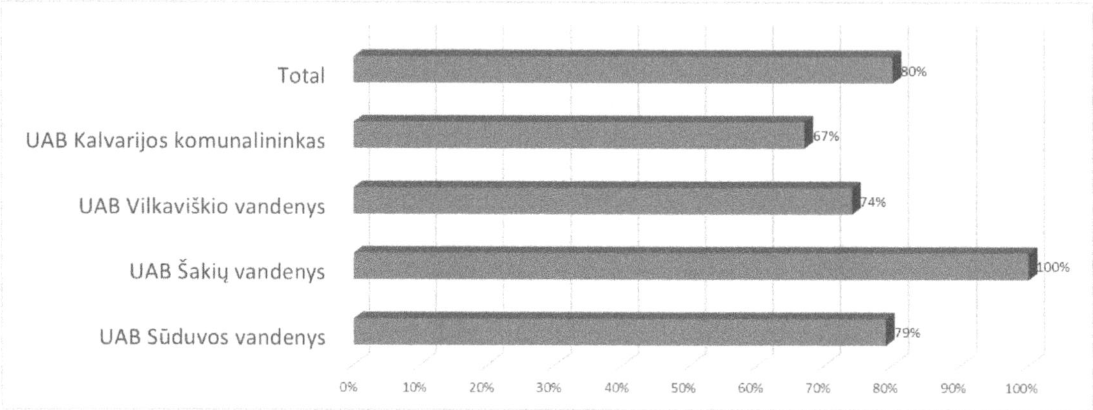

The majority of consumers receive drinking water and wastewater treatment services (76%); with the remaining being connected to either sewage treatment services or drinking water services (see Figure 6.11).

Figure 6.11. Different services provided for consumers – Marijampole region

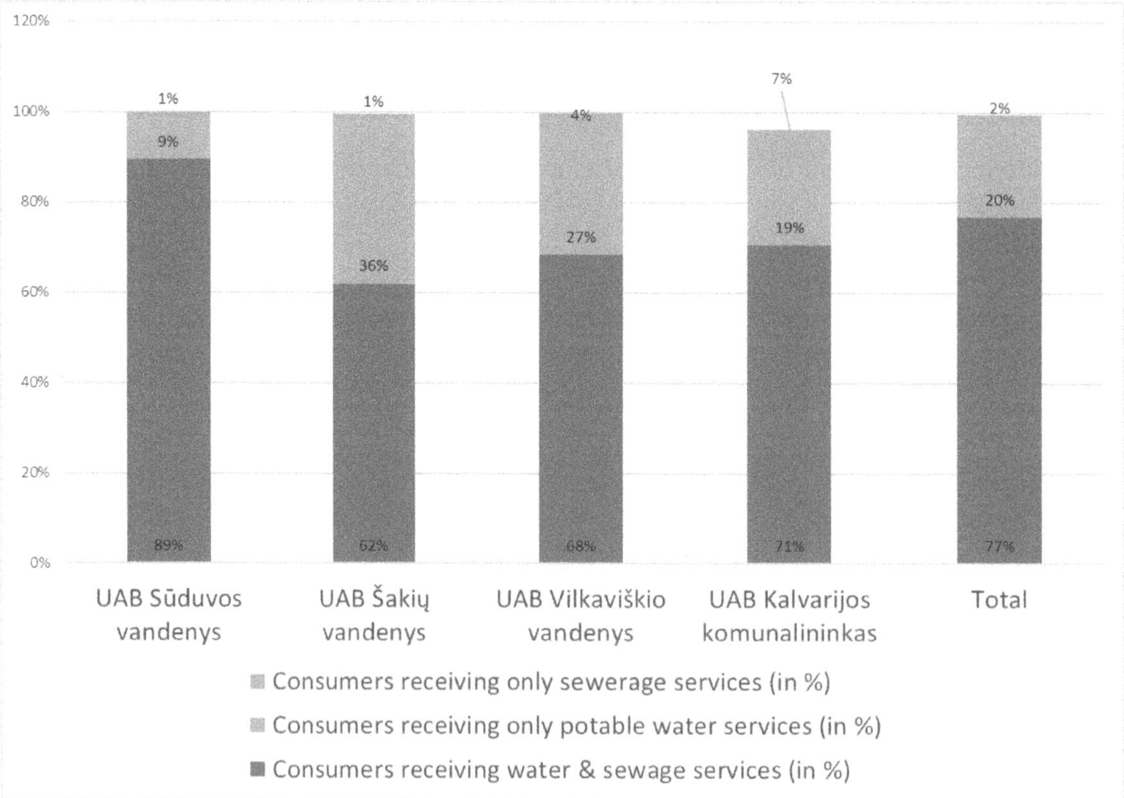

6.4.2. Key challenge 2. Losses in water supply service

In 2020, the volume of water extracted and distributed by the four companies was 4 067 thousand cubic meters. However, losses of Marijampole region water management companies accounted for an average of 29%, with the largest share of losses taking place in the water supply networks (see Figure 6.12).

Figure 6.12. Losses in water supply service - Marijampole region

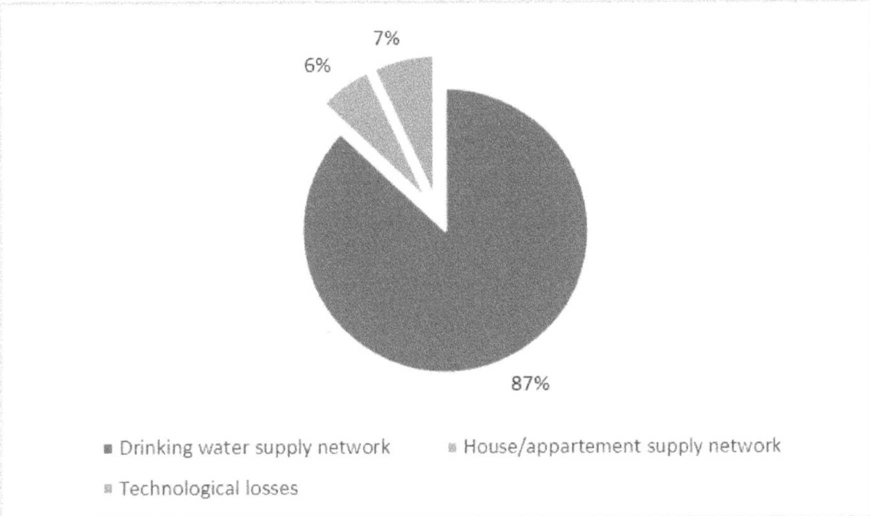

One of the biggest challenges faced by water operators in the Marijampole region is the old water supply network. The companies do not have any plans of the network and they rely on leakage reporting so they can fix the leak. According to the water operators, three fails in the water supply system are reported each day in the region.

6.4.3. Key challenge 3. Unknown level of wastewater treatment in the region

Data obtained in the context of this study relates to the volume of wastewater collected from households, (approximately) 6 902 thousand cubic meters (2020). However, no evidence has been found on the level of treatment and the number of treatment plants per municipality. It is not clear then how current treatment complies with existing environmental norms set by European directives.

According to the water operators of the Marijampole region, the WWTPs were constructed in the 80s and 90s of last century. However, due to the population decrease, renovation was done to downsize some of the plants so they could work efficiently and at lower costs. Furthermore, the wastewater is well treated, and the discharged water is tested quarterly or monthly, depending on the company.

6.4.4. Key challenge 4. Price disparities across urban and rural municipalities

Large water tariff disparities exist across municipalities (see Figure 6.13), in line with what happens at the national level: the lowest water prices are recorded in Marijampole, the largest municipality (in terms of population), an urban area with higher income levels, whereas the highest prices are recorded in the smallest municipality, a rural area with lower income levels. This can pose affordability challenges in the lower-income municipalities.

Figure 6.13. Water prices - Marijampole county

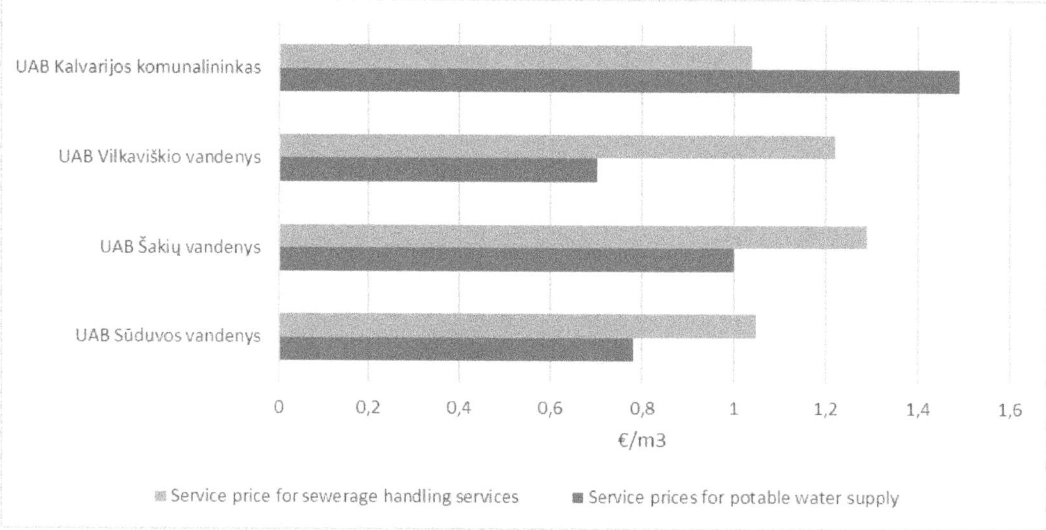

6.4.5. Key challenge 5. Importance of different cost categories and impact of rising energy prices

The four companies in the Marijampole region spent 8 million euros in 2020 (Figure 6.14). Employee costs alone represent half of the total costs, with energy costs representing 12% of these costs – a ratio that is likely to experience significant increase as a result of the current energy crisis.

As for the Kaunas region, water operators highlighted that the energy prices tripled in the last year, which made operation (including extraction, treatment, and distribution) of water challenging with the low prices. They also stressed that energy price increases are likely to limit (or postpone) maintenance as compared to what was originally planned with the set water tariff.

Figure 6.14. Cost categories for water operators - Marijampole county

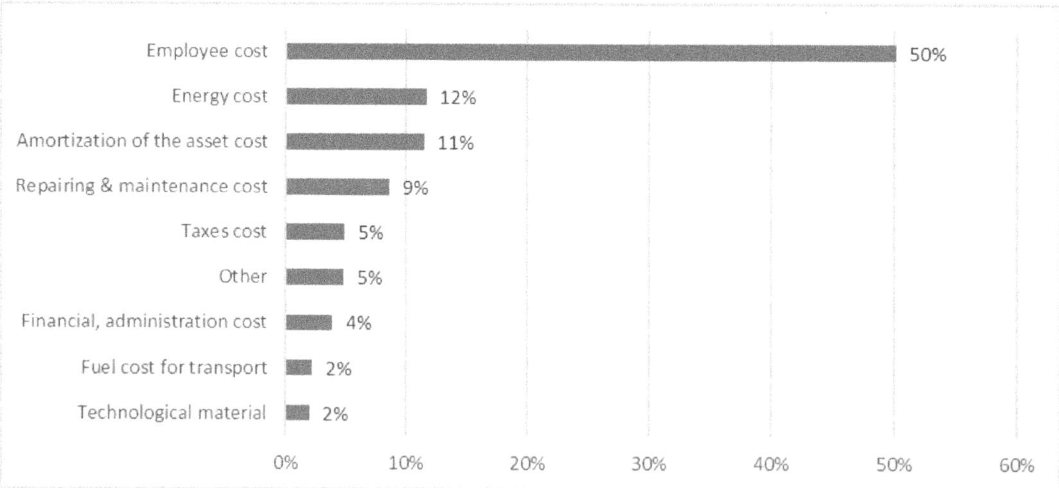

6.4.6. Key challenge 6. Diverse cost-recovery levels across municipalities

Only two out of four companies are managing to recover all their costs with revenues from water tariffs (see Figure 6.15). When all companies are combined, total revenues cover all costs.

Figure 6.15. Financial performance of water companies in Marijampole county

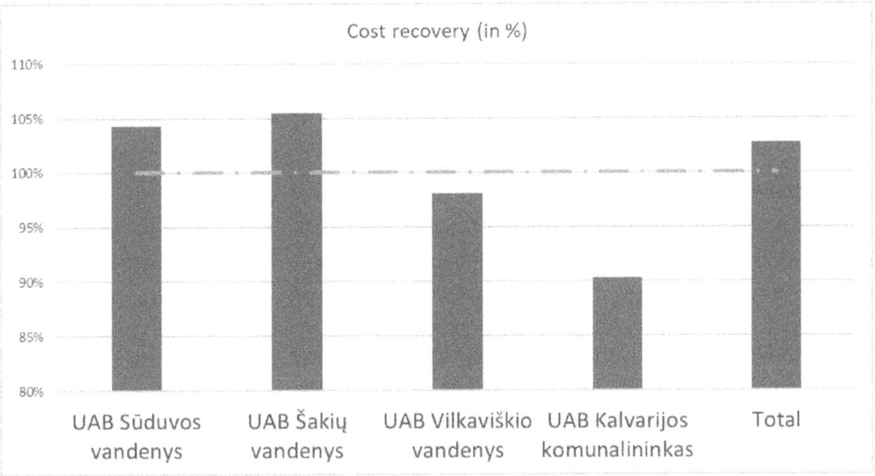

6.4.7. How consolidation can help address WSS sector issues in the two pilot regions

The above sections presented the main challenges/issues facing the different water companies in Lithuania, in particular for the Kaunas and Marijampole regions. Consolidation of the WSS sector in the two regions can contribute to addressing such challenges, and it can help in:

- Increasing the number of inhabitants connected to the water supply and wastewater treatment networks. In fact, the consolidation of different companies will lead to more cooperation between the different municipalities and thereafter to a better coordination in the infrastructure investments.
- Better (efficient) investment decisions which leads to economies of scale. The consolidated companies will be eligible to apply for collective funding and thereafter make better investment decisions – in relation to the water supply networks and/or to the wastewater treatment plants.
- Decrease in operation cost: although some cost components are exogenous, and utilities can do nothing to reduce them (e.g. energy prices), in other cases pooling some functions and activities can result in a cost reduction (e.g. through energy efficiency) – and this holds, for example, in reducing an important cost category such as personnel costs, as expertise might be shared among utilities. As shown in the next chapter, sharing functions is the focal point of consolidation.
- Improvement in water supply efficiency and decrease in leakage. This is due to a better organization of the work and sharing of functions.

6.5. Options for consolidation of the WSS sector in the pilot regions

6.5.1. Practical arrangements for consolidating the WSS sector: an overview

As mentioned in the previous chapter, in Lithuania the perspective of merging municipal companies into a regional company is encountering the resistance of municipal utilities – smaller municipalities fear their voice will not be heard after consolidation – and some utilities – larger ones are concerned they will need to increase tariffs to finance upgrade of least performing assets, affecting their original customer base. This poses a strong obstacle to the consolidation of the sector.

Finding the right practical arrangement for consolidating the WSS sector can be key in addressing such resistance. In fact, consolidation does not necessarily imply a full merger of all municipal utilities operating in a region, as different levels of cooperation can be realized through different organizational arrangements, and namely:

- **A special-purpose vehicle**—that is, a specific **cooperation agreement** between service providers who remain separate entities, with a well-defined scope such as managing a specific facility or sharing some functions. An example of this agreement is the SDEA, a public establishment of cooperation in the WSS sector operating in Eastern France (see Box 1 below);
- **A delegated contract** signed between the jurisdiction level in charge of service delivery and an operator, transferring all or most of operational responsibilities, but maintaining the original entities. Examples of this arrangement already exist in OECD countries, as summarized in Box 2 below.
- **A merger**, by which original service providers consolidate into a single entity and disappear.

These organizational arrangements can be seen as progressive, as they imply an increasing level of aggregation with municipal utilities having the largest independency in the case of cooperation agreement and reduced levels of responsibility in the case of delegated contract, as opposed to their full merging into one company in the upper level of consolidation – as also shown in the figure below.

These different practical arrangements were presented to workshop participants, stressing that merging is not the only solution, nor the unavoidable point of arrival of the consolidation process.

Figure 6.16. Practical arrangements for consolidation of the WSS sector

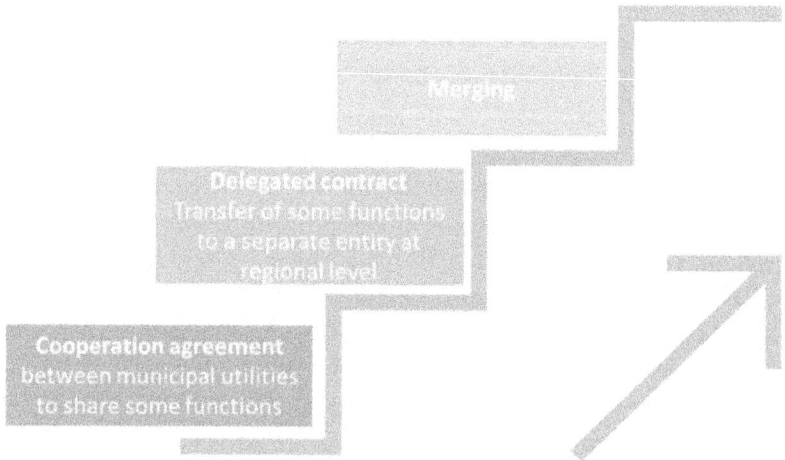

Box 6.1. Cooperation agreement between service providers: the SDEA in France

In France, *Syndicat des Eaux et de l'Assainissement Alsace-Moselle* (SDEA) is an aggregation of water utilities following a mandate (top-down) approach. The NOTRe Act mandated the progressive transfer of water and sanitation services competence from municipalities to integrated intercommunalities, with the purpose to achieve economic efficiency (through economies of scale), and solidarity (through economies of scope).

The SDEA is a public establishment of cooperation specialized in the water field and federates different municipalities/group of municipalities/Strasbourg EuroMetropol and the Bas-Rhin department. The idea from this federation is to have one establishment that manages drinking water production, river streams, reservoirs, and wastewater collection and treatment for all members of the federation. It comprises 737 municipalities and is administrated by local elected officials from different municipalities. The SDEA comprise three levels of governance, and namely:

- Global scale: bodies at the local scale include a General Assembly, a Board of Directors, a Permanent Commission, Thematic Commissions and Tender Commissions. This level is in charge of overall policy and economies of scale, adaptation of the common tool to the challenges, grouped purchases and pooling of financing capacities;
- Territorial scale: bodies at the territorial scale include Territorial councils and Contracts Commissions. This level is in charge of synergies, common projects, inter-perimetral consultations, pooling of local investments and sharing of best practices;
- Local scale: this level is administered by Local Commissions. It is in charge of proximity management, analytical financial management, definition of tariffs and financing, investment programs, awarding of work contracts and follow-up of local affairs.

Source: Series of ppt presentations provided by SDEA

Box 6.2. Delegated contracts: some examples from OECD countries

Several countries have separated water or treated wastewater production and the delivery of the service to customers:

- In Boston, a metropolitan authority consolidates water production and sewage treatment, leaving member municipalities in charge of system management.
- In Portugal, the government created a national water company in 1994. Municipalities in the same area were offered the opportunity to manage treatment plants jointly, while communes kept responsibility for operating water and sewer mains.
- In Australia, the 1994 reform planned by the Council of Australian Governments mandated the unbundling of former urban water monopolies, with bulk water production and sewage treatment organised at the regional level (by one public company) and retail water services at a more local level (by several water distribution companies). This choice paved the way for alternative water supply technologies (e.g. recycling and desalination).

Source: OECD project in Lithuania – Chapter 3 Issues paper

At the heart of the consolidation process: sharing of functions

No matter which organizational arrangement is chosen, the **sharing of functions** lies at the heart of the consolidation process for the WSS sector, in a view of reducing/ mutualizing costs and increase efficiency of operations. For example, employees training that can achieve a reduction in training costs per employee if trainings are jointly organized by utilities at the regional level; similarly, better unitary prices can be obtained if the procurement of goods and services (e.g. laboratory products) is done by all utilities together – and thus larger quantities are purchased at one time.

The number and types of functions that are shared among utilities can vary, from a "lighter" consolidation level to a "stronger" level, as some functions can be more easily shared than others in terms of transaction costs, administrative and organizational changes, and financial resources required. This also means that some functions could be easily shared in the short term, whereas other functions might need more time to be accepted and implemented – and, bringing this reasoning to the extreme, some functions might not eventually be shared even in the longer term. Functions that could be shared are listed in the table below, following an increasing level of complexity (from the easiest ones to the more challenging ones to be shared).

Table 6.2. Sharing functions among WSS utilities, from the least to the most complex one

Level of sharing complexity	Functions
	Training of staff
	Public relations and communication
	Customer care
	Procurement of products and services
	IT tools and systems
	Laboratory analysis
	Research and innovation
	Monitoring
	Technical expertise
	Application for funding
	Administrative management
	Financial management
	Application for funding
	Strategic investment planning
	Wastewater treatment
	Bulk water production

Participants to the workshops were presented with the full list of functions that could be shared, and they were asked to identify those functions that could be more easily shared – or, in other words, which functions could be shared in the short term, and which ones could be feasible but would require more time for implementing them.

> *Discussions with water operators highlighted that there is already a track record in mutualising functions of services in Lithuania, at municipal level or in other sectors, and in particular:*
>
> - *At municipal level, across sectors (WSS is not included): consolidation of public services (including customer services) in Kaunas city (see the Kaunas City service center);*
> - *In other sectors: solid waste management in the Kaunas District.*
> - *In the water sector: collection and treatment of sewerage sludge at the regional level in the Kaunas region; wastewater treatment in Kaunas, serving also small municipalities.*

- *Training of staff: it is carried out for all utilities at the national level by the National Association of Water Suppliers, which brings together all Lithuanian operators.*

However, size matters: larger cities (typically Kaunas city) have a higher capacity to mutualise multiple services at municipal level, or to lead mutualisation of some functions at district or regional levels, than smaller or rural districts such as Marijampole.

The tables below summarize the functions that could be shared as a priority in the Kaunas and Marijampole regions respectively.

Table 6.3. Sharing functions in the Kaunas region: outcomes of the discussion

Sharing functions in the Kaunas region	
Functions	**Advantages, opportunities, needs and challenges**
Laboratory analysis	These are areas where cooperation could work very well.
Research and innovation	More discussions are required to learn from current practices in that domain, identify topics and innovation of common interest, and then identify financial resources to support (common) research and innovation projects.
IT and knowledge management	Sharing IT systems would deliver common information and knowledge, facilitating cross-comparison. At present, several suppliers are serving municipal utilities with different products – and this also translates in higher costs born by the single operators. However, this would require upfront costs (purchasing software, training…) that would benefit from some sort of financial support.
Procurement	While demands can differ across utilities, there are opportunities to join forces and seek economies of scale for some substances and services (such as maintenance of solar panels). At present, joint procurement in Kaunas municipality (for municipal services) is working very well, and the same could be for joint procurement among water utilities.

Table 6.4. Sharing functions in the Marijampole region: outcomes of the discussion

Sharing functions in the Marijampoles region	
Functions	**Advantages, opportunities, needs and challenges**
Laboratory analysis	The facilities needed to carry out this type of analyses is costly, and often these are already in place in larger municipalities – thus, smaller utilities could make use of such facilities. They are discussing the possibility for having joint procurement of laboratory services, which are very expensive. However, the current procurement law would make this procedure burdensome (see also box below).
IT and knowledge management	Overall, the digitalization process started only recently, and it is still ongoing. At present, several suppliers are serving municipal utilities with different products – and this also translates in higher costs borne by the single operators. The possibility to share/mutualise experts with engineering and IT expertise was mentioned as a positive development that could support the management of the (smaller) water utilities of the region. However, this would require upfront costs (purchasing software, training…) that would benefit from some sort of financial support. Common databases might also allow for mutualizing customer service: at the moment, this function could not be mutualized as water utilities do not have access to other utilities' databases.
Procurement	While demands can differ across utilities, there are opportunities to join forces and seek economies of scale for some substances and services.

The ongoing revision of the Procurement Law is a common challenge and an opportunity at the same time. The procurement law is currently going through changes, so it could be an occasion to explore mechanisms to be put in place to make joint procurement possible. According to the current law on procurement, joint procurement, as well as the mutualisation of laboratory analysis and monitoring, could be put in place through a somewhat burdensome procurement procedure: it was suggested that this aspect of the law is amended to make mutualisation possible through a simple agreement between water utilities.

6.6. Making it happen: Practical steps towards implementation

6.6.1. Obstacles to consolidation and practical solutions

During the June workshops with municipalities and water utilities in the Kaunas and Marijampole regions, the reasons for resistance were explored, and some key concerns emerged. To make consolidation possible, these concerns need to be addressed. Main concerns and possible solutions (when available) are listed below.

Table 6.5. Selected barriers to consolidation and practical responses

Barriers to consolidation	Practical response
Utilities acknowledge consolidation is the forthcoming option for efficiency gains and financial sustainability. They claim they are fine and can manage consolidation. They point at municipalities as the institutions, which may oppose or delay the process.	This can be addressed through tailored governance arrangements, as illustrated by the SDEA.
For smaller municipalities, concerns about having their voices heard are a major political bottleneck.	It can potentially be addressed through tailored governance arrangements.
Overall, a lack of financial capacity was highlighted in both regions – and this is true in particular for utilities in smaller municipalities. Often, financial capacity of utilities can barely cover operation and maintenance of infrastructures – and in some cases not even maintenance. Sharing functions would require an initial investment (e.g. IT systems above) and, although this would be compensated by cost reduction in the medium term, utilities cannot sustain the upfront costs of setting up mutualization.	The discussions stressed the need to identify and clarify the scale (regional, national) at which mutualisation/the sharing of functions can best be carried out/supported.
The assumption that consolidation necessarily implies making water tariffs homogenous in the larger entity is a deterrent for action. It derives from the perception that homogenous tariffs result from an increase for selected customers, who will lose from the reform.	The case could be made that this assumption however is misleading: • Economies of scale can minimise the tariff increase after agglomeration • Affected customers are likely to live in the most prosperous part of the merged entity, and can afford a slight increase of their water bills • Homogenous tariffs are not a requirement for agglomeration. If it is desirable, it may be managed separately from mutualising functions or merging, and sequenced over a long period.

Of note: adding to the tariff setting formula selected indices and the possibility to reflect inflation or increases in selected costs (energy, labour, or construction) would facilitate utilities' responses to external shocks (as for the heating sector), without triggering a delayed and cumbersome tariff review, a point discussed in more depth in Chapters 4, 7 and 8.

6.6.2. Practical steps towards consolidation in the Kaunas region

- Mutualise functions with other local services in Kaunas municipality
- Develop a roadmap for the consolidation of selected functions (replicating the Kaunas City service center, but at sector level)
- Challenge applications for tariff revision as a response to the energy crisis. Use the opportunity to urge exploration of other responses benefitting from economies of scale.
- Question renovation and development plans, building on the benchmarking of business plans method proposed in Chapters 7 and 8.

6.6.3. Practical steps towards consolidation in the Marijampole region

- Mutualise functions, starting with procurement of laboratory equipment, testing and analytical capacities. The IT system could be mutualized in the longer term.
- Utilities in the region are not used to cooperate. Setting up a regional coordination body could be a first step for them to start working together towards sharing some functions. This would allow for discussing issues and possible solutions in a collective and potentially coordinated way.
- A uniform work organisation procedure would be useful as a basis for consolidation and sharing of (some) functions (e.g. information technology, procurement).
- Revive discussions between Marijampole and a neighbouring municipality about merging.
- Support discussion about sludge management at regional level. A decision is required as for the site that will receive the sewerage sludge.
- Revive exploration of sharing billing with a district heating utility.

6.7. In conclusion

The discussions in both regional workshops confirmed that merger is at best a distant option, if consolidation of WSS services should be based on voluntary initiatives. A more practical trajectory was considered, which aims at promoting some forms of consolidation by sharing, mutualising or coordinating functions. This can be a gradual endeavour, from functions that are comparatively easy to share or coordinate (e.g. training, procurement of some appliances or substances) towards coordination efforts which are more demanding (typically the development and investment plans).

Not all municipalities and utilities will advance at the same pace. The capacity to build on a large municipality, and a track record in sharing functions in other sectors, are assets. This confirms that the government (Ministry and economic regulator) have a role, ahead of setting up the appropriate incentives: supporting the emergence of some administrative hub or capacity at regional level can advance consolidation of WSS services in regions where such capacity does not exist.

Chapter 6 summarizes some relevant findings from previous outputs of this project, and it brings the reflection forward by providing recommendations on the way forward for consolidation of the water sector in the Kaunas and Marijampole regions in Lithuania.

Proposed options for consolidation and recommended practical steps are the result of targeted discussions with municipalities and water operators in the region: two workshops were in fact organized in June 2022 – one in the Kaunas region and one in the Marijampole region.

Chapter 6 findings do not mean to be exhaustive, nor representative for the entire country – and, in particular:

- The work for Chapter 6 has been carried out in a relatively short time, building on the evidence that was available. It is likely that more evidence (on the performance, on the state of the infrastructure, etc.) is available with the water supply companies (although not in a digital format which might make access and use challenging);
- The diversity of the two pilots in terms of the balance between urban and rural is an issue that is key to consolidation in large part of Lithuania. However, we acknowledge the limitation of the work with only two pilots that are very different but that might not cover all the diversity of Lithuania. Thus, the main conclusions of this report should not be extrapolated as such the main conclusions to any municipality like this.

The key messages included in this report are summarized below.

Key message 1. While the perspective of a full merger is encountering strong resistance, other "lighter" organizational arrangements could indeed be welcome by municipal water utilities and provide a pathway towards more efficient WSS services.

"Lighter" organizational arrangements would allow for the consolidation of the sector while maintaining existing water companies, although with different levels of responsibility and independence. These arrangements include: (i) cooperation agreements between providers with a well-defined scope; and (ii) delegated contracts signed between the jurisdiction level in charge of service delivery and an operator, transferring all or most of operational responsibilities.

Key message 2. No matter which organizational arrangement is chosen, the sharing of functions lies at the heart of the consolidation process for the WSS sector, in a view of reducing/ mutualizing costs and increase efficiency of operations.

The number and types of functions that are shared among utilities can vary, and some functions can be more easily shared than others in terms of transaction costs, administrative and organizational changes, and financial resources required. This also means that some functions could be easily shared in the short term, whereas others might need more time to be accepted and implemented.

The table below summarizes the functions that could be shared as a priority (i.e. in the shorter term) in the two pilot regions. In the Marijampole region, water utilities and municipalities also indicated a possible timeline for sharing functions, i.e. two functions can be shared in the shorter term (highlighted in the table with a green plus symbol), while another function can be shared in the longer term. In contrast, these time preferences were not provided by water operators and municipalities in the Kaunas region.

Table 6.6. Priority functions that could be shared in the two pilot regions

Priority functions to be shared	Kaunas region	Marijampole region
Procurement	Yes	+ (Laboratory analyses)
Laboratory testing and analysis	Yes	+
IT and knowledge management	Yes	Yes
Research and innovation	Yes	

Key message 3. Size matters! Larger cities – typically Kaunas city – have a higher capacity to mutualize multiple services at municipal level, or to lead mutualization of some functions at district or regional level, than smaller or rural districts such as Marijampole.

There is already a track record in mutualising functions of services in the Kaunas city, at municipal level or in other sectors; in the Marijampole region, water utilities and municipalities highlighted that they do not have the same capacity as a large city.

In addition, a lack of financial capacity to share functions was highlighted in both regions and this is true in particular for utilities in smaller municipalities. Often, financial capacity of utilities can barely cover operation and maintenance of infrastructures.

Key message 4. The assumption that consolidation necessarily implies making water tariffs homogenous in the larger entity is a deterrent for action.

However, homogenous tariffs are not a requirement for consolidation, and this needs to be made very clear when discussing with water utilities and municipalities.

Key message 5. The mutualization of functions and the practical steps recommended in this report will require facilitation support.

Chapter 6 outlines a “wish list” of actions that will not take place over night and on its own: rather, some facilitation will be needed so that representatives from water utilities can collectively agree on the way forward for mutualising specific functions. This facilitation support is essential for territories/regions with small (rural) water utilities such as Marijampole that are fully occupied with responding to, and solving problems, with limited capacity and resources for anticipating and setting the right conditions for efficient management.

7 Report with proposals for water pricing

Tariffs for water services can support consolidation, if properly set and if tariff reviews are adequately convened. The chapter focuses on depreciation methods for EU funded assets, decoupling consolidation from short-term harmonisation of water tariffs, and limitations to the role of water bills in financing of wider environmental policies.

7.1. Introduction

This chapter is Output 7 from the OECD project aimed at supporting the preparation of a roadmap for the consolidation of the water utility sector in Lithuania. As was noted in the earlier OECD Outputs,[1] further consolidation is viewed as a necessary feature of being able to deliver a sustainable and socially acceptable financing strategy for the future provision of water and sanitation services (WSS) in Lithuania.

The focus of this report is the arrangements for determining water tariffs in Lithuania. Consideration is given to the tensions that arise in the development and application of tariff setting processes between different policy concerns – including those associated with social and environmental outcomes – and some recommendations are presented. Attention is focused largely on four tariff setting considerations that look to be of particular importance to the development of pricing arrangements in Lithuania:

- The appropriate approach to providing for depreciation/capital maintenance in the tariff setting process
- The use of assumptions about water losses when tariffs are set
- The approach taken to disparities between the tariff levels charged by different companies and/or in different municipalities
- The extent to which WSS tariffs can be understood as funding wider environmental benefits.

The paper focuses on a specific set of issues related to how and when the tariff formula is applied. In relation to these issues, while there is some consideration of how incentives can be enhanced, the main focus is on how some of the policy priorities that have been considered in Lithuania could undermine incentives for efficient consolidation, and - given this - how that kind of negative outcome might be avoided. One of the key issue here is the policy focus on charges fully reflecting costs, which could be taken to imply that a depreciation allowance should be included in relation all assets (including EU funded assets): the Chapter sets out why an alternative approach to that (focused on the regulator providing conditional access to accelerated depreciation) would be preferable. Another is the policy focus on removing/reducing regional disparities, and it is highlighted that this could have an adverse effect on consolidation incentives.

A range of other issues that relate to tariff setting - and more broadly to approaches to economic regulation - are considered in Chapter 8, where a number of recommendations are presented in relation to benchmarking.

The current arrangements, and potential options for further development, are considered and assessed below in the light of relevant international experience. The relevance of considering international experience is enhanced by the fact that the overall economic regulatory framework for WSS in Lithuania shares a range of common features with those which apply in many other jurisdictions (for example, in terms of some of the responsibilities given to an economic regulator, and the broad ('building blocks') approach the regulator applies to tariff regulation).[2] Also, the broad question of how to meet WSS-related environmental challenges in financially sustainable and socially acceptable ways can be understood as one that all jurisdictions have had to, and will continue to have to, face to some extent.

At the same time, the feasibility and appropriateness of adopting different potential approaches will be heavily dependent on the specific circumstances that currently apply to WSS provision in Lithuania, and on how those circumstances have emerged over time. Given this, the report does not seek to provide a broad overview of international experience, as there would be a significant risk of such an overview being unhelpfully generic and of limited value. Rather, the approach adopted below is to focus attention on circumstances that apply, and the current and emerging challenges faced, in WSS provision in Lithuania, with international experience then drawn upon more selectively either to help highlight closely related experiences, or to illustrate potential options that look to merit particular attention.

In line with this, the report provides the following:

- An overview of some current and emerging challenges associated with the provision and pricing of WSS services in Lithuania that are relevant to the consideration of tariff setting options.
- A high-level overview of some of the proposed reforms (and reform objectives) that have been identified thus far.
- A brief overview of the current approach to setting WSS tariffs.
- A review of the current approach to determining the allowance for depreciation/capital maintenance requirements that should be provided for under the current tariff setting methodology, and the advantages and disadvantages of alternative approaches.
- A high-level consideration of some issues that are relevant to determining the appropriateness of assumptions with respect to water losses (including from leakage).
- A consideration of potential incentive issues associated with efforts to reduce price disparities between companies/municipalities.
- A discussion of how the use of WSS tariffs to fund broader environmental improvements can give rise to affordability and incentive issues that tend to emphasise the importance of broader regional consolidation (of one form or another), while at the same time potentially making that consolidation more challenging to achieve.

The final section of the report provides a series of recommendations drawing on the various assessments that are made throughout.

7.2. Current and emerging challenges

As was noted in Chapter 3, there is a significant level of agreement that the current arrangements for WSS provision in Lithuania are not sustainable.[3] There has been substantial investment in WSS infrastructure in Lithuania since its accession to the European Union, with this providing a wide range of benefits in terms of service quality and environmental protection. However, the delivery of these improvements has relied heavily on EU funding, with the Lithuanian Ministry of Environment identifying around 45% of WSS assets as having been created with EU funds.[4] The European Commission has indicated that financial support for the sector will be phased out, and therefore - looking forward - it will be necessary for a financially sustainable and socially acceptable financing model to be developed, based on prevailing – and expectations of future - WSS tariff revenues.

Substantial further investment will be required over time both to maintain (and where relevant replace) existing assets (including those assets that were funded using EU grants), and to enhance treatment processes where needed in order to meet current and future compliance obligations (for example, concerns over pharmaceutical concentrations may result in treatment requirements being introduced that aim to reduce associated risks of harm). This highlights the potential for significant tensions to arise over time related to the affordability and acceptability of associated WSS bill increases.

The severity of these tensions is illustrated by the Ministry of Environment's projections of the WSS prices that would be required – in the absence of efficiencies being secured through consolidation – for the sector to be financially self-sufficient. In particular, the Ministry's projections show that average prices in 2028 would need to be around ten times higher than current levels (as above, based the current industry structure) in order to be financially sustainable.[5] The scale of this projected price increase is driven by a number of key factors:[6]

- The need to maintain assets that were funded by EU grants.
- The need to maintain currently un-inventoried assets, and assets that are used for WSS service provision but currently owned by municipalities.

- The need for further enhancement investments to provide for compliance. In particular:[7]
  - The reconstruction of some wastewater infrastructure to provide for – and sustain - compliance with the Urban Wastewater Treatment Directive (UWWTD)
  - Wastewater treatment improvements in smaller agglomerations in order to improve the quality of water bodies (in line with Water Framework Directive (WFD) requirements)
  - Some drinking water infrastructure and treatment improvements to address quality issues (in line with Drinking Water Directive (DWD) requirements).

It should be noted, though, that this projection relates to average WSS prices across Lithuania. In practice, prices already vary significantly across municipalities – with the price in some areas more than 3 times that in others – and prices tend to be higher in municipalities with lower average wage levels.[8] Price disparities and affordability issues are expected to intensify as upward pressure is put on average WSS price levels.

Also, while the implications of the Covid pandemic on demographic changes remain unclear, pre-pandemic forecasts identified trends that would exacerbate the financial challenges to be faced. In particular, only one region in Lithuania (Vilnius) is forecast to have had population growth in 2050, and population is forecast to have declined by more than 50% in 2050 in 6 regions. Declining population levels can – absent other changes - result in relevant fixed costs being spread across smaller groups of customers, and can leave customers having to fund what has become over-sized infrastructure.

7.2.1. Consolidation and scope for efficiency improvements

The likely scale and nature of future investment requirements – as illustrated by the extent of the projected price increases referred to above - raises major concerns over the financial capacity of the WSS sector – in its current form – to meet the challenges that are faced. Alongside this, the current fragmented nature of the sector raises major concerns over the technical capacity of the sector to develop and deliver appropriate programmes of work in efficient ways. These concerns have underpinned the emphasis that has been put on the benefits that could be achieved through greater consolidation within the sector.

The economic characteristics of the sector (in particular, the scope for achieving economies of scale and density in the undertaking of relevant activities), and the fact that the WSS sector in Lithuania is still highly fragmented – with 64 public suppliers[9] serving a population of around 2.8 million[10] - strongly suggests that there may be scope to deliver substantial benefits through consolidation. This can be important for both the efficient delivery of services and planned investments, and the efficient identification and planning of future service and investment requirements.

There are a range of ways in which consolidation may provide opportunities to improve the efficiency with which services and planned investments are delivered, including potentially through:

- More efficient labour resourcing for, and scheduling and financing of, planned work such as enhancement projects (for example, the provision of new treatment technologies), asset refurbishments/replacements, and routine monitoring, repair and maintenance activities. Consolidation may allow for the smoothing over time of (through the use of a more coordinated approach across areas), and enhanced technical capabilities in relation to, what might otherwise by 'lumpier' requirements that are more difficult to finance and manage.
- More efficient approaches to managing unplanned/reactive work, such as may be required to address pipe bursts, sewer collapses, and other relevant incidents. The efficiency of these types of activities can have a significant bearing on a number of dimensions of performance, such as leakage, for example, by improving response times and capabilities.
- More efficient procurement of, and management of the cost risks associated with, inputs such as energy and chemicals.

- More efficient provision of customer-facing, administrative and support activities, where scale can offer considerable opportunities for both cost savings (e.g. through reduced duplication) and quality improvements (e.g. through the introduction of improved information provision processes).

The above list can be understood as largely taking service provision requirements and investment plans as given, and focuses attention on some potential ways in which the efficiency of delivering those requirements might be enhanced through consolidation. However, the likely scale and nature of the future WSS investment requirements in Lithuania makes it critical also to consider efficiency questions in relation to the identification and planning of future requirements. Importantly, there are likely to be different ways in which policy objectives associated with environmental requirements and service quality/access targets could potentially be tackled, and the decisions over which approaches are selected can be expected to have long-term implications for the cost, quality, and/or environmental consequences of service provision.

Determining the appropriate approach to the development and use of tertiary treatment processes – such as those used to reduce phosphorus concentrations in wastewater discharges – may be particularly challenging. Tertiary treatment can be very costly to introduce (in particular nitrogen removal), and the 'cost per population equivalent' of introducing and operating such processes can increase steeply (including by many multiples) as the size of the relevant treatment plant falls.[11] Given this, decisions related to the introduction of such processes can have a particularly marked bearing on costs in areas which are less densely populated. Also, the adoption of a given approach may have the effect of 'locking-in' a service provision model – and the funding implications associated with it - for many years, including, for example, because of the infrastructure maintenance or ongoing chemicals procurement costs that will be associated with some approaches.

Consolidation (of one form or another) may provide opportunities for significant efficiency benefits in relation to the identification and planning of appropriate responses to environmental requirements. This is particularly so because there may be significant benefits associated with the assessment of options in more coordinated ways across broader geographic areas, and because the effectiveness of options identification and appraisal processes may be heavily dependent on the availability of appropriate technical expertise, and this can be much more difficult to provide for at smaller scale (that is, there can be significant economies of scale in the provision of relevant technical expertise). These factors could have a substantial bearing on the efficiency of the approaches adopted in a range of different ways. For example:

- Beneficial opportunities to increase scale may be identified in a context where (as was noted above) unit costs can fall steeply as plant size increases (such that tertiary treatment may be introduced at one larger plant, rather than separately at two or more other plants, following appropriate network development).
- Alternative treatment approaches – such as those which use 'natural capital' solutions - may be identified as preferred given estimates of 'whole-life' costs and other sustainability considerations.
- There may be opportunities to explore whether the introduction of costly 'end-of-pipe' treatment options can be avoided (particularly at smaller sites) by delivering equivalent environmental outcomes in other ways. It is common, in a range of jurisdictions, for WSS companies to seek to contract with farmers in order to get them to adopt practices, which result in reduced concentrations of potentially harmful substances in water catchments. This kind of catchment management approach can, in some circumstances, provide substantially less costly ways of improving environmental outcomes than the introduction of relatively small-scale, complex tertiary treatment processes.[12]

There may also be significant benefits from adopting a broader (more consolidated) geographic perspective when other policy objectives are being considered. For example, the costs of increasing access to public WSS systems can be expected to differ markedly between areas, including - importantly - because of population density considerations. This may also point to there being particular benefit in effective options identification and development processes being undertaken when efforts are being made to achieve relevant policy objectives in areas with relatively low population density. That is, 'traditional' approaches (such a network extension) may prove very high cost on a per customer basis, and thus alternative approaches – including 'non-physical' network approaches – may merit careful attention.[13]

7.2.2. *Affordability, acceptability and deferral risks*

As was highlighted above, the bill impacts associated with appropriately addressing future capital maintenance and enhancement requirements may be considerable. However, the potential scale of these bill impacts will affect the affordability and acceptability challenges that can be expected to be faced if seeking to proceed with such plans. Given this, there is a material risk that appropriate investments may be deferred if the bill impacts of proceeding with them is viewed as likely to be 'too great'. This kind of deferral of investment might follow an explicit decision, based on an assessment of impacts, and consideration of relevant priorities. Deferral, though, could also emerge more passively, through understandable localised efforts to avoid, or at least limit the size of, bill increases (which may involve giving relatively limited attention to plans that could – if acted on – result in significant upward pressure).

The broader point here is that future tensions associated with bill affordability and acceptability will have to be addressed one way or another. If it becomes viewed as not feasible to increase charges sufficiently to fund investments that have otherwise been identified as necessary/appropriate, and if external sources of funding (such as EU or central government grants) are no longer available or are insufficiently large, then some scaling down of investment costs will be required. Addressing the efficiency issues highlighted in the above sections can be viewed likely to be critical in this context, as it can help reduce investment costs through efficiency improvements (i.e. by doing more 'now' for a given bill impact). The alternative in such circumstances is to scale back costs by cutting back on the scope of what is being delivered through deferring investments (i.e. doing less 'now' and leaving more for 'later').

There is typically some flexibility available in terms of the scheduling of capital maintenance over time and (subject to the legal requirements to which they may relate) the timetable for delivering enhancements. This can provide some degree of 'slack' such that a strategy of deferral may have little impact on efficiency considerations for a period. Also, given the extent of recent asset installations in Lithuania under the EU funding arrangements, a period of slack is in any case to be expected ahead of some growth in the need for more significant capital maintenance levels. However, extended periods of deferral can themselves potentially generate significant additional problems and efficiency challenges. In some circumstances, this may manifest itself through increased incidents of asset failure, which may then be costly to address. However, because of the long-lived nature of many WSS assets, there can be a significant time lag between significant asset degradation occurring and failure incidents arising. While this time lag can provide significant benefits in terms of the continuity of service provision in the short to medium term, it can also mean that potentially significant asset degradation can have occurred in a way that may be relatively non-visible for a number of years.

These considerations may raise only limited concerns when maintenance is viewed on an asset-by-asset basis. However, broader concerns typically relate to the potential for such deferral decisions to result in a broader and overall (regional, or sector-wide) capital maintenance 'backlog' that it is then not feasible or economic to address in a timely manner. A deferral approach can therefore result in significant problems being stored up for future years in inefficient ways, as instead of adopting a relatively 'smoothed' approach to the management and delivery of maintenance requirements over time (and across the relevant asset portfolio), it may result in clusters of lumpy requirements that may then be significantly more difficult to address, in terms of both cost and availability of resources and capabilities. Given this, addressing efficiency issues of the kind highlighted above can be viewed as likely to be critical both in order to try to help address bill affordability issues, and – in doing so – to help limit the extent to which deferral tendencies might generate additional problems to be addressed in future years.

The scale of the potential bill increase projections that the Ministry of the Environment has identified suggests that considerable bill affordability issues may arise even if only a portion of that increase were to be applied. However, large increases in charges for public services typically also raise broader legitimacy and acceptability questions for customers, that go beyond immediate issues of affordability, and – in line with this – it is common for regulated public service providers to have to show how they have tested and taken account of the acceptability of bill impacts that may be associated with their plans. This raises broader questions and challenges over how the purposes and outcomes (in terms of improved services and environmental conditions) of bill increases are communicated to, and response to the views of, customers over time, in ways that can help support the delivery of appropriate investments.

7.3. Planned water services sector reforms

The Ministry of the Environment has been developing reforms aimed at addressing the challenges the WSS sector faces. The following first sets out, and provides some initial comments on, the objectives the Ministry has identified, before describing – in broad terms – the main changes the reforms are currently envisaged as including.

7.3.1. The objectives of the planned reforms

The objectives of the planned water services sector reform have been identified as:[14]

- Reducing the disparities of prices for drinking water supply and wastewater treatment services and social inequality for the Lithuanian population.
- Ensuring implementation of national and EU requirements to provide quality drinking water supply and wastewater treatment services to the population.
- Transforming the drinking water supply and wastewater management sector from highly subsidized to self-sustaining and financially viable (full implementation of cost-recovery) – all drinking water supply and wastewater treatment companies operate efficiently.

The Ministry's identification of these high-level policy objectives looks to be a very positive step, as the objectives align closely to the key risks and challenges that are faced. In particular, it is notable that:

- As was noted above, the Ministry's WSS price projections highlight the extent to which affordability and social inequality issues can be expected to intensify over time. Finding ways of appropriately dampening and otherwise managing such effects may be critical to the success and legitimacy of reform efforts that could be expected to deliver longer-term benefits (including – importantly – in relation to affordability). As is discussed below, however, the specific ways in which price disparity issues are addressed merits careful attention, as such policies can – depending on how they are designed –undermine some efficiency improvement incentives in undesirable ways.
- The objective of ensuring the implementation of water and wastewater quality requirements can be viewed as recognising the significance of the deferral risks of the kind described above. That is, one way in which tensions associated with bill levels could be addressed is through an (implicit or explicit) approach of undertaking (potentially much) lower levels of capital maintenance work than would be needed to maintain appropriate levels of asset health, thereby degrading the levels of service that can be provided over time and storing up substantial maintenance/replacement requirements for future years. Clearly identifying the implementation of quality requirements as a policy objective (as the Ministry has done) highlights the importance of tracking progress in relation to the meeting of such requirements. As noted in Chapter 5, the Ministry may be well-placed to adopt an ongoing role focused on monitoring progress towards the achievement of, and continued compliance with, environmental (and other quality-related) obligations.

- The third objective recognises both the need for the sector to become financially self-sustaining, and that providing for this will provide a transformation in the efficiency of service provision. Providing a framework that facilitates and promotes this transformation is therefore central to the planned reforms. It is important that the tariff setting arrangements are consistent with this, but its achievement raises a broader set of questions in relation to the approach to policy development and economic regulation that are also addressed in other chapters.

7.3.2. The main features of the planned reforms

The Ministry has identified three main parts to the reforms:[15]

1. Strengthening the regulation of services:
    - New criteria for licensed activities and service quality requirements.
    - Operating a mechanism that applies when a licence is revoked.
    - Strengthening the role of the regulator.
2. Ensuring that all costs are reflected in the price of services:
    - Review and apply pricing methodology.
    - Ensure that assets (infrastructure) are owned by the company.
    - Carry out an inventory of assets.
3. Making better use of economies of scale by encouraging consolidation at regional level:
    - Subsidies to a regional enterprise for infrastructure investments.
    - Pricing tailored to regional companies.
    - Reducing administrative burdens.

Some of these different parts of the planned reforms (i.e. where they relate specifically to tariff setting) are considered in the sections below, whereas other parts are considering in other chapters. In particular:

- Issues concerned with how costs are reflected in prices (part (2) above) are considered in this report, which reviews aspects of the current tariff methodology.
- Issues concerned with the encouragement of consolidation (part (3) above) are considered in Chapter 3, but also in the assessment of benchmarking approaches provided in Chapter 8.
- Issues concerned with strengthening the regulation of services (part (1) above) are considered in Chapter 3.

7.4. The WSS tariff methodology

The economic regulator for WSS services in Lithuania currently adopts a form of 'building block' approach to determining allowed price levels that has been widely used internationally over many years. In broad terms, this involves determining price levels in a way that would be expected to provide a reasonable allowance for:

- Operating expenditure (opex);
- Depreciation of a defined Regulatory Asset Base (RAB);
- A return on the outstanding value of the RAB in the relevant period; and,
- Relevant tax requirements.

This provides a flexible framework that looks well-suited to addressing the range of issues the economic regulator may face in Lithuania. In particular, its use can include and be supplemented with, a range of initiatives related to incentive regulation, including approaches that have been developed for cost assessment and recovery, and for incentivising aspects of service delivery.

This section focuses primarily on two specific issues concerned with how the tariff methodology is, and could be, applied that have been central to discussions with stakeholders:

1. The asset base used for tariff setting, and in particular, the approach to setting depreciation/capital maintenance allowances in relation to:
   - EU funded assets; and,
   - Assets that are used for WSS services, but that are currently owned by municipalities and/or not yet adequately inventoried.
2. Assumptions about water losses when allowed unit prices are being set.

Before considering these matters, however, it is helpful to note some of the key different roles that the tariff setting process typically plays in relation to WSS services, as the advantages and disadvantages of some of the different potential approaches discussed below can differ significantly in relation to different roles.

7.4.1. Different roles the tariff setting process can play

The following roles/objectives of the approach to tariff setting are particularly relevant to consider in the current context:[16]

- **Cost recovery**: consistency with the recovery of efficiently incurred costs. Importantly, under a RAB-based approach, this will include some recovery of capex which was incurred in (and has accumulated over) previous years, to the extent that it remains to be recovered from customers.
- **The Financeability of future investment requirements:** providing a realistic and robust basis upon which utilities could actually fund investments that are likely to be viewed as appropriate and desirable.
- **Efficiency incentives**: providing incentives to deliver appropriate performance levels at efficient levels of cost over time.
- **Allowing for affordable, acceptable and equitable bills**: while this can clearly raise broader social and political considerations, it is important to recognise the different implications that different tariffs setting approaches can potential have in relation to these matters.

The relevance of these different roles is considered further below.

7.4.2. The treatment of EU funded assets

The current position (as provided for in legislation) is that granted assets, including importantly a substantial portion of assets that were funded by the EU, are excluded from the asset base for tariff setting purposes. Specifically, that means they are excluded from the RAB when allowed tariffs are being calculated, such that there is no allowance included in tariffs for the depreciation of these assets, and no allowance included to cover costs of financing capital that was used to provide for them.

The situation in relation to financing cost is straightforward: the utilities did not fund the EU granted assets and so do not face ongoing financing costs in relation to that funding. Given this, one would not expect any allowance for financing costs associated with past investment in these granted assets to be provided for in the tariff formula.

However, the situation with respect to depreciation is less clear cut. Concerns have been raised over the extent to which the calculation method (which excludes granted assets from the RAB, including for the purposes of calculating depreciation allowances) can be expected to provide a sustainable approach to funding necessary investments, and in particular the levels of capital maintenance that can be expected to be required over time in relation to those granted assets. The Ministry of the Environment's price projections illustrate starkly the extent of the impact the treatment of this issue could have on bill levels.

Those projections imply that average bill levels would be around five times higher than their current level if EU funded assets were included in the RAB for tariff calculation purposes.[17]

In practice, however, identifying the most appropriate approach to this issue raises a number of different considerations. In order to highlight this, it is helpful to compare the current approach used in Lithuania to two other standard approaches that have been adopted in a range of other jurisdictions and regulatory contexts, such that 3 different potential approaches could be pointed to:

1. **The current approach**: this can be understood as providing for no depreciation/capital maintenance allowance in relation to EU funded assets, and assets owned by municipalities/not yet inventoried, but with some depreciation allowance provided for other assets.
2. **Providing an allowance for current cost depreciation (CCD) in relation to all assets used to provide the relevant services**: this involves effectively determining depreciation requirements based on a forward-looking assessment of the average annual financial contribution required to maintain assets in a condition regarded as appropriate to allow for ongoing service provision. This kind of approach is typically applied by estimating the Modern Equivalent Asset Value (MEAV) of all relevant existing assets (i.e. the cost of providing an equivalent asset/basis for service provision),[18] and using this MEAV value – rather than the relevant RAB value – as the basis for determining depreciation allowances. On this basis, while gifted assets would have a zero RAB value, a positive depreciation allowance would be included in relation to them based on estimated MEAVs and relevant asset lives. This is referred to below as a 'full CCD' approach.
3. **Providing an allowance based on an estimate of average expected capital maintenance spend requirements over a given period**: this approach (which has been used in England and Wales over many years in relation to water 'infrastructure' assets), avoids the need to estimate MEAVs or asset lives, and instead focuses more directly on estimates of the costs of maintaining the long-term condition of the network. Those estimates of 'infrastructure renewals' costs are then included in the tariff formula as though they were a form of operating expenditure (opex). This is referred to below as an 'infrastructure renewals funding' approach.

It is notable that in a simplified long-term steady state context (where it is assumed that there is no enhancement, technological change, etc.), these approaches – on average - could be expected to result in the same allowance for depreciation/capital maintenance being included in tariff levels.[19] This is because, if (current cost) depreciation allowances have been set appropriately, then one might expect them to be equivalent to the average level of capital maintenance requirements over time, when we consider a simplified steady state context. However, when we move away from this stylised view to consider some of the practical challenges and circumstances that are typically faced, there is scope for the outcome of these different approaches to be far from equivalent. This is highlighted below by considering how the current approach used in Lithuania, and these two alternative approaches (a full CCD approach, and an infrastructure renewals funding approach) can be viewed as performing in relation to each of the different roles/objectives of the tariff setting approach that were identified above.

Cost recovery

All three of the approaches can be viewed as providing a coherent basis for cost recovery. In particular, they all provide a basis for the recovery of expenditure associated with capital maintenance, although the mechanism used differs in each case:

- The current approach used in Lithuania provides for cost recovery over time by adding capital maintenance spend to the RAB, such that a depreciation and financing cost allowance would be provided for under the tariff formula in future years until the relevant expenditure is effectively fully depreciated (and can thus be viewed as having been fully recovered). Also, it should be noted that the approach can be understood as consistent with providing for cost recovery associated with past capex, to the extent that there are residual amounts that stand to be recovered. That is, from a cost recovery perspective, the use of a zero RAB value for granted assets aligns with the fact that there are no outstanding amounts to be repaid in relation to those assets.

- Applying a full CCD approach would involve the same standard RAB addition approach being adopted as under the current approach, and thus provides for cost recovery in the same way. The overall levels of depreciation provided for would be (much) higher than at present, but this higher level (which is considered further below) does not relate directly to cost recovery considerations.
- The infrastructure renewal funding approach provides for cost recovery more directly by treating relevant capex (or at least an estimate of it) as though it were opex. This approach therefore avoids the need for cost recovery through RAB additions and subsequent depreciation (and financing cost) allowances, as the relevant investment requirements (or a smoothed estimate of them over a defined period) are funded directly from customer charges. Using this approach, relevant RAB adjustments would instead be limited to reconciling differences between actual infrastructure renewals spend, and the forecast level that had been provided for in prices.

The Financeability of future investment requirements

The three approaches differ significantly in terms of the conditions they provide for the financing of future investment requirements. In particular:

- The current approach provides a clear framework that can - in principle - be used to underpin the financing of new investment requirements, with that investment being funded to a large extent though borrowing against expectations of future additional tariff income that the RAB-based approach provides for. However, a key question concerns the extent to which – in practice - companies can be expected to be able to finance those investments that have been identified as appropriate, and to do so on sufficiently reasonable terms. In particular, over time, capex requirements can be expected to exceed the overall level of depreciation allowances, potentially by a large multiple. This implies that, under this approach, considerable levels of borrowing be required to support appropriate investments, with this raising questions over the likely borrowing capacity of different utilities, and the extent to which they are likely to be able to secure sufficiently favourable terms.
- The full CCD approach would (assuming it could be implemented) greatly increase the cash receipts of utilities, and in doing would either remove or considerably reduce borrowing requirements. The improved cash position this would result in may allow for more favourable borrowing terms to be secured, reflecting the stronger financial position of the relevant utilities.
- The infrastructure renewal funding approach provides a means of fully funding expected capital maintenance requirements from customer charges, and thus borrowing requirements would be limited to those associated with managing deviations between actual and expected requirements.

In line with the above points, concerns over financeability provides one key reason why some change to the current approach may be appropriate.

Efficiency incentives

The approach taken to the determination of depreciation/capital maintenance provisions in the tariff formula could potentially have a major bearing on the effectiveness of incentives to improve efficiency. The reasons for this include the following:

- Under the current approach, utilities would need to make the case for any new investment requirements (including capital maintenance) that would involve charges having to increase as part of the regulatory charge review process. This provides a clear basis for the scrutiny of identified capital maintenance requirements and of the efficiency of the cost forecasts associated with them. The need to finance capital maintenance through borrowing under this approach, can also be expected to focus attention on the potential for costs to be identified by the regulator as not having been efficiently incurred, as the ability companies have to service the debt they build up will be dependent on the extent to which they are able to actually add the capex they incur to the RAB. These factors can be viewed as tending to intensify the extent of focus one would expect to be put on efficiency assessments over time, because it may not be feasible for utilities to make progress with necessary capital maintenance unless they have performed adequately in regulatory review processes (in terms of demonstrating that there plans should be viewed as efficient).

- Adopting a full CCD approach could markedly change the financial landscape within which utilities and the regulator operate, and in doing so has the potential to materially weaken efficiency incentives. The primary reason for this is that – in the short- to medium-term at least – adopting a full CCD approach could have the effect of substantially relaxing the financial pressures that utilities might otherwise face. This follows because the depreciation allowance it provides for may exceed the actual investment requirements utilities face, with this then effectively providing additional financial headroom when costs are being managed.[20] While - in principle - this financial headroom could be used to build up a financial provision for when higher capital maintenance levels are required, there may be a material risk that headroom instead is effectively used to insulate the utility to some extent from the pressures for efficiency improvement that it may otherwise face. That is, there is a risk that the better financial position utilities would be in as a result of applying a full CCD approach would tend to allow a greater degree of deferral in relation to the achievement of efficiency improvements. The potential for this kind of efficiency incentive issue to arise (and how it might be mitigated) look to be key matters to be addressed if the adoption of some form of full CCD approach was being contemplated.
- The infrastructure renewal funding approach would not be expected to generate the kind of undesirable incentive effect described above, as securing the scope for raising additional funds through customer charges would remain (as it is at present) dependent on utilities adequately identifying the investment requirements to which it relates. Some dampening of efficiency incentives may arise as a result of utilities not having to raise funds from lenders (and thus convince those lenders of the credibility of their funding arrangements), but the approach maintains a clear link to – and a clear basis for regulatory oversight in relation to – identified capital maintenance requirements, rather than relying on separate CCD assessments based on existing assets.

Allowing affordable, acceptable and equitable bills

When the affordability and acceptability of bill impacts are being considered, relevant features of the three approaches include the following:

- Under the current approach, EU funded assets (or at least their value) – in relation to which no depreciation provision is included in tariffs – would over time be replaced by 'new' assets, the value of which would be added to the RAB, such that a depreciation provision would then be included in tariffs. When this replacement/renewal process is complete, the current approach would have effectively become a form of full CCD approach. This highlights the importance of timing considerations. That is, while the current approach can be viewed as already providing for convergence to a full CCD approach over time, the long-lived nature of many WSS assets is such that this convergence may only be achieved over a number of decades. The gradual nature of the associated adjustment to tariffs can be viewed as likely to have significant benefits in terms of the affordability and acceptability of bill impacts, at least in the short- and medium-term. As was noted above, however, there are separate questions over whether the associated tariff profiles provide an adequate basis for the financeability of identified investment requirements.
- By contrast, the introduction of a full CCD approach would involve a substantial immediate increase in tariffs (as illustrated by the Ministry of Environment projections referred to above). The extent of the affordability and acceptability challenges likely to be associated with such an approach (to the

extent that it would be feasible at all), would be expected to result in considerable attention being given to the adequacy of the justification for such a change, and in practice a number of potentially important limitations can be pointed to. The determination of depreciation allowances inevitably involves a range of approximations and assumptions being used, and their reliability and appropriateness can raise significant questions, including:

- **What assets values would it be appropriate to use?** This may be particularly important in a context where the identification and development of different, more efficient ways of providing WSS services look to be critical to the achievement of a financially sustainable set of arrangements, and where demographic changes may mean that the inherited set of service provision solutions may differ markedly from those that are likely to be most suitable going forward. Given this, there is a risk that valuations associated with existing assets may provide a poor basis for assessing appropriate CCD levels, and may materially overstate relevant asset values.[21]
- **What asset life should be assumed for depreciation purposes?** The assumed asset life will have a substantial bearing on the scale of the depreciation provision that is implied (under a straightforward straight-line approach). However, relevant asset lives can be difficult to predict, and there is a risk that understandable tendencies to try to adopt relatively conservative assumptions (in line with standard accounting considerations with respect to prudency) could result in the use of assumed asset lives that are unduly short (in that they may materially understate the scope for relevant assets to have longer economic lives). A relevant point here is that – given the financial pressures that appear likely to be faced in relation to managing future investment requirements – there may be significant benefits associated with efforts to extend the economic life of existing assets, including through the analysis of the risks of different types of asset failure, and the potential role that lower cost alternatives to 'full' asset replacement/refurbishment could play in the mitigation of those risks.

Put differently, there is a risk a full CCD approach could be applied in a way that effectively assumed customers should be paying to maintain (and over time renew) the current service provision model, in a context where substantial changes to that service model are considered likely to be required (including through some different forms of consolidation) in order to allow for lower costs of provision.

- The infrastructure renewal funding approach could also raise major affordability issues when new investment requirements are identified, as those requirements would be funded 100% from bills (as though they were opex). One feature of this approach is that such bill increases would only arise where new investment was being undertaken (rather than simply because of a decision to include a provision, as under the full CCD approach), and this may assist with efforts to improve the acceptability of the change, as it may be more straightforward to identify what the higher bills were funding. However, the often lumpy nature of capital maintenance requirements could give rise to significant bill volatility, with bills changing sharply to fund prevailing requirements, and this may raise major affordability and acceptability issues. Where it has been applied in England and Wales, an important feature of this approach has been its application to companies with relatively large and diverse asset bases, such that capital maintenance requirements can be managed across that portfolio in a way that allows bill impacts to be smoothed over time. However, the industry structure is more fragmented – as it is in Lithuania – the scope for managing bill impacts in this way (absent some form of consolidation – discussed further below) is much more limited, and as a result, significant bill volatility concerns can be expected to remain.

A broader issue that arises in relation to bill impacts is that of how inter-generational equity considerations should be taken into account. One view that could be taken here is that the full CCD approach (leaving aside the implementation and measurement issues noted above) provides an appropriate way of taking inter-generational equity considerations into account. In particular, it involves customers in a given period paying an estimate of the financial value of the assets that has been 'used up' in that period, and as a result provides for what is often referred to as 'financial capital maintenance' over time. However, it could be argued that this view is unhelpfully generic, and gives no particular consideration to the specific circumstances faced in Lithuania, which include substantial EU funding of assets.

A different way of approaching this issue would be to consider how (and how much) different generations of customers should be expected to benefit from the EU funding of assets. In high level terms, the benefits of EU funding to current customers could be summarised under the following headings:

1. **Environmental and service quality benefits**: the EU funded assets enabled substantial improvements.
2. **Institutional and structural benefits**: the funding has supported – and continues to support – developments that can be expected to improve the robustness and financial sustainability of the sector.
3. **Financial benefits associated with tariff levels**: current tariffs are much lower than they would be if the improvements had been funded based on customer charges.[22] In particular:
   a. Depreciation is only provided for in tariffs in relation to a relatively small portion of the overall asset base, and in line with this, prevailing capital maintenance requirements have been relatively low given that significant proportion of assets were only recently installed using EU funding.
   b. The allowance for financing costs in tariffs is much lower than it would be otherwise, including – importantly – because the RAB is much lower than it would otherwise be.

It is clearly intended that the improved environmental and service quality levels ((1) above) are maintained – and where necessary further enhanced – for future generations of customers. That is, the EU funding provided for a significant step improvement, and there is a clear policy objective to maintain and build on that higher level of performance going forward.[23] It is also clearly an objective to try to provide for enduring benefits through institutional and structural reforms ((2) above), as can be seen from the Ministry of the Environment's planned water services sector reform (summarised in an earlier section). The more difficult questions – in terms of passing on benefits to future customers – concern financial benefits associated with tariff levels ((3) above), and this inevitably raises distributional questions for political consideration. In practice, the key issue can be viewed as concerning benefits associated with the allowance for financing costs, given - in particular - the size of the RAB. The differences – in this respect - between the three approaches to depreciation/capital maintenance discussed above, include the following:

- Under the current approach, the financing cost benefits associated the EU funding of assets can be viewed as fully allocated to the cohorts of customers paying WSS charges over the short- to medium-term. In particular, each time an EU funded asset is effectively renewed/replaced, the cost will be added to RAB, and – other things equal - the RAB would increase. As a result, the allowance for financing costs in charges would also be expected to increase (assuming the WACC remains constant, and ignoring the impact of enhancements that may result in further RAB increases). The size of the RAB would keep increasing over time (as EU funded assets that had not been in the RAB were replaced by newly financed assets that are in the RAB) until all EU assets had been renewed/replaced, at which point – in principle, at least - a steady state would be reached, where the value of RAB additions related to capital maintenance would be broadly equivalent on average to the annual allowance for depreciation. After this point (which would only be reached after a number of decades, give relevant asset lives and assumed depreciation periods), there would be no direct ongoing benefit to customers from the EU funding assets.
- By contrast, a full CCD approach can be understood – on average and over time, at least – as locking-in the RAB value that applies when the approach is introduced (other than where there is enhancement). That is, if the depreciation allowance is set in line with average capital maintenance requirements, then over time the RAB increase associated with capital maintenance (on EU

funded, or any other assets) would be offset by reduction in the RAB that would otherwise occur such that the RAB remains broadly constant (again, ignoring the effect of any enhancement investment that may take place). This approach, then, can be understood as fully locking-in the lower financing costs benefit of EU funding for customers in all future periods, as a result of the higher level of depreciation allowances that it provides for (as opposed to under the current approach where – as described in the above bullet – the lower financing cost benefit would unwind gradually over the next few decades as all EU funded assets were renewed/replaced).

- The infrastructure renewal funding approach can also be understood as locking-in the RAB value that applies when the approach is introduced (again, other than where there is enhancement), because capital maintenance is effectively treated as an operating expense and thus not added to the RAB at all. As with the full CCD approach, then, this approach involves fully locking-in the lower financing costs benefit of EU funding for customers in all future periods as a result of the higher level of depreciation/capital maintenance allowances it provides for.

Summary and consideration of hybrid options

The table below provides a high-level summary of the above assessments that is intended to highlight where the main limitations of the different depreciation approaches look to arise (shaded in orange). As can be seen, none of the approaches look to raise particular concerns in relation to cost recovery. The key limitation of the depreciation approach that is currently adopted looks to concern the financeability of future investment requirements, as the approach relies on utilities being able to fund capital maintenance requirements primarily through borrowing (with relatively limited cash provisions included in charges). In line with the comments above, the current approach does not look to have major limitations when considered in terms of efficiency incentives or allowing for affordable, acceptable and equitable bills.[24] By contrast, neither of the other two approaches raise particular financeabilty concerns (because of additional cash availability they provide for), but both raise bill affordability and acceptability issues. As was highlighted above, the full CCD approach also raises concerns over potential effects on efficiency incentives.

Table 7.1. Highlighting where the main limitations of different depreciation approaches look likely to arise

	Some key roles/objectives of the tariff setting process			
Different depreciation approaches	Cost recovery	Financeability of future investment requirements	Efficiency incentives	Allowing for affordable, acceptable and equitable bills
Current approach				
Full CCD approach				
Infrastructure renewal funding approach				

The differences in these limitations raise the question of whether hybrid approaches could be used to draw on the benefits of different approaches to some extent. In particular, the following hybrid options could be considered:

1. A hybrid of the current approach and a full CCD approach; and,
2. A hybrid of the current approach and an infrastructure renewal funding approach.

The first hybrid option can be viewed as adopting full CCD approach with a glidepath for its introduction. As was highlighted above, the current approach can already be viewed as gradually providing for the inclusion of a depreciation allowance for all EU funded assets in the tariff formula, but as that process is driven by asset refurbishment/replacement activity, it can be expected to take a number of decades before it is complete. An approach that involved movement to a full CCD approach more rapidly than this, but that included a relatively lengthy glidepath period, might provide a way of sufficiently addressing limitations associated with financeability and affordability. In practice, though, it seems likely that the concern that the introduction of a full CCD approach decouples funding allowances from actual investment decisions, and as a result could have unwanted adverse consequences for the effectiveness of incentive regulation, would remain. More generally, it is notable that the introduction of a full CCD approach with a glidepath does not look to be a well targeted means of addressing the primary identified limitation of the current approach – the financeability of future investment requirements – as the basis for additional funding does not relate to future investment requirements (it relates rather to past investments that have already been made).

The second hybrid option - of the current approach and an infrastructure renewal funding approach - looks much more attractive, as it keeps attention focused on future investment requirements, and thus on the delivery of projects that can be expected to have tangible impacts on service and environmental quality. This option could be applied in a flexible manner that was adapted to the circumstances that were under consideration. That is, the base position could remain the current approach: with capital maintenance treated as new investment that is added to the RAB and funded through subsequent depreciation and financing cost allowances. However, there could be scope for depreciation on new investment requirements to be accelerated, where that could be shown to be necessary to allow for the financeability of the relevant project(s), and not to give rise to undue bill impacts.

From this perspective, the current approach and an infrastructure renewal funding approach can be viewed as sitting on a spectrum. The current approach includes no accelerated depreciation, whereas the infrastructure renewal funding approach includes fully accelerated depreciation: capex is fully depreciated in a single year and thus treated like opex. A hybrid approach would involve selecting somewhere on this spectrum between the two end points (such that there was some - but not full – acceleration of depreciation). There would be for this form of approach to evolve over time, and be adapted to differences in circumstances, so as to reflect the relative pressures and constraints associated with financeabilty and bill affordability/acceptability. For example, the current approach could be treated as the default position, but the opportunity to submit accelerated depreciation proposals to the regulator could be clearly highlighted, and expectations concerning the evidence that might be expected to support such proposals could be articulated (for example, in published guidance).

By keeping attention focus on the funding of future investment requirements, the approach could also be linked directly to the extent to which different forms of consolidation plans were being pursued, with greater scope for the acceleration of depreciation provided to utilities that develop such plans in a robust and credible manner. In line with the comments above, some forms of consolidation[25] may greatly enhance the scope for managing bill profiles over time as significant levels of capital maintenance come to be required in relation to what were EU funded assets. In particular, as well as potentially increasing the borrowing capacity of companies (and therefore their ability to fund future capital maintenance requirements without seeking additional revenues from customer charges through accelerated depreciation), consolidation can also allow for future capital maintenance and funding requirements to be managed across a larger and more diverse portfolio of assets, and thus allow for greater smoothing of associated work requirements and bill impacts. Regulatory decisions on the extent to which accelerated depreciation should be allowed could also take account of the utilities performance (i.e. evidence on the efficiency of its operations), with this providing a means of guarding against the risk that the allowing of accelerated depreciation could act to 'soften' the budget constraints that utilities would otherwise be expected to face, and dampen efficiency improvement incentives (in line with the discussion above). The use of incentive is discussed further later in this report.

7.4.3. The treatment of assets used for WSS services owned by municipalities and/or not yet inventoried

It will be important for there to be a clear identification and attribution of assets that are used for WSS service provision, but that are currently owned by municipalities and/or are not yet inventoried. This should allow for a clearer allocation of responsibilities, and better accountability, in relation to the management and maintenance of the relevant assets over time. However, it is not obvious that this would be expected to have any RAB implications. That is, unless there was clear evidence to contrary, it does not seem obvious why there should be viewed as being any past investments related to these assets that remain outstanding, and that WSS customers should now be treated as responsible for paying off. The inclusion of a zero RAB for these assets would align with the view that there are no residual amounts which stand to be recovered from WSS customers in relation to past investments, and that attention in relation to these assets should be focused on forward-looking questions concerning the identification, funding and efficient delivery of appropriate capital maintenance requirements.

When considering the question of how depreciation/capital maintenance provisions in relation to these assets should be taken into account in the tariff formula, similar issues arise to those that were highlighted above in relation EU granted assets. In particular, as with EU funded assets (and in line with the summary position illustrated in Table 1 above):

- The main limitation of the current depreciation approach concerns the financeability of future investment, as the approach relies on utilities being able to fund capital maintenance requirements primarily through borrowing, with relatively limited cash provisions included in charges (because cost recovery is assumed to be spread over a significant number of years).
- Adopting either a full CDD approach or an infrastructure renewal funding approach would address this financeability concern, but would have significant limitations associated with the affordability and acceptability of bills. The full CCD approach may also have a broader adverse effect on incentives for efficiency improvements.

In line with the comments above, there looks to be a strong case for adopting a hybrid of the current approach and an infrastructure renewal funding approach. As above, the current approach could be treated as the default position, but the opportunity to submit accelerated depreciation proposals to the regulator – as a response to identified financeability constraints - could be clearly highlighted.

7.4.4. Assumptions about water losses

The treatment of water losses in the tariff setting process has been raised as a particular area of concern by the Lithuanian WSS industry association. We understand the association to view the assumptions that are currently applied by the regulator when setting the tariff formula as being too stringent, in particular given the extent of losses that can occur in 'internal networks' on customer premises (such as those within apartment buildings) that the association considers not to be the responsibility of water utilities. This raises a number of specific questions that go well beyond the scope of this project, and we have not considered – and make no comment on – questions of detail with the respect to the current approach. However, the issue raises a number of broader points of regulatory principle and approach - that have also arisen in other jurisdictions and sectors – that we do provide some high-level comments on.

An initial point of note is that is it common for regulators to seek to set challenging but achievable targets when focusing on leakage levels (and more generally water losses).[26] This raises a broader question over what factors, objectives, principles, etc should guide the determination of a challenging but achievable target in relation to water losses. These broader questions can be very important for the legitimacy of regulatory decision making, but they can also affect the nature of the engagement that occurs within the sector over time.

We understand the WSS industry association to consider that the regulator – in determining its assumed level of losses – takes insufficient account of something the association considers to be a highly relevant factor: i.e. (as was noted above), the scope for leakage on 'internal networks'. Irrespective of the specific merits of this view, it raises a potential source of concern as when regulatory assessments are viewed as unreasonable and unachievable, confidence in the overall regulatory arrangements can be diminished, and in such circumstances utilities can tend to adopt less cooperative and constructive approaches than they might otherwise. This can result in significant resources being directed towards relatively unproductive activities, and tend to slow progress in the achievement of key policy objectives. While this raises general points concerned with regulatory approach, the apparent materiality of this issue (in terms of its potential impact as a result of charge determinations) suggests that there may be significant merit in seeking to resolve some of the tensions that look currently to be associated with this issue.

A key underlying issue here is the extent to which there is a shared (across the regulator, regulated companies and other stakeholders), accepted view of the current position in terms of actual leakage levels and – in broad terms – the factors that underpin them. To the extent it is not already being addressed by existing initiatives, there may be significant benefit - in terms of improving confidence in regulatory decision making - from efforts to better identify and clarify what is driving differences of view with respect to the underlying data on current levels and sources of water losses. For example, this could involve a consultation process that explicitly seeks to identify and – where possible using empirical evidence – evaluate the range of views that have been expressed on relevant factors. While such a consultation may be unlikely to resolve all material differences in view, it may be able to resolve some, and it can also provide a basis for explicitly showing where and how contrary positions have been assessed and taken into account.

One reason that this kind of process can be helpful is that regulators are often faced with relevant and material characteristics of the supply environments that different companies face, that can be expected to have both positive and negative implications for supply costs. For example, serving apartment blocks - rather than separate residences - can be expected to have some advantages from a WSS supply perspective (where a large number of customers are able to be served through a single connection point), that will sit alongside relevant disadvantages (including those that may be associated with leakage levels). Given this, it is common for factors that may be widely regarded as material to not give rise to any specific adjustment, because they are already viewed as being captured sufficiently implicitly, given the extent to which different factors (which when viewed in isolation would be regarded as material) can be expected to 'net off'. Stakeholders' perspectives of such trade-offs, however, may be heavily affected by the extent to which they have been articulated.

This may or may not be a relevant consideration in terms of how leakage assumptions are currently applied in a Lithuanian context. The broader point here is simply that, where successful, the use of the kind of consultation process described above can allow attention (and differences of view) to be focused on how the current position, and the identified drivers of losses, should be taken into account, rather than on what the current position is, and on what those drivers are. In doing so, it can help keep a greater degree of stakeholder attention on more constructive and productive questions.

When attention turns to this kind of 'how' question, articulating and testing reasoning through consultation can also potentially help encourage more constructive engagement with regulatory decision making (as well as most likely improving that decision making through the additional disciplines that it requires). It is common – in other jurisdictions – for 'boundary issues' to arise when leakage is being considered, as losses can be the result of leakage from pipes owned by water company customers, as well as from pipes owned by water companies themselves. This raises the question of the extent to which water companies should be held responsible for, and/or should face incentives in relation to, losses from pipes that they do not own or operate.

From one perspective, it may be viewed as straightforward that property owners should be responsible for losses that occur on their premises (and not be responsible for losses that occur elsewhere). For Lithuania, this perspective might imply that leakage from 'internal networks' (and its management) should not be treated as a matter for WSS companies, and its effect should be 'stripped out' of relevant assessments to the extent possible. However, levels customer-side leakage can have a material impact on a water company's costs of supply (to be recovered from all users), and therefore on the overall efficiency of the water supply system. It is typically important (and often central to their duties) for regulators to consider how overall system efficiency can be improved, and this raises questions over what incentives should be in place to encourage such improvements, and who should face them.

From this incentive perspective, it is notable that WSS companies may be relatively misplaced to identify and respond to losses from pipes that they do not own. They may have much better visibility in relation to where losses are arising (given metering arrangements, understandings of typical usage and loss levels, etc.), and to their economic consequences - as the economic costs of losses may be much greater than would be reflected to customers through the WSS charges they pay.[27] Given this, regulators can be expected to look to water companies to actively seek to encourage reductions in customer-side leakage - alongside efforts to reduce their own leakage levels – where that can be expected to deliver efficiency savings.

As noted above, we have not considered the details of the approach that is currently applied in relation to leakage (that the industry associated raised concerns over). The broader point here is simply that while the ownership boundary is clearly relevant to the assessment of WSS costs and associated allowances when account is taken of leakage levels, it does not – in and of itself – provide a clear-cut basis for concluding how customer-side leakage should be taken into account. Rather, given the effects that customer-side leakage can have on overall WSS costs, and that companies may be relatively well placed to influence levels of customer-side leakage – there is a well-founded case for considering some regulatory incentivisation of WSS companies in relation to leakage from pipes they do not own.

7.5. Reducing price disparities and potential incentive issues

The circumstances in some municipalities raise the question of whether the relevant WSS utility is likely to be financial sustainable - based on charges paid by the customers it supplies – even with the sorts of efficiency improvements that might be achievable through consolidation. Future demographic changes and changes to environmental requirements may exacerbate these kind of financial sustainability difficulties in some localities, particularly where there is a significant expected reduction in the size of what may already have been a relatively limited customer base.

This raises the prospect of larger, more financially secure utilities being deterred from consolidating with smaller utilities that face serious financial sustainability pressures (now and/or on the horizon), because such consolidation might be expected to end up with them having to cross-subsidise the smaller companies. There may be some circumstances where that does not raise a material barrier to consolidation. In particular:

- If the financial sustainability issues are relatively modest, then the scope for efficiency benefits may be sufficient to outweigh them.
- There may be other social, reputational and strategic factors that influence the appetite that larger utilities have for consolidation. For example, a company may be willing to bear some degree of cross-subsidy as part of the development of its regional coverage and reputation.

More generally, however, concerns over the sustainability of the funding model of some smaller companies would be expected to act as a material deterrent to at least some forms of consolidation, including – importantly – the development of integrated regional companies that take on responsibility for serving the smaller company's area. This raises issues that are relevant to policy efforts aimed at reducing price disparities between different companies/municipalities. In particular, cross-subsidy issues may arise where the reduction or removal of charge level differences between areas is treated as a policy objective, and - as was noted above - reducing the disparities of prices for WSS services for the Lithuanian population has been identified as an aim of the planned WSS sector reforms.

It is important to note that it is common in many countries for there to be uniform WSS prices to consumers over relatively wide geographic areas. As service provision costs can differ markedly within those areas –

depending on factors such as proximity to water resources, population density/sparsity, and so on - this kind of regional averaging of charges can involve significant embedded cross-subsidies. This kind of cross-subsidy – at least in relation to consumer pricing - is often viewed as relatively unproblematic, providing that some more appropriate locational signals are generated in other ways (such as, through the charges that must be paid to connect new housing developments to existing WSS infrastructure).

However, in Lithuania, there are currently significant differences between the charge levels that apply in different municipalities. Given that context, it is notable that a policy aim of reducing charge disparities could itself act to dampen incentives for regional consolidation. In particular, it would imply that customers from areas that currently have lower charges would – following consolidation - have to bear at least some part of the cost of charges being reduced (or of charge increases being more muted) in other previously high-charge municipalities. Therefore, while the achievement of lower levels of price disparity between areas would be a policy aim that is not out of line with practice in many in other jurisdictions, pursuing that policy could potentially have material adverse consequences for consolidation incentives.

This suggests that allowing flexibility in the approach taken to price differences in consolidation proposals may be highly desirable. In some circumstances, it may be relatively straightforward (given the opening price level differences, relative sizes, customer attitudes, etc.) for companies to identify a mutually acceptable glidepath that provides for price convergence over a relatively modest period of time. However, in other circumstances, scope to focus only on efficiency improvements and to not provide for such convergence in tariff levels may be important for the feasibility of a consolidation plan, and to ensure that customers from the (initially) lower charge area would not simply expect to be worse off.

7.6. The funding of wider environmental benefits

A common tension that arises in the consideration of WSS costs relates to the difference between:

- The costs of providing the water and wastewater services to the relevant set of customers; and,
- The costs the relevant water company faces in order to meet applicable environmental requirements.

Equity issues related to the first bullet can be viewed as relatively straightforward. The long-lived nature of relevant investments can inevitably raise some questions concerned with intergenerational equity (i.e. how should costs be shared between current and future cohorts of customers). Beyond this, though, the WSS customers that receive services from a given company can be readily identified (for the most part), and are typically expected to bear the associated service provision costs (subject to acute affordability issues of the kind noted above).

Equity issues can become more complicated, though, when the costs of meeting environmental requirements are considered (as in the second bullet above). A common approach is to simply treat any costs associated with meeting environmental requirements as though they are WSS service provision costs, and therefore as cost that should straightforwardly be viewed as to be borne by the relevant set of WSS customers. In some circumstances, however, this may not result in a close alignment between those being asked to pay the costs of meeting relevant environmental requirements, and those who benefit from the requirements being met. That is, there may be significant positive externality effects.

The extent of geographic consolidation can be highly relevant in this context, as it can affect how closely aligned the group that funds specific environmental improvements is with the group that benefits from them. For example, wastewater treatment plants can face stringent and very costly phosphorus removal requirements that relate to concerns over nutrient levels in receiving waters. It could be viewed that these requirements have widespread benefits across the population, including benefits associated with the meeting of government commitments made in international agreements. If there was a small number of large regional WSS companies in Lithuania, then it may be that there would be little practical difference between who bears the costs of, and who benefits from, phosphorus removal (with relevant costs shared across a broad range of customers from more urban and more rural localities). However, the fragmented nature of WSS service provision in Lithuania may mean that there is a risk of material disparities emerging between the set of customers who bear the costs of, and those who benefit from, some environmental protection measures provided by WSS companies.

The use of EU funds to support environmental improvements in recent years means that this potential source of tension will have been of limited relevance to date, as – to a large extent – the costs of meeting environmental requirements were not funded by the customers of the particular WSS companies to which those requirements applied (they were funded by EU grants). However, as those EU funded assets need to be maintained and replaced, and as other environmental requirements stand to be addressed, this source of tension can be expected to become more important over time.

In practice, the customers of a given company can be expected to both fund some environmental improvements that benefit others, and benefit from some environmental improvements that are funded by other customers (for example, as those other improvements may contribute to the achievement of national commitments, and in doing so confer widely dispersed benefits). The question arises as to whether the fragmented nature of the sector leaves some customers particularly exposed to funding wider benefits, and if that materially affects the financial sustainability of the relevant company. That might be the case, for example, if a company that served a relatively modest customer base was required to install and/or maintain tertiary treatment processes that – because of small scale – had a very high unit cost.

The starting point for Lithuania is again important here. That is, it is not unusual internationally to use WSS charges to fund initiatives that have a range of environmental benefits. But the fragmented nature of the WSS sector in Lithuania means adopting such an approach can potentially have significant distributional consequences: as there is a greater risk of misalignment between those who pay for, and those who benefit from, the environmental improvements being funded. Those distributional consequences may tend to imply that consolidation is very important (in order to more appropriately distribute the costs of environmental improvements) but also that incentives for such consolidation may be relatively limited.

In the Lithuanian context, a strong case could be made for some of the costs of achieving some of these environmental benefits to be covered through other means, at broader geographical scales, and independently from the water bill. Inspiration could come from a range of instruments in place in OECD and EU countries: they all ambition to make pollution costly for the polluters, in line with the polluter pays principle. They depend on the targeted pollution. In the case of agriculture, taxes on fertilisers can be appropriate; they best apply when fertilisers are purchased. In the case of industry and under some circumstances, extended producers' responsibility can be considered; this is for instance the case for pharmaceutical residues or other chemicals, which affect water streams and are not readily addressed through wastewater treatment. The recent workshops co-convened by the OECD and DG Environment on implementing the Polluter Pays principle in the context of the Water Framework Directive provides more evidence and examples (https://www.oecd.org/water/dg-env-economics-of-wfd.htm).

7.7. Summary and recommendations

This report has reviewed aspects of how prices for WSS services in Lithuania are determined, focusing on specific issues related to the tariff methodology that look to be of particular importance to the development of pricing arrangements. Overall, the report is consistent with and provides strong support for the broad set of reforms the Ministry of Environment has brought forward, and attention is focused on some specific options and issues related to how those reforms could be applied and implemented. As set out below, there are two main recommendations, and a recommendation that further consideration be given two issues as the tariff setting arrangements involve.

7.7.1. Recommendation 1: Retain the current approach to depreciation as the default position, but allow companies to submit accelerated depreciation proposals

This would keep attention focused on the funding of future investment requirements, and greater scope for the acceleration of depreciation could be provided to utilities that develop consolidation plans in a robust and credible manner. Regulatory decisions on the extent to which accelerated depreciation should be allowed could also take account of the utilities operational and financial performance, with this providing a means of guarding against the risk that the allowing of accelerated depreciation could act to 'soften' the budget constraints that utilities would otherwise be expected to face, and dampen efficiency improvement incentives, in undesirable ways.

7.7.2. Recommendation 2: Allow for some flexibility in the treatment of price disparities

It is recommended that flexibility is allowed for in terms of how price disparities between municipalities are expected to be reduced over time when consolidation options are adopted. Requirements for price convergence, or the expectation that price convergence may be introduced subsequently, may act as a deterrent to the bringing forward of some forms of consolidation plans (in particular those that would involve the agglomeration of companies across broader areas), as it may imply that some form of cross-subsidy will be introduced to the disbenefit of customers of the company that has lower prices initially.

7.7.3. Additional recommendation

It is recommended that further consideration is given to the following two factors in the detailed development and application of water pricing arrangements:

- When assessing the appropriateness of water losses assumptions (as part of the application of the tariff formula), consider the scope for WSS companies to influence customer-side leakage. As was highlighted above, companies may be relatively well-placed to help reduce levels of leakage (and the costs associated with managing them) even when that leakage occurs on networks other than those operated by the relevant WSS company.
- Consider the extent to which financial sustainability concerns (or the prospect of them arising) may be driven by requirements to fund broader environmental improvements that may have disproportionate effects on the prices paid in some WSS areas, and the extent to which this may undermine voluntary consolidation incentives and opportunities. To the extent that this is identified as a relevant feature in practice, give further consideration to the scope for, and potential, options that could allow the funding burden associated with meeting broader environmental improvements to be shared more broadly. Lessons can be learned from other European countries' experience, as captured in the recent OECD – DG ENV workshop on the Polluter Pays principle in the context of the Water Framework Directive (https://www.oecd.org/water/dg-env-economics-of-wfd.htm).

Notes

[1] OECD (2021), Reform of the water supply and wastewater treatment sector of Lithuania by consolidation of utilities: Output 3; featured in this report as Chapter 3.

[2] The Lithuanian economic regulator's approach to tariff regulation is considered in a later section.

[3] OECD (2021), Reform of the water supply and wastewater treatment sector of Lithuania by consolidation of utilities: Output 3 – Issues paper, p5-6; featured in this report as Chapter 3.

[4] The Ministry of Environment of the Republic of Lithuania (3rd November 2021), WSS sector in Lithuania Reform Investments, slide 6.

[5] The Ministry of Environment of the Republic of Lithuania (3rd November 2021), WSS sector in Lithuania Reform Investments, slide 7.

[6] The Ministry of Environment of the Republic of Lithuania (3rd November 2021), WSS sector in Lithuania Reform Investments, slides 6 - 7.

[7] The Ministry of Environment of the Republic of Lithuania (3rd November 2021), WSS sector in Lithuania Reform Investments, slide 3.

[8] The Ministry of Environment of the Republic of Lithuania (3rd November 2021), WSS sector in Lithuania Reform Investments, slide 4.

[9] Ministry of Environment of the Republic of Lithuania (2021) Consolidation strategy of WSS sector in Lithuania, slide 2.

[10] Acknowledging that water is supplied for 83%, wastewater is collected from 77% of population.

[11] For an illustration of this, see Figure 15 (p70) in: https://assets.publishing.service.gov.uk/media/5eda1e5ee90e071b734d2ca7/Northumbrian_Water_Reply_to_Ofwat_response_27.05.2020_NON-CONFIDENTIAL.pdf.

[12] A high-level overview of catchment management approaches that provides some early examples of its use in England and Wales can be found in this 2011 Ofwat document: https://www.ofwat.gov.uk/wp-content/uploads/2015/11/prs_inf_catchment.pdf.

[13] The relevance of alternative potential forms of consolidation is discussed further in the 'Incentives' section.

[14] The Ministry of Environment of the Republic of Lithuania (3rd November 2021), WSS sector in Lithuania Reform Investments, slide 10.

[15] The Ministry of Environment of the Republic of Lithuania (3rd November 2021), WSS sector in Lithuania Reform Investments, slide 11.

[16] Note that the focus here is on the way in which the overall level of allowed prices is set (through the determination of allowed revenues and associated allowed average price levels), rather than on the detailed design of the tariffs that different customers will face (with this latter issue often addressed through consideration of the appropriate structure (as opposed to average level) of charges).

[17] Based on the increase in 2020 average bills identified as resulting from the inclusion of assets and EU funds as being €10.52/m3, from a starting point of €2.63/m3 (The Ministry of Environment of the Republic of Lithuania (3rd November 2021), WSS sector in Lithuania Reform Investments, slide 7).

[18] This reflects the fact that it may be possible to provide an equivalent service in a different less costly way.

[19] Potential implications on financing costs are discussed below.

[20] In the short- to medium-term, CCD-based depreciation provisions may exceed actual capital maintenance requirements (given the relatively recent point in time at many assets were installed), and potentially by a significant amount. Where this occurs, the RAB would actually reduce over time (other things equal), and in principle – given the relatively low prevailing RAB values, and extent of EU funded assets – a negative RAB could result for a period, with utilities then effectively holding funds on behalf of customers for use in future periods.

[21] That is, in terms of the language used above, there is a risk that the MEAV of assets may be somewhat lower than currently recorded asset values, in circumstances where alternative, lower cost supply options could be used to deliver broadly equivalent services and service levels.

[22] The extent to which this is a realistic counterfactual is not considered here, as the focus on considering what benefits could/should be passed on to future generations of customers.

[23] See, for example, The Ministry of Environment of the Republic of Lithuania (3rd November 2021), WSS sector in Lithuania Reform Investments, slide 10.

[24] This is not to intended to imply that use of this approach would allow for all significant bill affordability and acceptability issues to be avoided. The point here is rather that the approach already provides for significant dampening of bill impacts.

[25] Some different forms of consolidation are considered in the incentives section below.

[26] The broader term 'water losses' includes leakage, but also reflects that there are some other sources of 'losses', such as where there is usage of water supplies that is unaccounted for (e.g. properties that are not registered for billing purposes).

[27] Put differently, water tariffs are unlikely to provide an effective signal to customers of the economic costs of leakage from the pipes that they own, and there is therefore a material risk that 'customer-side' leakage will – absent other interventions – remain inefficiently high, such that water supply volume requirements are inefficiently high.

8 Report with recommendations on benchmarking the performance of water utilities

Benchmarking – and some level of transparency more generally – can foster consolidation of water utilities in Lithuania. The chapter explores how mere cost comparison could be supplemented by the benchmarking of broader service performance measures and that of business plans and business planning processes. The latter in particular ensures that a range of consolidation options have been explored and duly assessed.

8.1. Background and objectives

This Chapter is Output 8 from the OECD project aimed at supporting the preparation of a roadmap for the consolidation of the water utility sector in Lithuania. As was noted in the earlier OECD Outputs,[1] further consolidation is viewed as a necessary feature of being able to deliver a sustainable and socially acceptable financing strategy for the future provision of water and sanitation services (WSS) in Lithuania.

The focus of this report is the scope to further develop WSS benchmarking arrangements in Lithuania in ways that can be expected to support the securing of efficiency improvements, including through consolidation. In line with this, some options for extending and enhancing the use of benchmarking are identified below in the light of relevant international experience. The approach adopted below is to focus attention on circumstances that apply - and the current and emerging challenges faced - in WSS provision in Lithuania, with international experience drawn upon selectively to illustrate potential options that look to merit particular attention.

Benchmarking can be focussed on different areas of activity, and the issues and options that are relevant to consider can vary between those different areas. This report considers the following types of benchmarking in turn:

- The benchmarking of costs.
- The benchmarking of broader service performance measures.
- The benchmarking of business plans and business planning processes.

The final section of the report provides a series of recommendations drawing on the various assessments that are made throughout.

8.2. The benchmarking of costs

The use of cost assessment approaches in the determination of allowed charges is central to the economic regulation of utilities. The use of these approaches can be highly relevant to consolidation incentives in Lithuania because they can provide a basis for the economic regulator to constrain the funds that companies are allowed to recover from their customers over time. The application of such constraints has the potential to incentivise companies to find ways of achieving efficiency improvements, including through consolidation approaches, in order to improve the financial circumstances they face, and can expect to face in future years.

The benchmarking of costs is an important tool that is available to regulators, and that can help with the identification of what cost constraints it may be reasonable and appropriate to apply, and of what an efficient level of costs should be regarded as in relation to a given area. Benchmarking can also be used to help promote a degree of comparative competition between utilities with different supply areas over time.

Regulators often apply benchmarking approaches at different levels of aggregation that can include:

- Totex benchmarking: i.e. the benchmarking of total opex + capex requirements.
- The benchmarking of 'base' totex (or 'Botex'): i.e. the benchmarking of total opex + capex, excluding expenditure on enhancements, such as the achievement of water quality improvements.
- Opex benchmarking.
- Totex, Botex or Opex benchmarking focused on particular business units/activities: e.g. water treatment, treated water distribution, wastewater collection, wastewater treatment.
- The benchmarking of the costs associated with more narrowly defined activities: e.g. pipe replacement costs, billing and customer support costs, etc.

There is typically benefit in adopting a pragmatic approach, considering multiple aggregation possibilities, depending on the availability and reliability of relevant data, and the complexities associated with drawing reasonable comparisons.

International experience has highlighted some of the complexities that can be faced when seeking to compare costs between areas when seeking to develop reasonably robust benchmarking models, and some frameworks that can help guide the development of cost modelling.[2] However, in practice, those complexities tend to be magnified when a set of smaller companies stand to be considered, as they do in Lithuania. That is, the average costs of larger, regional companies will reflect the fact that a portfolio of supply areas are being served, such that the higher costs that may be associated with serving some localities within a region remain not directly visible as they may be off-set by lower costs in some other areas. The modelling of the costs of larger, regional companies therefore needs only to be concerned with cost drivers where there is a material net difference between the companies under consideration once their overall portfolios of supply areas is taken into account. In a more fragmented context, of the kind faced in Lithuania, a segmented approach – which begins by grouping utilities into broadly comparable sets - looks likely to be much more appropriate than efforts towards broader comparative modelling.

That said, the similar tensions can clearly arise in the identification and specification of the criteria that should define what differentiates between segments: some definitions may tend to favour utilities in some areas – by making them appear relatively lower cost – while disadvantaging others. There tend to be no quick solutions to this kind of complex comparison problem, and the suitability of different segment definitions may vary materially depending on the relevant circumstances. Given these difficulties, there can be considerable benefit from focusing on seeking to establish effective processes through which the scope for different comparative bases for segmentation and assessment can be raised and tested, by – and in consultation with – stakeholders. In line with the comments below on the broader use of performance benchmarking, an important policy-level issue here concerns the extent to which utilities expect their future performance to be assessed through benchmarking in ways that could have material financial implications. Where that is the case, utilities may have significant incentives to seek to engage in processes aimed at developing and refining benchmarking approaches in order to determine how best –rather than whether – cost benchmarking may be applied.

8.3. Benchmarking a broader range of service performance measures

Attention so far has been focused on performance in relation to costs. While this is central to economic regulation, regulators typically also put considerable effort into providing for broader performance assessments, and associated incentives. One reason for this is simply that there are a broader range of measurable aspects of performance that can be expected to have significant relevance for the overall outcomes that are delivered for customers and environment. The monopoly nature of WSS services can mean that unduly limited attention would be given to these factors in the absence of some form of regulatory pressure, and that customers have limited access to information that can help them identify and compare the cost and quality of the services they are required to pay for. Where bill increases are required, this kind of lack of transparency and accountability can underpin significant customer acceptability problems, and make it more difficult to articulate – in credible ways – why bill increases should be viewed as justified, and as delivering demonstrable improvements.

An important additional consideration here concerns the risks of focusing incentive regulation on costs (benchmarked or otherwise) in a relatively narrow way. A standard concern in incentive regulation is that cost pressures may be resolved (deliberately or otherwise) through some form of 'under-delivery'. That is, one way in which a company may be able to out-perform a price control settlement (or lessen the extent of financial underperformance that might otherwise result), is to simply deliver less. This could manifest itself is through cost savings being made in ways that tend to undermine some aspects of service quality, and the risk of this has tended to be an important factor in the attention regulators in wide range of jurisdictions and sectors have given to the identification of service quality measures that can then be monitored alongside (or as part of the mechanics of) price control arrangements.

The transparency of performance information is a key consideration here, and the approaches that are adopted to providing for transparency – and, more broadly, for stakeholder engagement – provide an important part of the way that regulators typically seek to encourage performance improvements and guard against the deterioration of performance. The following section sets out some of the different ways in which transparency can help generate better outcomes from regulatory processes, before describing a particular example – the approach used by ERSAR in Portugal – that looks well suited as a relevant reference point against which potential developments to the transparency arrangements in Lithuania could be considered.

8.3.1. Recognising the scope of potential transparency benefits

Transparency requirements have been used as an important tool by many regulators internationally, and can help promote improvements in a wide range of ways, including by:

1. Improving company, and company owner, awareness of how performance compares with that of others in terms of those measures that are made available, and of what 'good' might look like.[3] This may, in and of itself, help to motivate desirable change by 'shining a light' on relevant disparities in relation to features of performance that may otherwise be receiving relatively limited attention (given other prevailing company and company owner priorities).
2. Improving customer, and other stakeholder awareness of the comparisons that are made available. This can increase the scope for customers and other stakeholders to challenge companies, and local governments, on their performance in ways that may create desirable pressures for improvement.
3. Increasing the quality and sophistication of performance comparisons that can be made (which can in turn magnify the impact of (1) and (2)). Important underlying issues here typically include improvements to the development of standardised ways in which information must be compiled, and made available. This can have a range of different dimensions, including because:

- With more comparative information being made available, companies can face strong incentives to seek to ensure that comparisons are made on a reasonable basis, in a context where observed performance differences for some measures may relate closely to differences in relevant underlying circumstances (such as the density of the population that different companies serve). That is, a context where there may be greater scope for undesirable inferences to be drawn from available comparative information can result in greater effort being put into refining the basis upon which it is viewed as reasonable to make such comparisons, which can provide a more robust basis for subsequent regulatory assessments.
- Transparency arrangements typically raise important questions over how potentially complex and extensive information on different aspects of company performance can be communicated in more accessible ways. In line with this, regulators often put considerable effort into the development of standardised and streamlined performance reports that can provide a relatively simple means for customers and other stakeholders to get a high-level view of WSS company performance across some key areas of interest (further comments on how this might be done are included below in the discussion of the Portuguese ERSAR example).

4. Extending the ways and enhancing the effectiveness with which the regulator can seek to use comparative information in its price review determinations, and its associated development of incentive arrangements.
5. Improving customer and other stakeholder awareness and understanding of the trade-offs faced in relation to the sector, and improving the credibility of company and other communications related

to those trade-offs (because those communications sit within a broader framework of information provision and challenge). This can provide a basis for better informed and more credible engagement with water customers in ways that can improve the likely acceptability of bill increases where that can be shown to be necessary for the delivery of valued improvements.

It is important to note that the information under discussion here concerns different aspects of the performance of monopoly public service providers. While there is likely to be some relevant performance information that it is appropriate to treat as confidential (for example, for security reasons), experience from other countries clearly shows that substantial levels of performance information can be made available while at the same time taking appropriate account of relevant confidentiality concerns. This is the case even where companies are privately owned (as in England), notwithstanding the potential for this to raise additional types of commercial confidentiality concerns.

Given the public service nature of WSS companies, and the broad range of benefits that can be associated with transparency requirements, there looks to be a strong case for adopting a presumption that the regulator is able to introduce transparency requirements, other than where companies are able to provide compelling reasons as to why that would not be appropriate.

In line with the above comments, there may be significant benefits associated with enhancing the transparency of – and the accessibility of, and prominence given to – WSS company performance information. ERSAR provides a useful example of what that kind of enhancement of transparency might look like, and its performance benchmarking arrangements are summarised below.

8.3.2. ERSAR as a helpful reference point

The approach to WSS quality of service regulation that has been developed and applied by ERSAR, the Water and Waste Services Regulation Authority in Portugal, looks to be particularly well suited as guide for considering ways in which it may be desirable for the Lithuanian service performance arrangements to be developed. It is notable, that the ERSAR quality of service arrangements are applied in a context where there are currently 263 water supply utilities, and 266 wastewater management utilities, all state or municipality owned.[4] ERSAR has described the goals of its quality of service regulation as being to:

- Protect the interests of users regarding the quality of service provided.
- Compare results between entities through benchmarking.[5]
- Guide entities towards efficiency and effectiveness; and,
- Consolidate a culture of providing information that is: concise, credible and easy to understand.[6]

These goals look to fit well with the circumstances faced in Lithuania, and the approach to quality of service regulation that ERSAR applies – which relies on the development of 'soft', reputation-based incentive – could provide a valuable complement to current regulatory activity. While it is notable that regulators in some other jurisdictions (including in England and Wales, and Scotland) have applied financial incentives to service performance metrics, the use of such approaches can generate further risks of unwanted effects arising, and the relatively limited regulatory use that has been made of such metrics to date in Lithuania strongly suggests that the consideration of such approaches would be premature at present. In any event, experience strongly suggests reputation-based approaches, focused on the provision of concise, credible and easy to understand comparative information, can have powerful incentive effects.

ERSAR operates an annual process that involves utilities submitting the required data, that data being validated and treated to provide for benchmarking, and utilities then getting a right of reply before the finalised data is then published and publicised (including through an App). The approach focuses on providing information on around 15 Key Performance Indicators for each service (i.e. water and wastewater), with indicators designed to reflect performance in relation to the protection of user interests, service provision sustainability and environmental sustainability. The specific KPIs to be used could, of course, be adapted to the Lithuanian context where appropriate. Also, it is notable that many of the KPIs used by ERSAR appear routinely in service performance assessments that are produced in a number of other jurisdictions, including, for example:

- Service interruptions (water supply).
- Main failures (water supply).
- Water losses (water supply).
- Flooding incidents (wastewater).
- Sewer collapses (wastewater).
- Compliance with discharge permits (wastewater).
- A customer complaints metric (water and wastewater).
- An affordability metric (water and wastewater).

The notable features of the ERSAR approach, therefore, are less to do with the specific indicators that it provides for collection of (because, as above, it is common for similar types of indicators to be collected in other jurisdictions), and more to do with the processes and approach through which that performance information is presented and communicated in clear, concise and accessible ways. For each performance indicator, companies are ranked and compared with their peers through the use of clusters, based on the different regions in which they operate, and the characteristics of the area (e.g. rural vs urban).[7] As can be seen in diagrams below, this is used to provide an easy to understand 'traffic light' based presentation of comparisons that allow for straightforward identification of those operators that are best performing, above and below average, and so on. The annual reports allow for comparison between expected and actual performance, and for performance levels to be monitored over time, with this assisting with the prioritisation of improvement opportunities.

Figure 8.1. Extracts from ERSAR service performance information

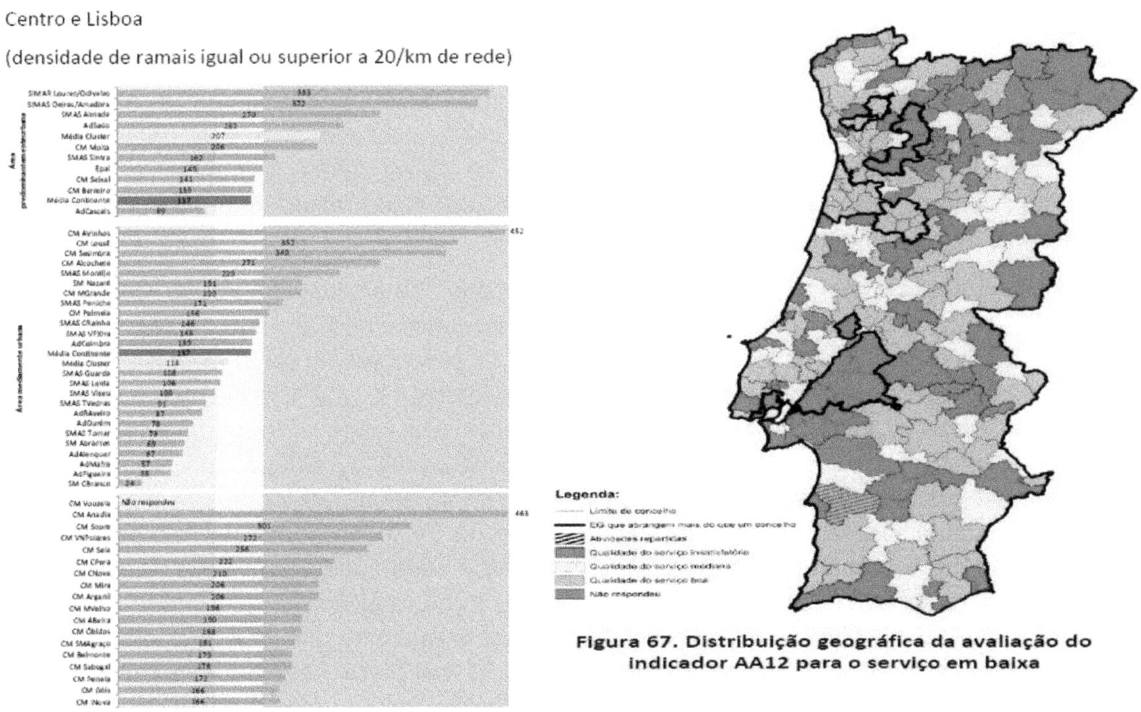

Note: In line with the comments above, the purpose of including these diagrams is not to emphasise the specific methods through which the underlying measures were calculated (and, in line with this, those methods are referred to in only high-level terms), but rather to illustrate the approach through which comparative performance information (once measured) is then presented and communicated.

In line with the comments above, the purpose of highlighting the ERSAR approach here is not to present the specific methodologies that are used to calculate and compare performance indicators as ones that should be considered for usage in Lithuania. Rather, the ERSAR example is intended to provide a useful reference point when considering how WSS performance data can be communicated in ways that can enhance the scope for comparative, reputational pressures to highlight better and worse performing areas, and in doing so to help make more visible where improvements may be both possible and appropriate. The adoption of this kind of approach could be tailored to reflect the relevant circumstances in Lithuania, with a range of underlying choices being required in relation to matters including:

- The specific KPIs that should be use
- How data should be audited
- How KPI information should be clustered and otherwise organised and adjusted when benchmarking results are being presented.

In line with the comments on cost assessment above, the most appropriate way to develop the specific performance benchmarking approaches that are to be applied will depend on a range of detailed and context specific matters that go well beyond the scope of this assessment, and is best viewed as something that would be expected to evolve over time. The ERSAR approach looks to provide a helpful reference point when considering the framework and processes within which benchmarking arrangements could be developed and applied. In particular, it focuses attention on trying to make available, and communicate, clear and easy to understand information on comparative performance. With this treated as an appropriate objective, attention can then be turned to the detailed and ongoing work that is likely to be needed to deliver on that. This is not a question of simply seeking to identify what the 'right' set of measures and underlying methodologies (e.g. for clustering municipalities) are as a stand-alone exercise. Rather, it is more a question of seeking to develop processes that can be expected to help provide ways of building and refining more appropriate approaches over time, recognising that this is challenging to do.

The challenges arise because there are different dimensions of performance that could be measured and compared in different ways, and decisions in relation to those dimensions and measurement and comparison techniques may imply materially different outcomes in terms of apparent relative performance. This tends to make the process through which methods are developed important, as that process can potentially help give legitimacy to the overall outcomes that result. A commitment to providing clear, concise and easy to understand performance information – one of the high-level goals that ERSAR identifies – is important here, because it makes it clear to stakeholders, including importantly WSS companies, that performance comparisons are going to be made and presented to the public in relatively simplified formats of the kind illustrated above.

Having made such a commitment, it is then important to consider the processes through which the specific performance measurement and comparison methods will be determined. But the context is then one in which all companies know that this kind of information will be produced in one form or another, and they know that how they are shown as performing is likely to be affected by the specific methodology choices that are made. Company interests, though, will clearly differ in a range of important ways, as relative assessments will show some as performing well and others poorly by comparison. This difference of interests across companies provides a valuable source of information and input, and the tension it can create between companies can be used by the regulator to try to help improve the robustness and reasonableness of the measures being generated. Again, the commitment to producing and publicising the comparative information is key as it can allow attention to be focused on more productive questions concerning how that information should be developed, rather than on the question of whether it should be developed, where company interests may be more aligned, in that there may be a general preference for limiting the extent to which there is broader emphasis put on company performance levels.

8.4. Benchmarking business planning

A different form of benchmarking that has been used internationally, and may provide a desirable means of seeking to encourage more efficiency-enhancing consolidation activity, relates to business planning processes. The following considers two options of benchmarking incentive that look to merit careful consideration:

- The first option focuses on how ambitious a plan is (according to the company itself and to the regulator)
- The second assesses the planning process, and in particular the adequacy of options appraisal processes: the regulator wants to ensure the company has explored a range of options (even though the selected one may look conservative).

Note that these options are not mutually exclusive and can be used in parallel.

8.4.1. Incentives to encourage the development of efficiency-enhancing consolidation plans

A number of regulators internationally – including the Essential Services Commission (ESC) in Australia,[8] and Ofwat in England and Wales[9] - have introduced forms of business plan incentives, typically to try to address concerns that companies may otherwise have an incentive to be unduly conservative in their planning, and to do too little to address the future challenges that are faced. Such approaches can be understood as effectively rewarding early movers for the information they provide in terms of the improvements that their plan presents as achievable. Where the company delivers on that more challenging plan, the outcomes can then form part of future benchmarking efforts that can increase the pressure on other companies to improve, while also providing a practical example of how that improvement may be achievable.

The PREMO framework

The approach developed by the ESC (the economic regulator of the Victoria water sector in Australia) is referred to as the PREMO[10] framework, and provides a useful reference point. Under the PREMO framework, instead of applying a uniform weighted average cost of capital (WACC) across companies, the allowed return on equity is varied depending on the level of 'ambition' shown in the relevant company's price submission. The diagram below illustrates how a higher return on equity is when setting allowed charges where the ESC identifies a plan as more efficient, with four different categories having been identified:

- Basic: where the submission is identified as reflecting stagnating or declining performance the allowed return on equity would be set at a level commensurate with the benchmark real cost of debt.
- Standard: where a slightly higher return on equity allowance is provided for to reflect that the submission is viewed as a good value proposition for customers but that represents a continuation of existing outcomes and cost efficiency targets.
- Advanced: a more ambitious submission that will generally commit to improved outcomes in terms of services, prices or both, and would receive a higher equity return allowance.
- Leading: where the proposals place the company as a sector leader on key aspects of performance.

Figure 8.2. Illustration of (real) return on equity allowances under the ESC's PREMO approach

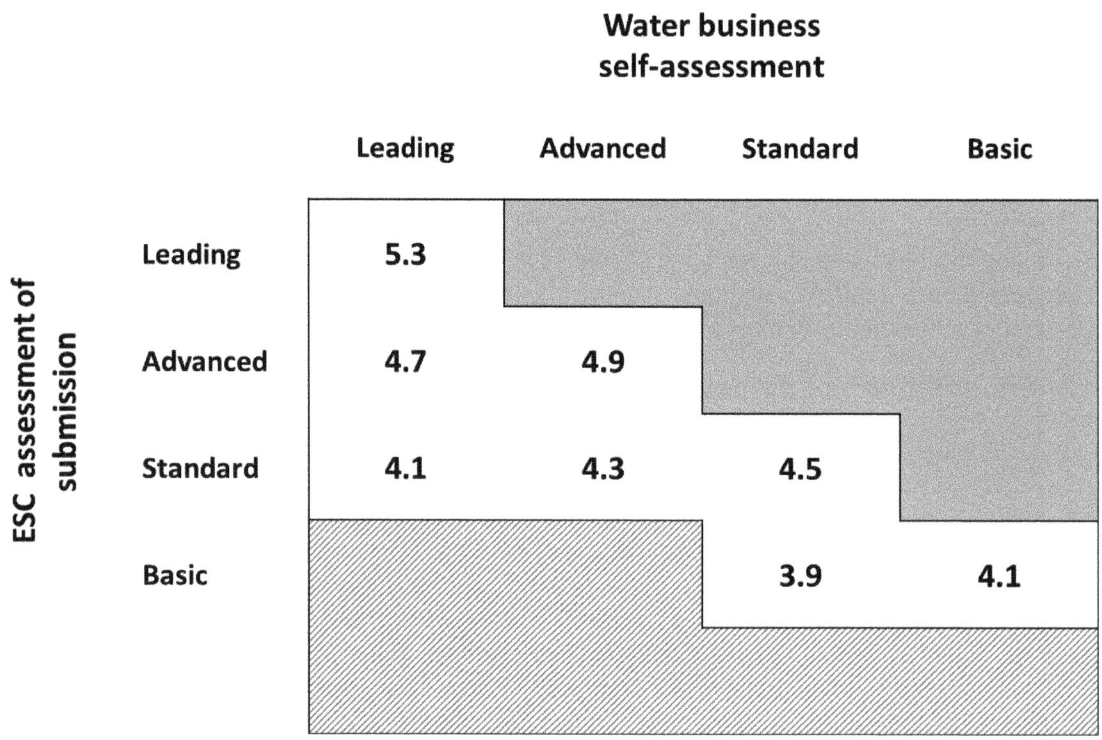

Source: Figure 2.1 in: https://www.esc.vic.gov.au/sites/default/files/documents/Water-Pricing-Framework-and-Approach-Final-Paper-Oct-2016.pdf

As can be seen in the diagram, the allowed return on equity is also made dependent on the company's own assessment of the level of ambition of its plan, with this intended to encourage companies to put forward their 'best offer'. In particular, it is notable that - under the approach – a company gets a lower allowed return on equity if ESC judges it as having a lower level of ambition than had been presented in the company's self-assessment. The ESC identifies the red shaded area as indicating where it reserves the discretion to adopt a different approach, such as setting a shorter control and/or requiring resubmission.

Some core features of business plan quality incentives

The PREMO approach provides an interesting example in part because of the clear and explicit way in which it adjusts the return equity allowance depending on assessments of level of ambition. At the same time, it includes levels of complexity (including the use made of company self-assessments) that seem unlikely to be necessary or well suited in the current Lithuanian context. In practice, this kind of business plan quality incentive approach can be viewed as comprising of three core features:

1. Scope for identifying company business plans as falling into more than one quality category.
2. Identification of the criteria that would be used to determine which quality category a business plan should be identified as in.
3. Explicit and credible up-front identification of how companies will be treated differently when identified as falling in one quality category rather than another.

The following considers how each of these features might be applied in an Lithuanian WSS context.

Identifying categories of business plan quality

The PREMO approach involves the regulator having to determine which of four 'quality' categories a price submission falls into: basic, standard, advanced, leading. Ofwat (the economic regulator in England and Wales) also used four categories – significant scrutiny, slow-track, fast-track, exceptional – in its review of price controls for the 2020-25 period, although in practice only allocated companies to three of those categories (with no business plans categorised as 'exceptional'). It is notable that in an earlier development of this kind of approach, the British energy regulator Ofgem applied a simpler categorisation that distinguished only between whether companies should treated as 'fast-track' - because their proposals had been identified as of 'high' quality and therefore appropriate to implement quickly - or 'slow-track' – because their proposals had been identified as of relatively lower quality and as requiring further, more detailed scrutiny. The use of four (rather than two) categories in the PREMO and Ofwat approaches can be viewed as a simple refinement of Ofgem's approach, that allows a further subcategorization of the 'high' (fast-track) and 'lower' (slow-track) quality categories. It is not obvious, however, that this further refinement would be particularly helpful if such an approach were to be introduced in Lithuania, at least in a first iteration. In particular, the use of additional categories increases complexity, and the burden that the regulator (in seeking to specify and apply the categories) and regulated companies (in seeking to understand and determine how to respond to the categories) can be expected to face, but may provide little additional benefit over a simpler two category approach.

Given this, the development of a two-category approach, where companies can explicitly expect more favourable treatment if categorised in the 'high quality' rather than in the lower quality category, looks likely to provide the most appropriate starting point for developing this kind of approach in Lithuania. That said, there may be a case for explicitly identifying the possibility of using two separate 'high quality' categories (with only one lower quality category), if there are some sources of additional benefit – for example, additional support from EU funds – that may be available in some circumstances but not others. Where this is the case, access to the additional support could be made conditional on achieving 'high quality' status in the regulator's business plan assessment, but would then involve some further hurdles having to be overcome.

Criteria for assessing which category a plan should be identified as in

For its review of 2020-25 business plans, Ofwat developed (ahead of company submission of business plans) a relatively extensive assessment framework that highlighted both the 'test areas' that were going to be explicitly assessed, and what the characteristics of high quality, ambitious and innovative plans would be likely to be in each of those test areas.[11] The test areas included a range of core priority matters such as securing costs efficiently, addressing affordability and vulnerability, and securing long-term resilience, and for each test area, Ofwat identified some questions it would be relevant to consider. For example, in relation to securing long-term resilience, the following questions were identified:

- How well has the company used the best available evidence to objectively assess and prioritise the diverse range of risks and consequences of disruptions to its systems and services, and engaged effectively with customers on its assessment of these risks and consequences?
- How well has the company objectively assessed the full range of mitigation options and selected the solutions that represent the best value for money over the long term, and have support from customers?

For a plan to be viewed as 'high quality', Ofwat identified that (among other things): the company will provide clear evidence that they have objectively considered and assessed the full range of resilience management options. For a plan to be viewed as ambitious and innovative, Ofwat identified that the company would need to present strong evidence that it has used robust, ambitious and innovative approaches to assess and mitigate risks to long-term resilience in the round.

Developing this kind of business plan inventive approach in Lithuania would not require the extent of development – in terms of assessment criteria and questions - that Ofwat undertook. However, some up-front specification of what the key test areas would be, and what sorts of questions would be expected to guide the assessment in those areas, is likely to be helpful both because it can give greater clarity to companies on what they can expect, but also because the regulator plans and delivers the subsequent assessments (by making it clear what practical steps that is likely to involve). When seeking to specify how companies should be assessed, it can be helpful to distinguish between the following:

- Hygiene factors: to what extent are there criteria that should be viewed as a necessary condition for any company's business plan to even be considered as potentially 'high quality' (such that the meeting of this criteria can be treated as a form of hygiene factor in the assessment process)? This may include reference to current performance levels and financial health.
- Other differentiating factors: given its strategic importance for the Lithuanian WSS sector, it would be expected that consideration of other differentiating factors would be heavily focused on the extent to which companies are bringing forward new consolidation options, and the extent to which they are able to demonstrate, robustly, that those consolidation options can be expected to be efficiency enhancing.

The relevance of different potential forms of consolidation is considered later in this section when some of the potential constraints to consolidation options emerging are considered.

The benefits of a plan being identified as of higher quality

Regulators have typically sought to provide for financial, reputational and procedural incentives to be associated with the identification of a company's business plan as 'high quality' within this kind of assessment framework. In line with this, in Lithuania, the development and submission of credible, efficiency enhancing consolidation plans could be encouraged in a number of different ways, including through:

- The use of a higher WACC in the tariff setting methodology than would otherwise have been allowed for (as is explicitly provided for in the PREMO approach).
- The explicit provision of some other form of financial reward: for example, access to grant funding or preferential borrowing opportunities.
- Greater scope for support with respect to financeability using accelerated depreciation (where that can be shown to be consistent with bill affordability and acceptability issues being sufficiently addressed).
- Scope for the price control to be determined for a longer period: in line with the comments earlier, this may be important in providing consolidating parties with an opportunity to share in the benefits of the plans they bring forward (particularly where there may be some time lag associated with the securing of those benefits).
- Presentation of the outcomes of the assessment in a way that can be expected to provide material reputational benefits for those associated with successful companies: the regulator can actively seek to highlight and publicise its assessments of 'high quality' proposals, and then use the companies actions as a positive case study to promote further change.
- Procedural benefits associated with less extensive review requirements, providing overall performance remains sufficiently 'on-track'.

The importance and implications of credibility

For business plan incentives to encourage companies to put more effort into developing efficiency enhancing consolidation plans than they would otherwise, attention needs to be given to the overall attractiveness of the rewards that are potentially on offer. The scale of financial rewards can be expected to be an important part of this, and to merit careful consideration by reference to the sorts of decision making that companies face (i.e. in terms of the risks they may be taking on if pursuing novel consolidation approaches). Another key factor, however, concerns credibility. Credibility can be enhanced to some extent through the publication of up-front information on available rewards, and the PREMO framework can be viewed as notable in this respect in terms of its clear articulation of the different WACC outcomes that can arise. However, interpretations of the relevance of reward information will be heavily dependent on perceptions of how the arrangements might be applied in practice. This can leave scope for a significant dampening of incentives to arise as a result of concerns over the likelihood of a company actually securing a reward even where it seeks to respond in appropriate ways through the development of consolidation plans. For example, a company may envisage a situation where it has developed a challenging and innovative consolidation proposal only for the regulator to classify it as somehow deficient and not meriting the 'high quality' classification, and the associated securing of the identified rewards.

To some extent, this kind of issue is inevitable with the introduction of a novel assessment mechanism, and given uncertainty over what plans might actually be presented to the regulator, it can be very difficult to address this kind of issue up-front, other than through the development and publication of the kind of a assessment criteria discussed above. However, in practice, much can be done to address this matter through the way in which the regulator engages throughout the process. Uncertainty (and the potential dampening of incentives) may be greatest where the regulator adopt a relatively arms-length approach to the process, such that – once its broad intended approach has been outlined – it is viewed as being for companies to interpret and respond to that approach, with the regulator's next key role in the process coming at the business plan evaluation and categorisation stage. Under this kind of arms-length approach companies may expect to be poorly sighted in terms of how well-aligned their plans are with regulatory expectations, and thus may heavily discount the prospect of actually securing the rewards that have been presented as potentially available. There may be a significant risk that the incentive arrangements have little impact, and indeed there may end up being little basis for the regulator to provide any rewards.

A different approach, though, would be for the regulator to be very clear up-front that it recognises this uncertainty (and the effects it could have), and is committed to seeking to work with companies to help reduce that uncertainty, and then to allow for rewards under the incentive mechanism providing it is presented with credible consolidation plans. Under this kind of more active approach, the business plan assessment process can be explicitly presented as an iterative one, in which the regulator will seek to provide guidance to companies who consider themselves potentially in contention for a reward, in order to try to resolve concerns they may have about misalignment of views. This can provide a situation in which there is limited remaining uncertainty over the final regulatory assessment (i.e. companies should have good sight of how their plans will be assessed) because of commentary the regulator has already provided along the way. In practice, this could be applied by adopting something like the following stages:

1. Clearly identify the hygiene factors (referred to above) that the earning of rewards would be conditional on: the development of these could include some engagement with companies that might be expected to bring forward consolidation plans to ensure the criteria are not unduly restrictive (while at the same time act as an appropriate initial filter).
1. Provide an explicit option for companies to check they have satisfied the hygiene factor requirements: this would not be a requirement, but would be expected to initiate a process of engagement with potentially successful companies.
2. Provide scope for companies to 'check-in' periodically on their developing plans, with the aim of identifying potentially material limitations (and where there are significant misalignments of view) at an early stage.

3. Where common issues are identified through the check-in process (for example, with respect to sufficiency of evidence on likely long-term impacts), the regulator could publish a brief update note in order to improve on the broader transparency of the arrangements.
4. Allow for early submission of draft plans on which formal feedback (with 'points to address') could be provided.

To some extent, the above can be viewed as similar to a form of procurement process in which – after an initial 'pre-qualification' phase – some ongoing negotiation and engagement is often an important part of ensuring that final 'bids' are well suited to the buyer's requirements. Although the context clearly differs here in some key respects, it is notable that there is scope for regulator and company interests to be relatively well-aligned, and the purpose of adopting something like this kind of more active engagement approach is to try to keep the scope for that high-level alignment clearly in mind for all sides, and to reduce the scope of unhelpful surprises to emerge (the prospect of which – in line with the above comments – may be viewed as a significant deterrent to the development of potentially beneficial plans).

8.4.2. Benchmarking of business planning processes: ensuring a range of (consolidation) options have been explored and duly assessed

The above has focused on how incentives based on the overall quality of company business plans might be used to encourage the development of beneficial consolidation proposals, in particular by seeking to reward plans that are identified as 'high quality'. However, a different form of incentive that also merits consideration (alongside the use of such approaches), involves providing scope for penalties to be applied as means of encouraging the more extensive and effective use of options appraisal methods.

The extent to which investment plans are based upon sufficient consideration of alternative potential options – including options that involve consolidation – is likely to become an increasingly important factor over time and raises questions over the appropriate scope of the regulator's cost assessment activities. A distinction can be drawn between:

- Identifying how desired outcomes are best met (i.e. the choice of approach); and,
- Identifying the efficient cost of delivering the approach that has been selected.

A narrow cost assessment exercise may focus only on the second bullet point above. However, there may be substantial scope for efficiency improvements associated with the first bullet, particularly where there may be opportunities to deliver services in more coordinated and consolidated ways that enable greater economies of scale benefits. In line with this, there may be some benefit in seeking to directly target the sufficiency of 'how' assessments.

When considering ways of addressing this, it is helpful to distinguish – in principle – between the following two types of assessment that a regulator might undertake:

- Providing for detailed, expert reviews of the options appraisals that companies have undertaken.
- Assessing whether companies have undertaken appropriately robust options appraisals processes.

Historically, many regulators have tended to adopt the first 'expert reviewer' role (or have appointed engineering consultants to undertake it on their behalf). However, this can involve the regulator effectively taking on responsibility for demonstrating why a given assessment by the relevant company should be regarded as not sufficiently well founded, by reference to the regulator's own assessment of alternatives. Such an approach can be resource intensive as it will often require considerable detailed work in relation to specific matters where the regulator inevitably has relatively limited information and expertise. This can then put significant limitations on what it is realistic to expect the regulatory review process to achieve (given, in particular, relevant information asymmetries).

The second role noted above seeks to address matters in a different way by taking a step back and focusing regulatory attention on the adequacy of the options appraisal processes that companies have undertaken, rather than on the detailed analysis and findings of the specific appraisals they have produced. From this perspective, it is viewed as for companies to demonstrate to the regulator that they have conducted appropriate options appraisal processes, and if companies are unable to do that sufficiently, then that – in and of itself – could be treated by the regulator as a basis for some form of penalty to be applied (through making a downward adjustment to the cost allowance the company).

Ofwat has adopted this latter kind of approach in England and Wales in some of its stand-alone (i.e. not benchmarked) assessments of proposed investments, where it has applied the following approach:[12]

- If a company provided evidence that a lower cost option was available but gave no reasons as to why it was rejected, Ofwat would use the lower cost option when calculating the allowed costs.
- Where a company has not provided evidence that its selected option is optimal (i.e where there is insufficient evidence that the potential for using alternative, lower cost, options was explored and assessed), Ofwat would apply a 20% reduction to the company's proposed cost estimate, intended to protect customers from the risk that a potentially sub-optimal solution was being adopted.

On the face of it, this kind of approach might be viewed as relatively arbitrary, in that it could result in a substantial gap between the amount a company has identified as needed to deliver on a specific project, and the amount the regulator allows to be recovered through charges, without the regulator having explicitly identified that the lower amount should be viewed as sufficient. However, the regulatory approach can be understood as intended to incentivise companies to ensure that high quality options appraisal processes have been undertaken (and that the company can demonstrate this), in a context where the quality of the appraisal processes is viewed as potentially having a substantial impact on costs that may be recovered from customers over many years.[13] The approach can therefore be understood as having risk-based foundations, in that companies that seek to proceed with highly material projects without having undertaken an adequate options appraisal process can be viewed as exposing customers to significant risks of funding inefficient investments.

Ofwat's penalty-based approach is applied in a context where it sits within a broader set of reward and penalty arrangements that private water companies are subject to. The different context in Lithuania may mean that such an approach would be unlikely to be feasible or desirable. However, an alternative to applying this kind of downward adjustment to allowed costs would be to effectively not accept the relevant part of the price control submission, and to send it back to the company to address the limitations in its assessment of options. That is, the regulator could be viewed as introducing a form of assessment 'gateway' that companies must successfully pass through in order to secure funding for significant new investment projects. If the company has not shown that relevant options have been appropriately taken into consideration, then that part of the price control application could get stripped out and sent back.

This may provide a more practical and appropriate means of proceeding in Lithuania, with the regulator providing some guidance on what is expected in terms of options appraisal including in terms of the consideration of consolidation options. In this way, evidence of having conducted an adequate options evaluation process could effectively become treated as a condition of a successful application for relatively large-scale requests for the recognition of new investment costs in the tariff formula. The availability of practical evidence of potential consolidation options – including from pilot study activity – can be of considerable importance under such an approach. In particular, such evidence provides a concrete basis upon which a regulator could question the adequacy of a company's consideration of options, as it can look for evidence that the lessons from the pilot study have been recognised, and that the potential relevance of those lessons have been explored and tested. By making pricing assessments in other company areas dependent, to some extent, on the consideration that has been given to pilot study evidence, the regulator can effectively raise the prominence and importance of that evidence, and increase the scope of the likely impact of pilot study activity.

8.5. Summary and recommendations

This Chapter has sought to identify potentially desirable developments to benchmarking arrangements in Lithuania, with a particular focus on the scope for encouraging efficiency improvements through consolidation. It has considered – drawing, where helpful, on examples of international experience – some ways in which the identification and achievement of WSS efficiency gains might be further encouraged through the use of different forms of benchmarking. The key points that have been identified are summarised below through the identification of recommendations and suggestions concerning how the current arrangements could be developed so as to help tackle the key WSS challenges that are likely to be faced.

8.5.1. Recommendation 1: Commit to developing a Service Performance Incentive framework

- Commit to develop, make publicly available and publicise a KPI framework that provides concise, credible and easy to understand comparisons between companies, using the Portuguese ERSAR approach as a guide.

The development of this kind of framework has the potential to deliver substantial benefits by providing more robust protection of customer interests, and guiding companies toward the use of more efficient and effective approaches, using reputational incentives. A key starting point would be a commitment to the adoption of such an approach so that industry attention could be focused on how that would be best achieved (rather than whether performance comparisons should be made more prominent).

8.5.2. Recommendations 2: Develop incentives that focus on the benchmarking of company plans, and planning processes

- Develop guidance setting out how the economic regulator would enable companies that present credible, efficiency-enhancing consolidation plans to share the benefits they result in, through the treatment of consolidation costs, and commitments concerning how rapidly future efficiency savings will be reflected in allowed prices.
- Develop guidance setting out regulatory expectations with respect to companies being able to demonstrate that robust options appraisal processes have been undertaken in the development of capex plans, and how capex applications will be treated where a company is unable to adequately demonstrate that.

These proposals directly target key aspects associated with encouraging the bringing forward of efficiency enhancing consolidation plans: the extent to which companies can expect to benefit from bringing forward such plans (given the scope for 'ratchet effects' to otherwise undermine such incentives); and the risk that companies do not adequately explore or consider different ways of addressing outcome requirements when developing their capex plans. Examples from Australia and the UK provide useful reference points.

Notes

[1] OECD (2021), Reform of the water supply and wastewater treatment sector of Lithuania by consolidation of utilities: Output 3; featured in this report as Chapter 3.

[2] See, for example: https://www.severntrent.com/content/dam/stw-plc/our-plans/Severn-Trent-water-cost-modelling-framework-Final.pdf.

[3] The identification of appropriate indicators is discussed further below.

[4] With direct management, delegation or concession operating models used.

[5] The selection of specific indicators is discussed below.

[6] The extracts from ERSAR reports shown below illustrate how this has been done through the use performance comparison charts and a map-based comparison of performance between utilities using a traffic light system.

[7] Some brief comments on the development of clustering approaches are provided below.

[8] https://www.esc.vic.gov.au/sites/default/files/documents/Water-Pricing-Framework-and-Approach-Final-Paper-Oct-2016.pdf.

[9] See, for example: https://www.ofwat.gov.uk/regulated-companies/price-review/2019-price-review/initial-assessment-of-plans/.

[10] The terms PREMO comes from the different identified elements of the assessment process: Performance; Risk; Engagement; Management; Outcomes.

[11] A detailed description of Ofwat's assessment approach is provided in: https://www.ofwat.gov.uk/wp-content/uploads/2017/12/Appendix-13-IAP-FM.pdf.

[12] See p54-55 of: https://www.ofwat.gov.uk/wp-content/uploads/2019/12/PR19-final-determinations-Securing-cost-efficiency-technical-appendix.pdf.

[13] It is notable that, in presenting its approach, Ofwat highlighted that options can range considerably in cost, and pointed to companies as having provided evidence that there could be a 35% difference in cost between reinforcing as opposed to replacing a main.

www.ingramcontent.com/pod-product-compliance
Ingram Content Group UK Ltd.
Pitfield, Milton Keynes, MK11 3LW, UK
UKHW051504290926
15471UKWH00008B/1398

9 789264 601109